IN THE WEB OF CLASS

D1565786

The American Social Experience Series

GENERAL EDITOR: JAMES KIRBY MARTIN

EDITORS: PAULA S. FASS, STEVEN H. MINTZ,
CARL PRINCE, JAMES W. REED & PETER N. STEARNS

Portrait of a Street Boy, 1892. Charles Currier Collection, Library of Congress.

IN THE WEB OF CLASS

*Delinquents and Reformers
in Boston, 1810s–1930s*

ERIC C. SCHNEIDER

NEW YORK UNIVERSITY PRESS
NEW YORK AND LONDON
1992

NEW YORK UNIVERSITY PRESS
New York and London

Library of Congress Cataloging-in-Publication Data
Schneider, Eric C.
In the web of class : delinquents and reformers in Boston,
1810s–1930s / Eric C. Schneider.
p. cm. — (The American social experience ; 22)
Includes index.
ISBN 0-8147-7933-6
1. Social work with juvenile delinquents — Massachusetts — Boston —
History. 2. Juvenile corrections — Massachusetts — Boston — History.
3. Child welfare — Massachusetts — Boston — History. 4. Poor children —
Massachusetts — Boston — Social conditions. I. Title. II. Series:
American social experience ; 22.
HV9306.B7S36 1991
364.3′6′0974461 — dc20   91-27617
CIP

New York University Press books are printed on acid-free paper,
and their binding materials are chosen for strength and durability.

Manufactured in the United States of America

c 10 9 8 7 6 5 4 3 2 1

Contents

List of Illustrations

Preface

I remember as a youngster standing in line at the Rhinelander boys' club, clutching my quarter and awaiting my turn at the hot lunch. The Rhinelander boys' club was an outpost of the New York Children's Aid Society that still served a working-class clientele in the largely German and Irish Yorkville of the early 1960s. The food was filling, if not interesting, but I soon discovered that for $0.15 I could buy a slice of pizza and have a dime for candy, which, if not as filling, was more satisfying. The boys' club also had a number of recreational programs, but I preferred playing stickball with my friends. Certainly in my case the institution failed to provide an alternative to the freedoms of street life.

For a time, I also lived at a home operated by the St. Vincent de Paul Society. My aunt, with whom I grew up, worked as a housekeeper, and my ability to live with her depended in part on the families for whom she worked. Like the families discussed in this book, she used the home as part of her family strategy, to tide us over a difficult time until she could find more suitable employment.

We also had our encounters with family court, although not because of my delinquencies, which were fairly minor and went undetected. My aunt had received custody over me and reported upon occasion to the court. As an immigrant with limited education, she was somewhat in awe of the court and we always endeavored to put on a good face in our visits with the judge. Fearful of being labeled a spendthrift and losing custody of her child, she asked for as little money as she could and endured investigations of her personal matters with as much dignity as she could muster without appearing disrespectful.

Despite her involvement with social welfare institutions, my aunt disdained people on public welfare. The dole was the resort of those unwilling to work, and "the projects," the home for those unable to manage by themselves. Always present was the assumption that people on welfare were somehow inferior. I grew up internalizing the difference between what nineteenth-century reformers called the worthy and the vicious poor.

The suspicion of welfare and the welfare state that is so much a part of our contemporary consciousness is a historical artifact and the result of generations of historical experience. I do not pretend to excavate that experience, although I believe it is the product of both harsh encounters with welfare institutions and the emphasis on individual, moral responsibility for poverty espoused by reformers. I seek to understand how welfare institutions, reformatories, and the courts helped shape the lives of the working class, and how the working class shaped the history of these institutions.

My own history has undoubtedly shaped this book. To the degree that my sources have allowed, I have viewed reform from the perspective of its clients, for whom I have a good deal of sympathy. Following the conventions of most historians, I have drawn my periodization from the actions of reformers, but I have not assumed that they were the only actors on the set. Rather I have interpreted reformers as engaging in a dialogue with their clients and responding as much to clients' actions as to currents in reform thought or to religious or scientific beliefs.

This book has its own history and one of the pleasures of finishing it is the opportunity to acknowledge the many people who have helped me. At Boston University, I worked with Sam Bass Warner, Robert V. Bruce, and Aileen Kraditor, and most of what I know about my craft is due to them. My fellow graduate students—Susan Benson, Linda Hansen, Barbara Hobson, Peter Holloran, Larry Metzger, Marc Miller, Susan Reverby, Susan Walton, and Paul Wright—shared insights and made learning a pleasure. Brian Gratton, Susan Porter, and

Lynn Weiner read the manuscript twice, which is a testimony to both friendship and endurance.

The Chester Avenue Seminar read many of the chapters, and my book would never have been completed without it: Len Braitman, George Dowdall, Brian Greenberg, Svend Holsoe, Emma Lapsansky, Cindy Little, Randall Miller, Marion Roydhouse, and, with special thanks, David Allmendinger. Alan Kraut and Nancy Tomes in their brief sojourns in Philadelphia also became friends and valued critics.

The staffs of the Boston Children's Services Association, especially Jan Straw, the Boston Juvenile Court, especially the Honorable Francis G. Poitrast, the Division of Youth Services of the Commonwealth of Massachusetts, the Ellis Memorial Center, the Boston Public Library, the Congregational Library, Schlesinger Library, the Harvard Law Library, and the interlibrary loan staffs at Boston University, the University of Delaware, and the University of Pennsylvania all deserve thanks.

As an administrator, I enjoy neither summers nor sabbaticals in which to write. However, Diane Dailey Frey secured three hours of library time for me during most weeks of the year, which, together with late nights and naptime on weekends, allowed me to finish the book. My children, Alex and Ben, have always played a game called "going to work in my study," and I hope to make it up to them.

My largest debt is to my wife, Janet Golden. Since the time we met on a picket line at Boston University, our personal and intellectual lives have become intertwined. She is a model friend, scholar, and partner who has taken time from her own work to comment on countless drafts of the manuscript. She makes everything possible.

As for any errors of fact or interpretation, mea culpa, mea culpa, mea maxima culpa.

Introduction: The Web of Class

We have never dealt successfully with our troubled children. We lock them up, put them on probation, place them in foster care, or keep them at home and utilize home visitors and social services—the limited possibilities have all been tried before and failed. Efforts to reform delinquents have faced three stumbling blocks. The first was the definition of the problem itself. Reformers repeatedly described social problems as cultural in origin and overlooked or downplayed the impact of social structure. According to this view, delinquency stemmed from character deficiencies, and reformers focused on providing delinquents with new cultural values while ignoring issues of economic inequality, power, and class.[1] Second, the effectiveness of even cultural reform was hampered by the political economy of welfare. The fear of dependency has shaped Anglo-American welfare policy since the early nineteenth century, and the provision of assistance has been dictated by the doctrine of "less eligibility"—a person receiving assistance should live no better than the worst-off participant in the marketplace. The corollary for delinquents was that they could not be treated more favorably than nondelinquent children. Finally, reformers underestimated the ability of delinquents and their families to manipulate social welfare/juvenile justice agencies for their own purposes. Delinquents refused to be the passive "beneficiaries" of reform, and they and their parents used social services in unexpected ways.

The cumulative result was a social welfare/juvenile justice system that did not aid or reform very many.

Historians have studied delinquency and institutions for the delinquent in a number of ways: as part of intellectual history (focusing on important reformers to analyze changing conceptions of delinquency), as part of the study of deviance (analyzing the characteristics shared by institutions for deviant populations), as part of the educational system, in institutional biographies, or in studies of a particular aspect of juvenile justice, such as the juvenile court. But historians have not studied the relationship between delinquency prevention and social welfare, they have not investigated how institutions and programs for juveniles interacted and came to form what later generations have termed a system, and only rarely have scholars considered the impact of delinquents and agency clients upon the actual function and organization of institutions.[2]

This book attempts these tasks by analyzing how public and private programs for juveniles developed out of efforts to reform social welfare. It traces the emergence between 1815 and 1935 of a juvenile justice "system" out of a maze of public and private, voluntary and coercive, male- and female-oriented, and Protestant and Catholic organizations, and it examines the interaction among reformers, institutional officials, delinquents, and their families.

The best way of analyzing the development of a wide range of institutions and agencies, especially given the time period covered, is through a case study. Boston is a logical choice, given the availability of records and the opportunity to locate this work in an extensive body of scholarship. Boston had unique characteristics, but its public institutions were among the first of their kind and its private social welfare agencies prided themselves on being flagships in their field.[3] While Boston was not the world writ small, to the degree that reformers elsewhere aspired to national standards, they did so according to standards made in Boston.

The themes of this book can be illustrated by the case history of Margaret Kern and her family. Between 1910 and 1927, when they were studied by the Harvard Law School's Crime Survey, the Kern family came into contact with twenty-two different social welfare agencies, including the Judge Baker Foundation (a mental health clinic) and the juvenile sessions of the Roxbury Municipal Court (a district court in Boston). The Kern case history reveals the level of cooperation among social welfare and juvenile justice agencies and between the public and private sectors. The case history also shows the extent to which social workers were able to intervene in families, and how an appeal for aid enmeshed a family in the social welfare network. It is apparent from Mrs. Kern's fear of public institutions, not only those for delinquents but even public hospitals, that working-class people were aware that public institutions guarded the boundaries of their communities by establishing who was deviant.[4] At the same time, private institutions offered the chance of social mobility to those who adopted the mores of the dominant culture.[5] One can also see the limits on welfare agencies' power and the success of family members in using agencies for their own ends. In sum, the case history highlights the ways in which social welfare helped pattern the experience of class while also illustrating the ability of clients to maneuver within that system.[6]

The Kerns' involvement with social welfare began with an appeal for relief in 1910. Mr. and Mrs. Kern had moved to the Boston area from New Hampshire in 1899 with their two sons, and they had had three additional children by 1910. Mr. Kern, who as a child had been committed to the New Hampshire State Industrial School for theft, worked as a house painter and in a shoe factory. His drinking, a bad back, and his inability to find steady work led the family to request assistance. Mrs. Kern made a very favorable impression on the social worker from the Family Welfare Society, who found her "charmingly independent" for her reluctance to apply for aid. While wary of accepting charity, Mrs. Kern was willing to use social welfare agencies for her own purposes, namely to strengthen her hand within the family. In 1913, she asked the Massachusetts Society for the Prevention of Cruelty to Children to force her husband to support his family, reportedly saying that she wished "he would either stay away or work while he is there." Mrs. Kern thought that her husband was somewhat in awe of the "Cruelty," as the SPCC was popularly known, and she believed that a stern warning would frighten him into working. Apparently it did, for Mr. Kern obtained a job in a shoe factory, but his employment was short-lived. Two years later, in 1915, both the

Brookline Friendly Society and the Red Cross provided assistance to the family, to which two more children had been born, while Mr. Kern was unemployed and the two oldest sons were in the army. Mrs. Kern's problems with nonsupport continued, and in 1917 she obtained a formal separation agreement under which Mr. Kern was to provide five dollars a week for her and their five younger children. Mr. Kern disappeared shortly thereafter.[7]

Margaret Kern's odyssey through the world of social welfare and juvenile justice was just beginning. Apparently neither of her oldest sons provided any support for their mother and siblings, and Mrs. Kern supplemented a small mother's pension check by keeping a male boarder. However, his presence aroused suspicion, and Mrs. Kern was warned to choose between her check and her boarder. Still "charmingly independent," she decided to keep the boarder. Despite the professionalization of social work, well under way by 1920 and credited with undermining the moralism of volunteer friendly visiting, Mrs. Kern was judged according to traditional moral standards. The boarder's sex, not boarding per se, aroused comment and led to an investigation. Mrs. Kern's aid was still governed by the criteria that divided the worthy from the unworthy poor.[8]

Mrs. Kern's children led to her subsequent encounters with social welfare agencies. Women such as Mrs. Kern had few economic options, and she chose to work as a domestic. She rose early to travel by several trolleys from her home to her suburban cleaning jobs. Most days she returned after 6 P.M. and, like many working mothers, she had to leave her children alone after school, and they soon got into trouble.[9] Sixteen-year-old Harriet and one of her girlfriends liked to wait around the trolley-car barns and flirt with the conductors. The police brought her into court in 1921 for being saucy and having a disreputable companion—not one of the adult conductors, but her girlfriend.

While adults sometimes were charged with contributing to the delinquency of minors, child-savers generally saw the girls themselves as a community menace and targeted them for arrest and intervention. Generally, this meant meetings with a probation officer and attendance at a girls' club or industrial school in order to provide some form of supervised recreation, although girls thought to be sexually active were frequently incarcerated.[10] Harriet's case was settled without a hearing and the court ordered her to join a girls' club, but intervention came too late, for Harriet was pregnant. She eventually gave the infant up for adoption and found a job as a ward maid in Boston City Hospital, but this ended her delinquency only temporarily.

Gerald Kern, fifteen years old, was the next child to be arrested. First, he was brought to court for gaming on the Lord's Day (probably shooting dice or playing cards on the street) and placed on probation. Later the police accused him of stealing a dog, but the court dismissed the complaint for lack of evidence. However, Gerald was neither working nor attending school at the time of his arrest, and the court took his old gambling case from the file and placed him on probation. (The juvenile court sometimes filed cases without a finding if a delinquent met the terms of probation. Then, if the juvenile was suspected of further delinquency, the old case could be reactivated and a delinquent sentenced without having to file and prove new charges.) Two years later, in 1924, the police brought Gerald to court for singing and loitering in the park, and Gerald, as a repeat offender, agreed to be sent away to the George Junior Republic, a private institution for delinquents that emphasized inmate self-governance.[11]

Gerald Kern, like many of the working-class children entrapped in the system of welfare agencies and the courts, had never been convicted of any real crime. He had committed status offenses—acts that would not be considered criminal if committed by an adult—and was incarcerated largely for being poor and without supervision. It is also significant that he went to a private institution; by the twentieth century, incarceration in the public reformatories was reserved for repeat or serious offences. The juvenile court that sentenced Kern was the climax of the child-saving movement, for it maximized cooperation among private and public institutions and shuffled delinquents among them. Its flexibility, lauded by Progressive era observers, permitted a judge to keep delinquents loosely supervised almost indefinitely, and, in Kern's case, created a record that permitted his incarceration for mischief.

The two younger Kern children, Abby and Lena, also attracted the attention of the welfare agencies. Abby, fourteen, began truanting in 1924, but the Roxbury Neighborhood House, a social settlement that the girls attended occasionally, sought to keep a warrant for her arrest from being served. However, the settlement worker changed her mind after discovering that Abby had been associating with a bootlegger who received police protection and used young children to sell his booze. The truancy complaint offered an opportunity to have Abby placed on probation, and the Neighborhood House offered to oversee Abby's activities.

Most settlement houses acted in a similar fashion, seeing the court as part of the social welfare network and sharing their concern over the leisure-time activities of working-class youth. Working girls' clubs, supervised dances, and athletics were staples of the settlement house social agenda for youth. Social and settlement workers also lobbied for restrictions on public amusement parks, nickelodeons, dance halls, and other commercial entertainments that catered to working-class youth. But by cooperating with the court, the settlement helped blur the line between private and public and voluntary and coercive institutions. As a result, neighborhood residents sometimes saw the settlement as an alien, even hostile, institution imposed on their community by out- siders. Instead of attracting working-class children into a bourgeois cultural world, the settlement made them wary of reformers' inten- tions. Quick to sense condescension or suspect duplicity, working- class adolescents attended these institutions but did not necessarily respond to their message.[12]

Twelve-year-old Lena also got into trouble by becoming a truant. The Family Welfare Society arranged for an interview at the Judge Baker Foundation, where the psychiatric team found her to be men- tally normal, but discovered that she masturbated and suffered from "sex ideation." They recommended that she be placed out and the Children's Aid Association, another private social welfare agency, tried to persuade Mrs. Kern to have Lena placed in a foster family. While the social worker who investigated Mrs. Kern found her to have a nice, maternal air about her, she reported that the home was clut- tered and not particularly clean. While it may not be surprising that a tired domestic with five children would turn her attention to things other than housekeeping once she arrived home, for social workers the state of the house remained an index to moral worth and maternal ability. The lax housekeeping, together with the records of her other children, suggested that Mrs. Kern would continue to have difficulty managing Lena. Nonetheless, Mrs. Kern refused to surrender her daughter, and the Children's Aid closed the case.[13]

The two older Kern children, Harriet and Gerald, experienced further problems around this same time. Harriet apparently drank heavily and picked up men, and in 1924, pregnant again and unsure of the child's paternity, she quit her job. Meanwhile, in an all too common pattern, Gerald learned more about delinquency while incarcerated. Although he wrote home that he enjoyed the George Junior Republic, Gerald broke into a store with another boy and stole money and shoes. Fortunately, both crises passed quickly. The Family Welfare Society refused Gerald's request for bail, but one of Mrs. Kern's employers agreed to furnish the money. Gerald was allowed to remain at the institution and eventually earned a position of trust as sheriff of the community, and planned on attending college upon his graduation. Harriet was determined to keep her second child and through the Catholic Charities found a place as a domestic in a family that allowed her to do so. Two years later she married and, although she and her husband separated for a while, they reunited and were reported as doing well.

Both Harriet and Gerald can be considered successes. Harriet was redeemed by marriage and domesticity, while Gerald sought individual advancement through education. It is likely that Harriet would have married regardless of the intervention by social welfare agencies, and the outcome of her case says very little about the ability of agencies to persuade working-class youngsters to adopt bourgeois values. However, Gerald's transformation from a youthful loiterer to a potential college student probably would not have occurred without assistance. Gerald was preparing to leave the working-class world and whether or not he attended college is less important than his desire to do so. The decision represented the adoption of a new worldview that emphasized future orientation, thrift, and individual gain, and sacrificed group solidarity for social mobility.[14] Gerald had internalized the values of a bourgeois culture, perhaps more so than other graduates of the George Junior Republic, who had more modest goals of acquiring respectability and who were notably unsympathetic to organized labor and loyal to their employers.[15] Private institutions, with their ability to work intensively with a small number of select clients, provided one of the few vehicles for effective cultural reform.

Abby and Lena remained the chief causes of alarm to social workers. A janitor at the settlement house reported that both girls engaged in sex delinquencies. Lena was accused of being immoral with several boys, while Abby had a steady boyfriend by whom she had become pregnant. Abby married two month before giving birth, but Lena was too young for this traditional road to respectability. The Baker Foundation examined Lena again and tried to explain the seriousness of her behavior, but she countered that girls were unable to have babies before they were sixteen. The consulting physician discovered vaginitis and a discharge, but noted that she "has not been injured" by her contacts. That is, her hymen was intact and, since penetration determined the degree of delinquency, social workers decided that any commitment to an institution would have to be voluntary. At a case conference all agreed that the girl was a candidate for the State Industrial School for Girls at Lancaster, but Mrs. Kern rejected the notion out of hand.[16]

Like the other public reformatories, Lancaster labeled the deviant and established the limits of acceptable behavior. By the 1920s, inmates guilty of sexual offenses dominated the inmate profile of the Lancaster school, and Mrs. Kern undoubtedly knew of its reputation when she shunned the suggestion to have Lena committed there.[17] Without evidence of "complete" intercourse, the conferees believed the Roxbury district court, unlike the Boston Juvenile Court, would not commit Lena to Lancaster.[18]

As in the nineteenth century, a girl's sexual experience was the single most important fact in determining how institutions treated her. Lena's school principal ordered her expelled because he believed she would taint the other children. Lena then attended another school, where she was placed in the class for the mentally retarded. Although tests had shown her to be of normal intelligence, sexual deviance was taken as prima facie evidence of mental defect.[19] Lena quickly proved too restless to remain in the class, and was transferred back to her original school. The welfare agencies and the schools were in a quandary: Lena's mother refused to have her placed out or institutionalized, and Lena, while disruptive, did nothing to warrant a court appearance.

The only avenue open to the social welfare agencies was to develop a case of neglect against Mrs. Kern. Mrs. Kern had indicated several times that she would send Lena to the Daley Industrial School for Girls, a Catholic boarding school, if she could afford the five dollars weekly tuition. The school did not wish to accept a girl accused of sex delinquency, however, and recommended that Mrs. Kern send Lena to the House of the Good Shepherd, a Catholic institution that, among other things, reformed prostitutes.[20] This Mrs. Kern refused to do for the same reason she refused to consider Lancaster. The SPCC and the Children's Aid decided to trick Mrs. Kern into providing evidence of neglect. They agreed that the social worker from the Children's Aid Association would make an appointment for Mrs. Kern at the Daley Industrial School. If she did not show up, the SPCC would file a neglect complaint with the court. The plan fell through, however, when Mrs. Kern, shrewder than the social workers thought, refused to allow the Children's Aid to make an appointment for her. Lena's record ends with this stalemate.

The lengths to which the social welfare agencies were willing to go and the ultimate futility of their efforts are equally impressive. Poor people approached social welfare agencies reluctantly because the results of their encounters were so uncertain. Financial assistance, if it were forthcoming at all, involved interference in private life, inspections of the home, questions about employment and personal habits, and possible reports to state agencies or the courts. An appeal to the social welfare network was an index of a person's desperation. Yet, despite their obvious power, the social welfare agencies could do little in the Kern case. Hemmed in by the law and rules of evidence and the customs of a democratic society, social welfare agencies were reduced to foolish plots. Agencies did not always agree on goals, and judges did not necessarily interpret evidence in the ways social workers thought they should, nor did judges follow the recommendations made by social welfare agencies for the disposition of cases.[21] Social welfare agencies cooperated extensively with juvenile justice institutions, but it is easy to exaggerate their power and impact upon families.[22]

While Mrs. Kern and the SPCC struggled over Lena's future, the youngest daughter, Millicent, became ill with a heart ailment. Admitted to the City Hospital, she stayed only for a few days before Mrs.

Kern took her home against medical advice. A social worker had recommended that Millicent be transferred to the almshouse hospital and Mrs. Kern refused. " 'I told her that if she came to get [Millicent] to take her there, she would do it over my dead body.' " Mrs. Kern tried to have Millicent admitted to a private hospital instead, and her employers agreed to pay the bill. However, the hospital refused to accept the girl, on the basis of unspecified social reasons. Mrs. Kern believed she had been blackballed because of her refusal to listen to the City Hospital social worker and her insistence on taking her daughter home. As a result, the girl, despite her illness, was either at home, playing on the street, or taken to work with her mother. It is not known what happened to her.[23]

One might well argue that Mrs. Kern acted irresponsibly, neglected her children, and jeopardized their well-being for her pride. Certainly that was the social worker's perspective. Rather than placing Lena in Lancaster, as was advised by the Judge Baker Foundation as well as several different social service agencies, Mrs. Kern kept her at home where she was almost certain to get into further trouble. She also refused to have Millicent hospitalized anywhere except at a private hospital, even if allowing her to remain at home threatened her health. These factors, together with the history of her other children, suggest a portrait of someone overwhelmed by her difficult life and unable to command the respect and obedience of her children.

Yet there is another side to Mrs. Kern. Several social workers, not all of whom were friendly to her, described her as being maternal, shrewd, and intelligent. Her employers thought highly enough of her to offer to bail her son out of jail and to support her daughter's hospitalization. The Harvard Crime Survey investigator admired Mrs. Kern for her independence and refusal to tolerate the petty slurs and demeaning investigations into her private life by social workers. Her older daughters gained respectability and Gerald appears to have internalized the values and culture taught at the George Junior Republic. Mrs. Kern's horror of public institutions reflected her awareness of their ability to label their inmates. Mrs. Kern's strategies for the survival of her family, seen only obliquely through the eyes of others, suggest the craftiness and strength of the "powerless" in their confrontations with authority.[24] She sought to gain whatever advantage she could from the social welfare agencies while attempting to maintain her dignity and defend her family against their intrusions.

In the 1920s, the fundamental choices facing the working class remained limited. Although real wages had increased since the nineteenth-century, working-class families remained vulnerable to unemployment, illness, accident, death, or the desertion of a spouse.[25] They could work for low wages, send their children out to earn, beg, or steal what they could to contribute to the "family economy," borrow from relatives or neighbors, subsist on the minimal support provided by social welfare agencies, or require some combination of these sources at different times in their lives. The very poor, such as Mrs. Kern, spent their entire lives ensnared by social welfare agencies.[26]

One is struck by the cost of Mrs. Kern's relationships with social welfare agencies, which added tremendously to the burden of being poor and did little to relieve its misery. Mrs. Kern wrote numerous letters, made many court appearances, endured frequent visits by social workers, fretted over agency plans for her children, had her affairs discussed with neighbors and with private and public agency representatives, and in the end had to solve many of her problems herself. Social welfare agencies determined Mrs. Kern's experience of class as much as her work as a domestic did.

Social welfare and juvenile justice institutions also defined the experience of class for working-class children. Boys, such as Gerald Kern, entered into the juvenile justice system by committing minor offenses, frequently "crimes" of a working-class street culture or petty larceny, while sexual activity, such as that of Lena Kern, remained the main form of female deviance, long after the supposed liberalization of sexual mores. Working-class children were judged delinquent because they were caught violating bourgeois conceptions of proper adolescence—through their use of the streets for leisure and economic purposes, their independence from adult authority, or their illegal activity.[27] The outcome of a delinquent's experience with social welfare institutions depended upon luck and gender as well as class. Gerald may have been exceptional—college remained an exclusive institution in the 1920s[28]—but the George Junior Republic fostered his aspirations for upward mobility. Most working-class youths were encouraged simply to seek respectability, which for women was defined as marriage, for men as participation in the marketplace at whatever position, for whatever wage.

If the Kerns had lived a century earlier, they would have had a far different encounter with charity, but no more palatable choices. The same could be said of each subsequent era. One way to understand the organization of this book is to see how the Kerns might have fared in each of the periods covered.

Charity, although simpler and more personal in the 1820s, also was more overtly moralistic. As is discussed in chapters 1 and 2, one of Joseph Tuckerman's ministers to the poor might have left a religious tract for Mrs. Kern to read, and, especially since she was Catholic, urged her to attend Protestant services and made relief contingent upon doing so. A well-do-to family might have provided Mrs. Kern with some sewing or laundry work and visited periodically to offer spiritual and moral guidance. Public authorities might have threatened Mr. Kern with the House of Industry if he begged money and idled away his time in taverns, but no agency or court would have interfered with his patriarchal rule of the family. Gerald Kern would have been subject to incarceration in Boston's House of Reformation, with an eye toward teaching him obedience and discipline, but few institutional settings existed for girls. If children escaped institutionalization, no clubs existed to supervise them, police courts were reluctant to try them for minor offenses, and the poor relocated with startling rapidity, making the opportunity for an extended encounter with a social welfare institution unlikely.[29]

At midcentury, the experiences of the Kern children would have changed more than that of Mrs. Kern herself. One alternative to incarceration was placement in a private farm school or in a Protestant farm family. Massachusetts reformers developed these programs, which I refer to as domestic reform, in response to the failure of congregate institutions, particularly Boston's House of Reformation. This is discussed in chapter 3. In addition, Massachusetts modeled the Lancaster School on the "family plan," and rebuilt the State Reform School for Boys along the same lines. The difficulties of applying domestic reform to public institutions are considered in chapters 4 and 5.

The arrival of large numbers of Irish Catholic immigrants (and the eagerness of Protestant agencies to take immigrant children and put them in Protestant homes) spurred Catholics to organize a parallel social welfare system. Although started in bitter rivalry, Catholic institutions had by the 1880s become relatively well integrated into the emerging social welfare system. As seen in the Kern case, Protestant and Catholic agencies referred clients to one another and the state cooperated with both. This is the subject of chapter 6. Also by the 1880s, reformers tried keeping families together if possible, and friendly visitors would have dropped off religious tracts and assisted Mrs. Kern in finding work as a domestic or in a garment factory. Home libraries, industrial schools, and settlement houses tried to control children's leisure time and provide alternative environments to their homes. These institutions provided edifying reading materials, military drill, and woodworking lessons, designed to teach thrift, precision, and order to an industrial working class. These developments are reviewed in chapter 7.

In the 1920s, the Kerns found that public and private, Catholic and Protestant, coercive and voluntary institutions cooperated extensively. Police and court officials, settlement workers and school authorities, psychiatrists and social workers, even janitors, discussed the Kerns' activities. At the same time, delinquency had become the province of experts using psychological language and concepts. The juvenile court, in the name of therapy and with the help of the diagnoses of the mental health clinic, sentenced delinquents such as Gerald Kern to probation, foster care, or the reformatory. Chapters 8 and 9 examine these trends.

Historians have generally studied class by analyzing workers and employers. However, persons excluded from the workforce because of sex, age, illness, or disability had their experience of class patterned by institutions other than the shoproom or the factory. Class was also defined in the relationship between donor and beggar, Sunday school teacher and student, home visitor and the visited, settlement worker and adolescent, judge and delinquent, reformatory superintendent and inmate. Furthermore, workers experienced seasonal layoffs, the effects of the depressions that ravaged the economy, mechanization that eliminated skilled jobs, and treks in search of work, which could leave them or family members dependent on some form of charity at least for a time. Accidents, death, or illness disrupted the family, leaving children vulnerable to the temptations of street culture and the intervention of charity workers.[30] Social welfare institutions formed the strands of a web of class that helped form the cultural and class identities of working-class youth. By encouraging adaptation to the values of the dominant culture, by reinforcing fear of dependency, and by institutionalizing and labeling deviants, welfare and juvenile justice institutions helped shape the working-class world.

PART I

The Creation of Private and Public Charity

I~N~ the early nineteenth century, reformers in both the United States and England sought to redefine the relationship of the poor to society. Welfare reform in both countries reflected the ideas of Adam Smith and Thomas Malthus, as reformers sought to cut subsidies to the poor and bring charity in line with the demands of the free market. Malthus, with his claim of having discovered the laws of population growth, was particularly influential. Relief, he argued, sustained the poor artificially and kept them from learning self-discipline—especially delayed marriage and reproduction—or from suffering the misery and famine that were the consequences of overpopulation. In England, the revision of the Poor Laws in 1834 limited outdoor relief (aid given to the poor in their homes), established the poorhouse with a regimen of strict discipline as the centerpiece of welfare policy, and announced the doctrine of "less eligibility." In the United States, most notably in New York and Massachusetts, public commissions on welfare promoted reforms along the same lines.[1]

Relief certainly seemed in need of reorganization. Boston, like the rest of Massachusetts, based its system of poor relief on the Elizabethan poor law, in which aid was linked to "settlement" (each community was responsible only for its own poor). However, this system did not work particularly well, even in the eighteenth century, as the surplus population in a stagnant agricultural economy moved about in search of work. Colonial wars also unloosed streams of refugees, who had little inclination to return home but who possessed no legal settlement in Boston. The municipal almshouse served as the refuge of the poor, but it was itself a problem. The almshouse mixed the aged, the young, the ill, and the insane together with able-bodied beggars and drunks, who presumably could work, and inmates constantly escaped. Other indigents received aid in their homes, but Boston's Overseers of the Poor were popularly elected and dispensed charity as a form of patronage, making a careful examination into the conditions of recipients unlikely. In sum, it was a costly, chaotic system, poorly designed for the eighteenth-century town, and utterly unable to handle the problems of the nineteenth-century city.[2]

Reformers read Malthus in this context and set out to remake the world of charity in the early nineteenth century. Private reformers—moral entrepreneurs—adopted one part of the Malthusian program: moral reform. They created voluntary societies to instill in the poor the self-discipline that would make poor relief unnecessary. Municipal authorities followed another, complementary path and created new public institutions to deter pauperism.

CHAPTER I

Moral Entrepreneurs and the Invention of the Reformable Child

The moral entrepreneurs were urban missionaries seeking to awaken the souls of the unchurched poor. They did not intend to organize welfare or to undertake the cultural transformation of the poor. But they confronted increasing destitution and the poor besieged them with requests for aid. Eventually forced into relief-giving, the missionaries organized a social welfare bureaucracy in order to prevent impostors from taking advantage of them. However, the missionaries' efforts largely failed. Unable to distinguish between the worthy and the unworthy poor, or even to settle differences among themselves, they turned instead to the children of the poor. They hoped to prevent pauperism by teaching children self-restraint and self-reliance.[1]

The missionaries were entrepreneurs in two senses: they defined a set of social problems and they created the enterprise of reform. The moral entrepreneurs discovered the extent of poverty, delinquency, and class differences in the early nineteenth century, they publicized the existence of social problems, and they established organizations to combat them.[2]

The Moral Instruction Society

The Society for Moral and Religious Instruction of the Poor (1816) was Boston's first urban missionary society, and it embodied the hope that moral reform might eradicate poverty.[3] Other groups had organized to relieve the economic distress brought by the Embargo and the War of 1812, but the Moral Instruction Society was the first to propose converting the poor rather than offering relief to a specific group such as widows or seamen. Established by business and professional men, including Pliny Cutler, a merchant and manufacturer and one of the wealthiest men in Boston, Henry Thurston, a well-to-do lawyer, Charles Cleveland, a broker, and Samuel Armstrong, a publisher, the Society investigated prostitution and urban vice and pressed religious tracts on the poor.[4]

The Society did not enjoy much success. They literally preached to the converted—the unchurched poor showed little interest in their work. As early as 1821 the Reverend Samuel Jenks, the Society's secretary, reflected in his diary that while some advances in ministering to adults had been made, they were "small & the prospect dim." Jenks believed he had failed to convert anyone and he wondered if "the Lord has rejected my labours." The missionaries' inability to attract an audience to their services led them to begin the "painful" duty of home visiting. The Society's female visitors, who repeatedly knocked at the doors of the most "ignorant and heedless" families, concluded, "we find some whom in charity, we think pious." If this condescension is typical of missionaries' attitudes, it is not surprising that few among the poor converted even while they besieged the Society with requests for assistance.[5]

Eventually, the Moral Instruction Society succumbed to conflict with the poor, who exchanged promises of conversion in order to get aid. Handwritten comments at the end of the 1830 report quote one of the Society's missionaries: " 'Am more and more convinced that there are very few virtuous and suffering poor.' " Such suspicions led the Society to complain that home visiting involved missionaries "with a multitude of cases merely secular" that they were not well equipped to handle. Some found themselves deceived by professional beggars with whom "the city is infested." The Society argued that its missionaries were not "*ex-officio* overseers of the poor." Reluctant to visit the homes of the poor, unwilling to provide relief, especially during a depression, and fearful of being taken in by impostors, the Society suspended its work in January 1838. Converting the poor—and reshaping their culture—proved more difficult than anyone had imagined.[6]

Joseph Tuckerman and the Ministry to the Poor

Not every missionary effort fared as poorly as did that of the Moral Instruction Society. Joseph Tuckerman, Charles Francis Barnard, and the other members of the Ministry to the Poor found a warmer reception when they visited the homes of the poor, no doubt due to their obvious sympathy. Tuckerman wrote, "I am received with great kindness and affection in the families in which I visit." However, even the ministers to the poor eventually doubted their ability to transform the poor morally. By the 1830s, Tuckerman and his ministers exhibited frustrations with the poor similar to those experienced by the Moral Instruction Society.[7]

Joseph Tuckerman presents antebellum moral reform's most humane face. He deserves reinterpretation, for he was not simply a forerunner of modern social service work, an apologist for entrepreneurial capitalism, or an advocate of harsh measures to control the poor. Tuckerman wrestled with the moral problems presented by a free market economy and he developed a range of responses to poverty and delinquency, including the first social welfare bureaucracy. Tuckerman's career represents both the possibilities and the limits of antebellum moral reform.[8]

Tuckerman was the best-known urban missionary in antebellum Boston. The son and grandson of wealthy merchants, he received a B.A. in 1798 and an M.A. in 1801 from Harvard. He spent the next twenty-five years in relative obscurity, as pastor to a small congregation in Chelsea, Massachusetts. Suffering constantly from poor health, Tuckerman began to look for an alternative to the strain of maintaining his congregation. In 1826, he heeded the call of his friend and mentor, William Ellery Channing, and "retired" to the post of minister to the poor in Boston. At the age of forty-eight, Tuckerman entered the career that brought him renown.[9]

Tuckerman always admonished his audience to treat the poor with respect, arguing that all men were children of God. He maintained that "the poorest, the lowest, the most degraded is the brother, and the fellow immortal of the richest, the most intellectual, the most cultivated, the most virtuous." In fact, society had as much to fear from the "licentiousness of wealth" as from the growth of pauperism. While he devoted far more attention to the latter, Tuckerman never lost his belief in the spiritual equality of man.[10]

Unlike his contemporaries, Tuckerman rarely blamed the poor for their poverty. In the late 1820s temperance became increasingly central to the bourgeois definition of character, and reformers perceived intemperance as the most important contributor to poverty. Yet Tuckerman argued that intemperance was a symptom, not a cause, of destitution. To be sure, he had little sympathy for idlers who wasted money on drink, and he believed that it was absurd to speak of the constitutional rights of those who refused to support themselves. Nonetheless, he maintained that persistent unemployment could lead to drink or even to crime. He blamed "society" or its "more favored classes" for the poor's intemperance more than the poor themselves. The poor had to learn to save their wages for hard times, but the "wise" had to teach them self-restraint.[11]

Tuckerman was equally sympathetic to others among the poor who were normally considered morally defective. He argued that young prostitutes were like children, "wayward and passionate, impatient of restraint; and vain, giddy and light-minded," who had grown up in conditions "too perilous for human virtue." Tuckerman did not absolve prostitutes of moral responsibility, but like the women evangelicals who organized rescue missions, he argued for a more sophisticated understanding of the class and gender relations that led to prostitution.[12] Tuckerman described professional beggars as "more sinned against than sinning." Given that they were treated as outcasts, owned nothing but the clothes they wore, and existed without friends or family, he asked, "is it surprising that they are debased and shameless; alternately insolent and servile?" In sum, at the beginning of his career as an urban missionary Tuckerman resisted the emerging bourgeois consensus that tended to equate poverty with vice, and it is likely that his views helped him gain an audience among the poor.[13]

Tuckerman's career also shows the limits of antebellum moral reform. His belief in the spiritual and moral equality of individuals, whatever their social condition, did not translate into other forms of egalitarianism. And despite an acute economic analysis of the causes of poverty, Tuckerman remained convinced of the inviolability of the laws of the free market.

Tuckerman accepted a hierarchical social order; nothing in his background prepared him for anything different. He used the social relationships in his former Chelsea parish to illustrate his goals for his ministry. Tuckerman believed that rich and poor had met before the church door, exchanged greetings, and then proceeded to the proprietary pews or the free seats "without the slightest feeling . . . that distinction of condition was thus implied between them." Restoring personal relationships between rich and poor did not mean erasing social distinctions. Tuckerman assured his readers that he wished to raise the degraded spiritually, and "not above their accustomed employments . . . nor above contentment with a very humble external condition." Tuckerman, whatever his sympathies for the poor, did not object to inequities of wealth and power and to the ordering of life by the marketplace.[14]

Tuckerman remained bound by the constraints of political economy in his analysis of poverty. He observed the economic disruption caused by mercantile capitalism, including the utter dependence of the unskilled wage worker upon his employer, the use of technology to displace labor, the inability of journeymen to become masters, and the poor's reliance on child labor for support. While artisan republicans used these facts to criticize capitalism, Tuckerman could not conceive of an alternative to the marketplace. He perceived structural problems in the economy, but there his analysis failed him. While he urged employers to keep up their wages as long as possible during economic downturns, he also noted that violation of the laws of political economy only hurt the poor. Subsidized housing, employment programs, and soup kitchens attracted "idlers and vagrants" from the country and created more problems than they solved. After discussing the economic causes of poverty, Tuckerman fell back on the Malthusian argument that the only real way to change the condition of the poor was "*by improving their characters.*" Tuckerman's failings were those of nineteenth-century classical liberalism.[15]

Changing the character of the poor meant having home visitors instruct them in bourgeois values. The poor, Tuckerman commented, indulged their appetites and sometimes were "intemperate, filthy, wasteful and improvident." They suffered from low wages, "but not half as much as from a misapplication of the wages they receive." Only home visitors could teach the poor to live without relief by training them to practice "forecast and economy" and to "exercise a present denial in view of a future good." Character reform, as much as the hope for religious conversion, underlay the work of Tuckerman's Ministry to the Poor.[16]

By the 1830s, Tuckerman had organized a small army of home visitors through the Ministry to the Poor. Tuckerman's first recruit, Charles Francis Barnard, was the most notable, for he took the ministry in new directions in his work with children. Barnard was born to a wealthy merchant family in 1808, and attended Harvard College and Harvard Divinity School before joining Tuckerman in 1832. The following year, Frederick Gray, born in 1804 and raised by his wealthy grandmother, gave up his partnership in a publishing house to join Tuckerman's ministry. Robert Waterston, born in 1812 to a merchant father, apprenticed himself at age fifteen to a Boston merchant, before leaving commerce for the Harvard Divinity School at the instigation of William Ellery Channing. He joined the Ministry to the Poor in 1839, a few months before his marriage to the daughter of former mayor Josiah Quincy. The Ministry to the Poor consisted of well-connected, energetic men in their mid to late twenties, who left the business world to devote themselves to careers in moral enterprise.[17]

The Ministry to the Poor was a religious bureaucracy that brought moral reform to hundreds of poor families. In reviewing the accomplishments of his lieutenants in 1838, Tuckerman found that Charles Francis Barnard visited 248 families, totaling 445 adults and 708 children. Over seven hundred children and adults attended Barnard's weekly services, while 542 children had enrolled in his Sunday school, with its forty-eight female and twelve male teachers and five assistants. Frederick Gray visited 230 families, enrolled 362 pupils in his Sunday school, and had thirty-eight teachers instructing the two hundred students in his sewing school. John Sargent, who had joined Tuckerman's ministry in 1837, visited three hundred families and counted 130 children in his Sunday school. Although it is difficult to estimate the number of children and families affected by the Sunday schools and urban missions, it is clear that after the public schools, they served as the most important institutional mechanisms for transmitting cultural values.[18]

In their meetings with the poor, Tuckerman and his ministers encountered the same demands for relief as had the visitors of the Moral Instruction Society. Out of their conflict with the poor emerged new efforts to organize welfare. After six years as a minister to the poor, Tuckerman became a leading exponent of Malthusian welfare reform, and public and private welfare in Boston reflected his influence.

Pauperism and the Organization of Charity

Tuckerman's experiences convinced him that Boston's charities had been too generous and had actually encouraged people to rely on welfare. As early as 1829 Tuckerman began calling for cooperation among charitable organizations in order to weed out undeserving applicants for aid. The deserving poor—those who could not support themselves because of illness, accident, temporary misfortune, or age —had a moral right to relief and could be aided most effectively by private sources who were aware of their problems. Others did not deserve to starve but, in keeping with the latest in Anglo-American reform thought, should find relief only in the municipal workhouse.

Tuckerman did what he could to make the workhouse the centerpiece of public welfare in Massachusetts. As the leading expert on poverty, he was appointed to the Massachusetts Commissioners on the Pauper System, whose report he wrote in 1832. Tuckerman took the extreme Malthusian position, arguing that all state relief should be abolished, with local overseers of the poor having the authority to compel anyone seeking aid to live in the workhouse until all assistance was repaid. In discussing paupers, Tuckerman shed his earlier sympathy for the poor and employed the moralistic language and categories of his contemporaries, with his environmentalism fueling his moralism. Just as home visitors might uplift the poor, paupers threatened to corrupt them. Therefore it was necessary to combine the workhouse and the elimination of public relief with the organization of private charity and home visiting.[19]

The Association of Delegates from the Benevolent Societies of Boston was Tuckerman's vehicle for organizing private charity. In 1833 Tuckerman asked the various ministers working with the poor to meet. Eventually, representatives from other charitable agencies were included as well, and they formalized their organization in 1834. They agreed to divide the city into districts for visiting, to exchange information about the poor, and to adopt rules to coordinate their giving.[20] They resolved to assist only families whose children were enrolled in school, to provide aid after a "personal examination" of the home, to give in-kind, rather than cash, assistance, and to adopt the principle of less eligibility that kept assistance below the lowest wages paid in the marketplace. They agreed that intemperate persons would not be relieved and that their families could receive in-kind relief only in dire emergencies. By restricting aid to the worthy and linking it to careful home examinations, private agencies hoped to convince the able-bodied poor that their choices were between the marketplace and the workhouse.[21]

The delegates from the benevolent societies proposed to eliminate professional beggary through interviews and cooperation. Agents gave out tickets to the poor, directing them to the Association's office for an interview. Before recommending that an agency assist an applicant, the office compared information from the interview with that collected from the member agencies. Home visiting remained at the heart of the system, both for giving advice to the poor and for collecting or verifying information about them.[22]

Tuckerman did not perceive the difficulty in combining home visiting, which was still intended to restore relationships between the wealthy and the poor, and the prevention of pauperism. He continued to insist that the Christian visitor "look upon every man, in every condition, as his brother," and that his goal was the instruction and salvation of "*each* and *every one*,"[23] but his aims were at odds with his methods. The prevention of pauperism demanded that a visitor be suspicious of an applicant for relief, at least until an investigation took place. In a situation hardly conducive to Christian brotherhood, a visitor had to inquire into a poor person's character and apply standards of "worthy" and "unworthy" in determining eligibility for aid. Conflict with the poor had led to the organization of charity and undermined moral reform.

The effort to organize charity soon foundered. Agencies were unwilling to surrender autonomy and were unable to agree on whether to provide assistance in specific cases. Even Tuckerman acknowledged that there were certain cases that he would not turn over to an association and would continue to assist privately. Apparently other delegates were equally adamant about keeping some cases. Moreover, when cases were discussed, delegates disagreed on how to apply standards of moral worth. One society would argue that a family was unworthy of aid while another "thought they were deserving, and continued to relieve them." Dissension led some agencies to drop out of the Association and the drive to register the names of the poor faltered. The spirit of the Association was kept alive by the Boston Society for the Prevention of Pauperism, which eventually evolved into an employment agency, but the successful organization of charity remained a task for a later generation to accomplish.[24]

The failure of the Association suggests the problems inherent in trying to divide the poor into the worthy and the unworthy. In a preindustrial world where employment in virtually all trades was seasonal, where alcohol was part of all social transactions, where work and leisure were not sharply delineated, where men and women migrated from country to town and back in search of work, and where the economy was advanced enough to produce periodic depressions, it was simply not possible to distinguish between a "professional beggar" and a laborer wanting work but needing relief in order to survive. The missionaries tried to apply subjective criteria objectively. It was easy to agree that sloth, intemperance, promiscuity, and lack of foresight were signs of a deviant character, but less easy to determine the measure of deviance in a given individual. Tuckerman's refusal to hand over some of his cases, and the delegates' inability to agree on who was a pauper, suggest the impossibility of applying the concept in practice. "Pauperism" may have been useful in organizing the world intellectually, but it offered little help in organizing charity.

Still, pauperism was a useful concept. It explained the increase in poverty without jostling reformers' belief that they lived in a benevolent, prosperous world kept well ordered by the marketplace. It invited the respectable poor to join in condemning the not-so-respectable, while all the poor were warned that the poorhouse was a possible fate of those who shunned bourgeois values. Finally, pauperism explained reformers' conflict with the poor. The poor who pretended to convert, who sought to deceive the missionaries at every turn, could be dismissed as paupers rather than be seen as men and women grasping at any source of survival.

The conflict engendered by almsgiving proved to be too heavy a burden for some missionaries to bear. Charles Francis Barnard expressed sentiments that must have crossed the minds of others. He noted, "I am getting to be more distrustful of myself,—my feelings, —the appearances of things,—and feel that I must use all means . . . of ascertaining the true character and the real claims of those who may apply to me." Barnard had become weary of the conflict with the adult poor over relief: "I meet with continual disappointment among the objects of my ministry. They deceive me in every point to get assistance from me, and, worse than all, they lead me into false hopes as to their moral and spiritual advancement."[25] Optimism wilted in day-to-day conflict with the poor, leading even the most generous to question moral reform, to believe in pauperism, and to find Malthus's harsh doctrines appealing. In order to escape the conflict over welfare, moral entrepreneurs invented the reformable child.

The Creation of Juvenile Reform

The inability to organize relief-giving, or to avoid it altogether, helps explain the appeal of programs for children. Children were poor through no fault of their own and reformers recognized that delinquents were made and not born. If reached early enough, they could still be taught the lessons of self-control and self-improvement that were lost on their parents. Belief in the plasticity of children's natures reinforced reformers' sense of poor children's vulnerability to slum environments and made child-saving all the more urgent.[26]

Tuckerman capitalized on the emerging concern with childhood by contrasting the absence of home life among poor children with the ideal of a tidy, comfortable home presided over by a nurturing mother. Poor children seldom washed, were dressed in dirty, tattered clothes, did not attend school, ate irregularly, drank liquor, and were "now caressed with the extravagance of intoxicated affection, and now beaten with the extravagance of intoxicated anger." They went out foraging for food or fuel, were encouraged to beg, and were illiterate and immoral. If taught at all by their parents, they learned to become "more wary, more cunning, more artful." At an early age these children became "deceivers, profane, lewd, and dishonest." The relations between parents and children were a parody of those in the bourgeois Christian home, with children "every day deceived by their parents," and parents in turn deceived by their children.[27]

Poor children were also not prepared to work. According to reformers, they were used to the independence of street life and the irregularity of day labor. When too old to beg, they worked as messengers, porters, pin setters in bowling alleys, or peddlers of penny papers and trinkets. They labored just long enough to acquire spending money for "vicious indulgence" and were never apprenticed to learn a trade. They were therefore unused to discipline and inclined to resist an employer's authority. Without intervention, they would become the inmates of prisons and workhouses.[28]

The moral entrepreneurs supported a range of institutions designed to interrupt the flow of recruits into the ranks of the unworthy poor. Among the most important were the public schools. As early as 1816, the Moral Instruction Society had advocated creating public schools, and Joseph Tuckerman and the Boston Society for the Prevention of Pauperism lobbied for "intermediate" schools for children who, for reasons of age and illiteracy, were excluded from the public school system. After several false starts, in 1838 the city established four intermediate schools, which provided rudimentary skills and lessons in self-restraint and hard work—the staples of a "moral education."[29]

For the most difficult children, reformers advocated the creation of a juvenile reformatory. The Moral Instruction Society had noted the need for institutional provisions for delinquent children in 1823, while Joseph Tuckerman had nothing but praise for the municipal House of Reformation after it was established in 1826. The reformatory provided a way to train poor children so that they could be apprenticed in a trade. Tuckerman argued that it was the only appropriate place for "vicious" children.[30]

Private institutions supplemented public ones, and Sunday schools undoubtedly reached the largest number of children. Sunday schools were organized along the Lancastrian plan, thought most efficient for the education of poor children. Here the model was the message: the Lancaster system embodied hierarchical organization and discipline. The teacher instructed the head monitor, usually an older student, who then passed the lessons on to the assistant monitors. The assistant monitors kept order and drilled the younger pupils in their lessons. Students exchanged places frequently, as the teacher rewarded the diligent by advancing them to the front of the classroom. Appropriately, the Sabbath schools reported their accomplishments in the number of pupils taught, the lines of Scriptures recited, the quantity of hymn verses sung, and the number of answers given in catechism. The purpose of the schools was manifestly religious, but the subtext included lessons in self-discipline, industry, and individual enterprise in an effort to counter the moral laxity of preindustrial or "traditionalist" cultures, which had presumably shaped the children. Success, as the Moral Instruction Society assured the supporters of its Sunday schools in the 1820s, meant that the lower classes would "cease to exist."[31]

The Sunday schools were not foisted upon a reluctant working class by an entrepreneurial elite.[32] The large number of pupils attending Sunday schools indicates that they met a real need. Reported enrollment reached thirteen hundred in fourteen schools in 1827, a pattern similar to that found in other cities. The poor were not manipulated into attending school, nor was manipulation the intention of Sunday school founders and teachers. Parents enrolled their children to gain an understanding of basic religious tenets, for educational benefits, and to participate in a common Protestant culture. Founders and teachers devoted their time, energy, and fortunes to Sunday schools because they saw them as God's work.[33]

It is a mistake, however, to ignore the class dimension of Sunday schools. Sunday schools reflected the power relationships of the larger society. The organization of the schools—funded, supervised, and sometimes taught by members of the entrepreneurial class—the structure of the classes, with their rigid Lancastrian principles, the lessons themselves, with their emphasis on order, discipline, and self-restraint, the subordination of poor children in worn clothes, reciting at attention before well-dressed visitors and board members—all reinforced the lessons of class.

At the same time, the lessons of class were not the only ones learned in Sunday school, especially since students forced the schools to meet some of their needs. For some students, the Sunday schools provided a way of learning to read and write without interfering with work. The Moral Instruction Society's teachers found themselves teaching literacy as much as religion. In order to attract pupils, the schools also provided gifts or entertainment. Children enrolling in several different schools might receive shoes from one and clothing from another. When a school offered prizes to pupils for bringing in new students, attendance at other schools dropped. The school with the reputation for the most generous Christmas celebration or the best summer picnic also attracted the largest number of enrollees. The students also shaped the history of the Sunday schools, and eventually the missionary groups were forced to consolidate. The Moral Instruction Society petitioned the city to take over the secular education of the poor, because it was too burdensome, while it merged its Sunday schools with a larger citywide effort that coordinated activities among the schools.[34]

The Ministry to the Poor proved more creative than the Moral Instruction Society in its activities for children. Charles Francis Barnard's Warren Street Church provided an antebellum forerunner of a settlement house program. The church offered sewing classes for girls, evening school two nights a week for children who worked, an "infant school" at which working mothers could leave their toddlers, a library and reading room, and music lessons for the children. He organized an annual floral procession on the Fourth of July, in which children paraded through Boston wearing garlands and singing hymns, and he trooped street urchins through the Boston Atheneum, a private library normally the preserve of blue-blooded businessmen and scholars, to gape at the statuary and paintings.[35]

Barnard received both acclaim and criticism. He broke with the Hollis Street Church and later with the Benevolent Fraternity of

Churches because of his unorthodox style and their jealousy over his success in attracting young parishioners. Some critics simply dismissed him as the "dancing parson." So many wealthy children attended his services that he was forced to require written permission from parents in order to forestall charges of raiding established churches. Yet the list of his backers—Patrick Jackson, Abbot Lawrence, Nathan Appleton, Charles Jackson, William Prescott, and others—was a who's who of New England mill owners and entrepreneurs. Barnard persuaded doctors, lawyers, wealthy matrons, and businessmen to teach his classes and serve as role models, and he encouraged children from different backgrounds to mingle in his "Children's Church."[36]

Barnard fostered the same hope for relationships between rich and poor as did Tuckerman and the other missionaries. It is unlikely that any degree of class mixing actually occurred in his church other than the pupil-teacher relationships common to Sunday schools. Nonetheless it is apparent that Barnard was an unusual reformer. Barnard's obvious romanticism and his iconoclasm suggest a personal charm that many youngsters probably found appealing. Certainly Barnard found his work with children far more rewarding than his ministry to the adult poor. He wrote, "I have almost wept for joy in the streets on noticing their [children's] manner of approaching me, on hearing the sweetest tones of their voices subdued and mellowed to the accents of truest affection." Like other charismatic reformers, who were the most successful in conveying the lessons of bourgeois culture to delinquent and poor children, Barnard seemed able to overcome bureaucratic inertia and class difference. He had the advantage of working with a selected group of youngsters who came voluntarily to this church, but still his accomplishments were considerable.[37]

Although reformers did not realize it, they were recreating the distinction between the worthy and the unworthy poor, only at a younger age. Efforts among voluntary societies focused on recruiting poor children to Sunday schools and recreational and vocational programs, where they could be exposed to the values of individualism, self-restraint, thrift, and industry—the cult of self-improvement—that characterized the rising bourgeoisie. But children were no more passive than their parents, and reformers created institutions for those who proved to be too difficult for voluntary societies to handle. The public reformatory—like the workhouse for the adult poor—underlined the message delivered by the moral entrepreneurs. The reformatory confined "vicious" children, those who willfully rejected the exhortations to reform. Moral entrepreneurs invented the reformable child, while public institutions defined the deviant one.

CHAPTER 2

Public Welfare and the Public Reformatory

Malthusian welfare reform relied upon deterrence, and deterrence was embodied in the workhouse. The workhouse magnified the fear of dependency by isolating and labeling the dependent. It reinforced the message of the moral entrepreneurs that dependency stemmed from individual moral flaws and that the poor had to learn the values of a bourgeois culture. And the philosophy of welfare that placed the workhouse at its core came inexorably to shape reform efforts for delinquents.

Massachusetts' first reformatory, Boston's House of Reformation (1826), was part of Mayor Josiah Quincy's "system" to restrain idleness, vice, and crime. Quincy envisioned a city rationalized by the marketplace and swept clean of madmen, the infirm, vagabonds, prostitutes, beggars, drunkards, and delinquents. Such deviants would be physically and symbolically isolated in a group of imposing institutions, the House of Industry for paupers, the House of Correction for adult criminals, and the juvenile reformatory, all located on the distant South Boston Bay. Poverty was placed on a par with criminality and the lines of deviance drawn for Bostonians of all classes to see.[1]

A second Boston mayor, Theodore Lyman, was also concerned about pauperism, but he linked it to the increasing Irish population in the city. In order to ready poor children for steady employment,

Lyman endowed a "manual labor school" that became the second public reformatory, the State Reform School for Boys (1848). Determined to learn from the problems of the municipal House of Reformation, state planners separated the reformatory from other institutions for the deviant and selected the rural community of Westborough as its site. However, the history of the House of Reformation was repeated at the state reform school: a brief period of humane conditions and decent treatment gave way to overcrowding, brutality, and inmate resistance. Ethnic and religious difference, the legacy of poverty, and the dictates of less eligibility confounded public efforts to reform poor children.[2]

The Problem of the Pauperized Poor

Josiah Quincy and the moral entrepreneurs took the fear of dependence that was an integral part of republican ideology and redefined it. According to classical republicanism, dependence resulted from economic relationships. Servants, apprentices, the landless, women, and the young lacked the basis for participation in political life because of their dependent economic positions. Capitalist development threatened to expand the number of the dependent by reducing the independent artisan to a wage earner, and artisan radicals used republicanism to form a powerful critique of capitalism. However, the moral entrepreneurs provided an alternative explanation for dependence. In their view, the free market liberated individuals to pursue their self-interest and it rewarded ability, but it also accentuated individual responsibility for failure.[3] While recognizing that temporary economic setbacks caused some individuals to need relief, most moral entrepreneurs argued, as did Quincy, that dependence was the consequence of idleness, drink, and moral disability. And just as mercantilism distorted the natural operation of the market, government interference in welfare simply worsened poverty and created paupers. The only source of real relief was character reform, not social reform. Quincy took this one step further. Unlike the moral entrepreneurs, he did not attempt to instruct the poor in bourgeois values. He created institutionally the paupers who could be condemned by all, and he invited all groups, regardless of class, to join in opposition to pauperism, and to divide the world between the respectable and the vicious.

Quincy began his assault on pauperism with an investigation of the Massachusetts relief system. State payments for poor relief had more than doubled between 1801 and 1820, and Quincy chaired a legislative committee that found the increasing cost due to the large number of "state's poor" and to the prevailing practice of poor relief. State's poor did not have a place of settlement to which they could be returned, and the state treasury funded their upkeep. Therefore towns had no particular reason to economize or to deter the unsettled poor from applying for aid. As for the settled poor, Quincy denounced the tradition of aiding them in their homes, which he believed subsidized vice. He linked poverty and dependence with moral failing, and charged that recipients traded food, coal, and clothing for liquor. Like other Anglo-American welfare reformers, Quincy believed that any form of welfare sapped initiative. The poor first thought of relief as a right, then they depended on it as steady income, and finally it destroyed the "stimulus to industry and economy." The only solution was to make relief as unattractive as possible. In so far as a relief system was necessary, it had to be based on deterrence: all outdoor relief had to be abolished and almshouses transformed into houses of industry, where the able poor would be forced to work for their support.[4]

Boston also found the cost of relief oppressive in the early nineteenth century, and the town meeting appointed Quincy chairman of a committee to investigate pauperism. Not surprisingly, the committee's findings reflected the opinions of its chair. "Indolence, intemperance and sensuality," the report concluded, accounted for two-thirds of the city's poverty. Aiding the poor in their homes was wasteful and liable to abuse. The alternative, the Boston almshouse, was too small to permit the classification and segregation of its inmates. No one worked and the poor were not even restrained: during their weekly strolls about town, they visited friends, begged, drank, and stole from local shopkeepers. The almshouse neither reformed nor deterred the poor, nor did it mark them as different, as object lessons for the working population about the consequences of failing to adopt a bourgeois culture. Only a house of industry could avoid becoming a "resort of idleness," and the town meeting voted to build one.[5]

The issue of pauperism resurrected Josiah Quincy's political career. The Federalist blueblood had served in Congress and then in the state senate, but he was a maverick even for the fluid politics of the time. The Federalist caucus snubbed the renegade aristocrat in 1820 by refusing to renominate him for the senate and including him only as a candidate for the lower house. He ran last among the Federalist candidates, an indication of his waning popularity. However, Quincy remained in the public eye as the author of reports on pauperism and crime. After Boston incorporated as a city in 1822, a coalition of Republicans and shopkeepers willing to buck the Federalist elite and wanting a government based on economy and free market principles turned to Quincy as their candidate for mayor. His expertise, his maverick political stances, and his lineage made him an obvious mayoral candidate, and his welfare reform proposals probably appealed to most taxpayers. Although Quincy lost the first election for mayor, he won in 1823. Once in office he moved quickly to confront the urban problems with which he had become identified.[6]

When Quincy took office, the city's House of Industry stood empty, mocking his vision of it as a hive of industrious paupers. The Overseers of the Poor, an independent board left over from the town government, resisted mayoral encroachments on its power and refused to end outdoor relief or to relocate the poor from the almshouse to the new structure. Curtailing welfare costs was not necessarily in the Overseers' interests, since they distributed relief as patronage. The Overseers' actions also suggest that they did not define poverty as deviant or seek to isolate the poor from the rest of society. The struggle over the House of Industry and outdoor relief represented an attempt to assert mayoral power and to destroy the political base of the Overseers. It also signified the enaction of a new conception of poverty and dependence.

Quincy eventually broke the Overseers' power. When the Overseers persistently refused to transfer cases to the House of Industry and went so far as to release a group of inmates who were about to be sent there, the mayor seized a portion of their budget. Later Quincy sold the almshouse out from under them, after the voters rejected Quincy's proposed restructuring of the Overseers' legal authority. When the Overseers declined to give a public accounting of their expenditures, the City Council passed a series of resolutions that ended the Overseers' authority over indoor relief. After 1825, the able poor broke stones at the House of Industry, while the Overseers controlled a dwindling budget for outdoor relief.[7]

Quincy's dispute with the Overseers also stemmed from his ideas about deviance. The Overseers operated the almshouse as a refuge for the poor without inquiring into the source of their poverty. Their lax policies indicate that they did not see the poor as particularly alien or in need of restraint or discipline. Quincy, on the other hand, had an entirely different framework for interpreting poverty and he believed that only the workhouse conveyed that vice and its consequence, dependence, would not be tolerated. Quincy was at odds with both artisans and aristocrats who did not share his market philosophy. Thus he concluded in his report on the Boston almshouse that it was not sufficient for the Overseers of the Poor to be men "in easy circumstances, prudent, intelligent and humane." Rather, they had to be "bred to business," and accustomed to dealing with men "in the laborious walks of life."[8]

Quincy shared his conception of deviance with the moral entrepreneurs, other civic officials, and a rising business class. The Moral Instruction Society and, eventually, Joseph Tuckerman and the ministers to the poor endorsed combining visiting and moral reform with a punitive public welfare system.[9] Reformers in New York, Philadelphia, and Baltimore responded similarly to increasing welfare costs in the late 1810s and early 1820s. Living in port cities with rapid population turnover, an accumulating proportion of poor people, and little economic growth, they believed it essential to restrict outdoor relief, to classify and instruct the poor, to deter applications for aid, and to segregate paupers in institutions. These men believed that existing welfare policies undermined the work ethic, encouraged reproduction among the poor by violating natural law, and subverted efforts to teach the poor self-discipline and self-restraint. Malthus and the marketplace reigned.[10]

Quincy's victory over the Overseers of the Poor marked only the initial success of his effort to define deviance through institutions. The mayor turned next to the House of Correction. Quincy had noted in his report on the Boston almshouse that the bridewell, a secure facility within the almshouse, was barely large enough to incarcerate unruly paupers, and had never served as a house of correction, as originally intended. Therefore in 1823 Quincy reorganized the Boston jails and began constructing a separate House of Correction adjacent to the House of Industry. The building stood vacant for a year after its completion, because of expenses incurred in other city projects and the reluctance of the sheriff and the Overseers of the House of Correction to give up the convenient downtown jail for the remote new facility in South Boston. To make use of the new structure, Quincy opened a portion of it to house juvenile offenders in 1826. Juveniles and adult criminals continued to share the same quarters until 1836, when the city opened a separate building for delinquents. By the end of his mayoralty in 1828, Quincy had physically and symbolically isolated the poor, criminals, and delinquents in what city residents referred to as Boston's Botany Bay. The reference, with its echo of British penal policy, suggests the success of Quincy's campaign.[11]

The House of Reformation

The lines of deviance, however clearly drawn around adult paupers and criminals, blurred considerably around delinquent children. Quincy wanted to reform delinquents, not to label them. His city swarmed with "idle and vicious children," at least some of whom could be saved from growing up paupers and criminals if restrained and educated in the proper environment. When the House of Correction stood completed but vacant, it made sense to use it as a juvenile reformatory.[12]

The House of Reformation reflected the dual functions of restraint and reform. It was a congregate institution, architecturally similar to the factories, prisons, workhouses, and hospitals erected in the early nineteenth century, with large dormitories, group workshops, and a common eating hall. Like these institutions, its success depended on the imposition of order. In the first report in 1827, the directors described how children took their places at the dinner table, ate in silence, and at the end of the meal, rose in order of the numbers assigned them and marched back to their quarters. According to one visitor, who observed the boys at their recitations, they compared favorably to the "Prussian parade at Pottsdam." Yet at the same time,

Reverend E. M. P. Wells, the superintendent, imbued the reformatory with his reformist spirit. A charismatic reformer, Wells through force of will and personality was able to dominate the institution, initiate reforms, and seize the public imagination.[13]

Quincy's choice of a superintendent suggests his belief in the possibility of reforming children. Eleazar M. P. Wells was born in Hartford, Connecticut, in 1793, to parents of modest means. Wells, who was expelled from Brown University for refusing to inform on a fellow student, studied for the Congregational ministry before receiving orders in the Episcopal Church in 1826. Josiah Quincy appointed Wells superintendent of the House of Reformation in 1827, and Wells used the position to establish himself in Boston reform circles.[14]

Wells emphasized education as well as industry. When he took over the reformatory a year after it opened, he ended the practice of leasing the boys' labor to local tradesmen. Under the supervision of manufacturers, the inmates had caned chairs, made brass nails, soled shoes, and woven baskets. Conflict was inherent in the system, as boys resisted being exploited, while the entrepreneurs became exasperated at the boys' "depravity and indolence," and swore at and occasionally beat them. Wells believed in education and, while the boys still worked, he reduced their hours to five and a half per day. The boys also spent four hours in school and had several hours for play, in which the youthful superintendent sometimes participated. Wells appears to have been completely dedicated to his task, even going so far as to sleep on a cot in the dormitory, with the keys to the school under his pillow, in order to secure "perfect purity and order."[15]

The most extensive account of Wells's superintendency appears in Alexis de Tocqueville and Gustave de Beaumont's study of American penitentiaries. The prominent Frenchmen noted that Wells adopted a trust system and expected the inmates to grade themselves, while forbidding them to inform on one another. At the end of the day, each child reported whether he had been good, bad, or average and the results were tabulated at the end of the week. Wells divided the inmates into three "bon" and three "mal" grades on the basis of this moral bookkeeping, with those in the highest grade having considerable privileges. They could go to Boston unescorted, swim or sail in South Boston Bay, and wear their Sunday dress clothes during the week. They served as monitors, supervising other inmates in their tasks, held keys to various parts of the institution, took charge of the marketing, and rang the bells, which signaled changes in activity. Children in the lowest grade were kept in solitary confinement, forbidden to talk, fed bread and water, and sometimes were handcuffed and blindfolded. In the case of a serious offense, a child faced a trial by his peers. Tocqueville and Beaumont praised Wells's administration and compared the House of Reformation favorably to similar institutions in New York and Philadelphia, where children worked longer hours, received less education, and were subject to harsher discipline.[16]

The reform school taught the lessons of an emerging bourgeois culture. Attentiveness to time, enforced by the bell ringing that signaled the start of a new activity, industriousness, promoted by the tasks inmates performed for the institution, self-discipline, taught by the self-reporting of offenses, regularity, learned through the unvarying schedule, and future orientation, suggested by the system of rewards promised those in the higher grades, were supposed to replace the values boys brought with them. Naturally these lessons, to the degree they were learned at all, could only be digested slowly. Inmates spent an average of two to five years in the reformatory, followed by an apprenticeship.[17]

Vocational training prepared boys for apprenticeships either to urban tradesmen or to farmers. A report by the Inspectors of Prisons in 1838 listed forty-three shoemakers, thirty-two farmers, twenty-one mariners, seven blacksmiths, and five ropemakers among the 135 boys apprenticed since the school opened. Shoemaking and the maritime trades were mainstays of the Massachusetts economy, as was agriculture, which had the added bonus of removing boys from the urban environment. The emphasis on vocational training became more pronounced after 1832, when E. M. P. Wells resigned.[18]

Wells was forced out of his superintendency because under his administration the reformatory violated the principle of less eligibility. The immediate issue was the cost of the reformatory. The City Council criticized Wells's replacement of the inmate leasing system with a more expensive educational program. They charged that the boys should have been subject to rigorous moral and physical discipline, and that the institution had strayed from simple utility and devoted too much to frills. Economy was more important than Wells's apparent success with delinquents. Josiah Quincy recalled that five-sixths of the 414 inmates under Wells's administration were reformed, but the City Council decreed that the reformatory was not to be a finishing school for the poor.[19]

The controversy over Wells's superintendency reveals a debate over the meaning of reform that went beyond simple matters of cost. City officials had to choose between two versions of reform: one based on education, the other on manual labor; one expensive, the other supposedly cost effective; one emphasizing self-restraint, the other imposed order. Not only did Wells's system deprive the city of earnings from labor contracts, but it also supplied boys more education than did the public schools. Children under the age of fifteen who worked in factories had to attend school three months per year, according to legislation passed in 1836, but the law contained no enforcement mechanism and did not affect many children. School attendance for all children between eight and fourteen did not become mandatory until 1850, and well after that date attendance was haphazard and confined to three months per year.[20] It is no wonder that few public officials shared Wells's enthusiasm for reform based on an educational program that appeared to reward pauperism. Reformatory inmates, almost by definition the children of the vicious poor, could not be given advantages the children of the laboring poor did not have. To do so undermined the deterrent function of institutions. The reformatory was not an avenue of upward mobility; it was part of a system to prevent vice, crime, and pauperism. At best, it would graduate law-abiding citizens prepared to be shoemakers, farmers, or carpenters.

After Wells's departure, officials instituted a stricter regimen based on manual labor, which in turn provoked resistance. In 1836 the boys made 850,000 brass nails per day for a local contractor while their time in the classroom declined. Discipline and overcrowding became a problem. A city investigating committee reported that the beds nearly touched each other in the dormitory, a situation thought conducive to group masturbation and possibly to homosexuality. Windows had to be nailed shut to prevent escapes, and the administration worried about violence. The Inspectors of Prisons found the boys dirty, neglected, noisy, rude, and dominated by a "spirit of insubordination and misrule." As an investigator wrote in 1840, "there are few boys who would not rather be censured by their officers than be nicknamed *sneak* or *spooney* by their comrades." Instead of inmates divided among themselves and vying for attention from the superintendent, inmates presented a solid front of resistance to authorities.[21]

The House of Reformation also came to house more serious offenders. Between 1826 and 1847, 981 children were jailed in the reformatory. Of these, 44 percent were charged with larceny or some form of theft; 25 percent with being "stubborn," a catch-all "crime" designed to give the court leverage over delinquent youth since no specific offense had to be proven; and 20 percent were vagrant. The types of offenses committed did not change much over time, but the records suggest that less delinquent children were being diverted away from the institution. For example, of 440 boys committed in 1851–52, 39 percent had prior arrest records and a quarter had previous commitments. As the City Council claimed, the reformatory had become a prison for young criminals.[22]

Decline seems an almost inevitable part of any institution's history. Charismatic reformers are replaced by bureaucrats, difficult cases accumulate, the racial or ethnic characteristics of inmates change, making them seem more alien to taxpayers and legislators, facilities age and funding becomes scarce, and reformers themselves move on to other issues or develop more effective techniques for reform that undermine established institutions.[23] But the decline of the House of Reformation did not occur because of some natural history of institutions. It can be traced to specific policy differences over how to treat the delinquent children of the poor. Wells's policy of reforming delinquents through education and the internalization of new cultural values was too expensive and violated the principle of less eligibility. With cultural reform rejected, no alternative policy existed to replace it; delinquents were not offered training but were employed simply to keep them busy and to reduce the cost of their institutionalization.[24] What had started as an attempt to reform delinquents became instead a juvenile version of the workhouse.

The experience of girls in the House of Reformation diverged significantly from that of boys. Their number always remained small and discussions about the institution generally ignored gender. When visitors described children's uniforms, they mentioned the white pantaloons and blue jackets and caps worn by boys, but no one commented on the girls' dress. Discussions of work hours and apprenticeships focused on male trades, while descriptions of the bon and mal grades seem applicable only to boys. Furthermore, while the vicious children featured in reformers' writings did not have any specified sex, the language used to describe them and their fate—marauders who might wind up on the gallows—indicated that reformers were thinking primarily of boys.[25]

The near invisibility of female delinquents stemmed from the ambivalence of male municipal authorities in confronting girls who were actually or potentially sexually active. Most male reformers echoed the thoughts of Tocqueville and Beaumont that "the reformation of girls, who have contracted bad morals, is a chimera which it is useless to pursue." Such sentiments kept the number of female inmates small and helped make the House of Reformation one of the least desirable institutional alternatives for young girls.[26]

The reformatory's earliest admittances illustrate the problem faced by institutional officials. After the reformatory opened in 1826, one of its first inmates was a young prostitute. The directors admitted her only after repeated requests by the police court and they decided to keep her strictly segregated from the other inmates. This girl's inclusion was a sign of things to come: one-fifth of the thirty-five girls accepted between 1826 and 1831 were sent for being "dissolute," which usually meant a sexual offense. For example, G. H., age fourteen, ran away from home and was discovered living in a brothel by her parents, who had her committed to the reform school. Good behavior led to a placement in a farm family, but after only two months, G. H. ran away. She returned to the brothel, where she was arrested, and the court recommitted her to the reformatory.[27]

Despite their willingness to accept G. H. after two stays in brothels, male municipal officials were ambivalent about reforming sexual offenders. Only a few girls were admitted each year and all, regardless of offense, lived a cloistered existence. Never numbering more than twenty-six, they had separate quarters from the boys, studied under different instructors, and during the religious observances attended by both sexes, the girls stayed in a room above the chapel and listened to the preaching and singing through a hole cut in the floor. For girls, the reformatory was a workhouse from the start. They worked so steadily at domestic tasks for the institution, including sewing the trousers and jackets worn by the boys, that they were given little time for school or for outdoor recreation.[28]

The reasons for this harsh environment were never explained but can be surmised. Keeping the girls constantly supervised offered the only possibility for quarantining the morally contagious. The directors claimed that girls who had been guilty of sexual offenses corrupted the other girls, with the "contagion" spreading from one inmate to the next. The boys were also at risk, since walls were "not thick enough, vigilance . . . not active enough" to prevent contact between boys and girls. The presence of a sexually active girl was communicated to the boys through her air and manner, even if no words were spoken, and awakened their "animal nature." Admitting the failure of their policy, the directors ordered all the girls in the reformatory released in 1840.[29]

The girls' wing reopened once it had been "cleansed," with the directors resolving to exclude streetwalkers and former brothel inhabitants and to admit no girl older than twelve. (The new requirements would have prevented G. H.'s admission on both counts.) But age and history were not adequate predictors of moral character. Most girls had no tell-tale history of prostitution; they were arrested on parents' complaints as stubborn, or brought in by city missionaries or police as vagrants or for petty theft. Reformatory officials could only guess as to a girl's purity, and apparently they guessed incorrectly. In 1842 the department again released all its inmates.[30]

Not surprisingly, the directors became leery of admitting any girls. In 1843 a single inmate remained in the female wing, and the city closed it so that its space could be used for the boys. The city began using a part of the House of Industry as a girls' reformatory, and so the reformatory literally became subsumed into the workhouse. The new situation was far from ideal. In 1851, the directors reported only five inmates, despite complaints of an increasing number of wayward girls in the city. While the girls in the House of Reformation apparently had corrupted the moral health of each other and the boys, the older female inmates in the House of Industry now threatened to do the same to the girls. By the 1850s, public policy was in shambles.[31]

This attempt to reform delinquent girls failed because of the conception of female deviance embodied in the reformatory. "Moral contagion" was not only a problem with girls—boys also learned to become more adept at crime while institutionalized, but no one suggested that they be released. Official policy reflected a belief that boys' criminal acts did not corrupt their core being in the way that girls' criminal acts did, especially since those acts were sexual. Illicit sexual acts unfitted girls for moral motherhood and threatened to ruin not only the girls themselves but also their future families. Male municipal officials simply did not know what to do: Did the reformatory exist to preserve young girls' sexual security? If so, how could sex offenders who might corrupt the other inmates be identified and kept out? and what could be done with the young girls found in brothels or on the streets? It was easier to concentrate on boys.[32]

Institutions run by women offered only slightly better solutions. These were private organizations and the inmates were, at least ostensibly, voluntarily committed. However, a minority were referred by official agencies or the police, and this probably involved some coercion. The most common institutions, prostitute refuges or "Magdalen homes," largely adopted the same conception of female deviance found in the reformatory. For example, Boston's Penitent Females' Refuge, with its female directors and staff, offered superior conditions to the reformatory and house of correction and welcomed inmates regardless of their past experience. But it was severely regimented and required a lengthy stay before placement in domestic service. It defined deviance in moral terms and it kept women steadily at work washing, ironing, weaving, cleaning—the same tasks that made prostitution seem a viable alternative to domestic service. It was basically a private form of the workhouse, and more inmates escaped than left by any other route. A more unusual alternative, the Temporary Home for Fallen Women, attempted to meet prostitutes more on their own terms. It provided religious and social services, and it did not require a particular length of stay. The managers allowed repeat offenders to return to the home, perhaps encouraging women to use it as a "half-way house" to get out of prostitution. Nonetheless, few women adopted the evangelical religious tenets that the managers thought essential for their reform. So while a range of institutional alternatives existed for girls and women who wanted, needed, or were compelled to leave the streets, it was a fairly narrow one, with the House of Reformation occupying its lower end.[33]

By the 1840s, in response to the intractability of the inmates and increasing numbers of foreign-born poor, reformatory officials began to describe delinquency as a nearly insoluble problem. They placed the blame on the parents, presenting the home life of these children as the inverse image of the Victorian ideal. Children inhaled "rum-tainted breath" from their mothers, heard curses and blasphemy from their fathers, grew up in filth and disorder, learned to speak by imitating profanity, developed intellectual skills by practicing deceit, and became thieves before they understood the meaning of private property. It was better, officials maintained, that such children die in their cradles. These were the unworthy children of the unworthy poor.[34]

The State Reform School for Boys

The appearance of large numbers of foreign born among the poor required new measures to interrupt the growth of pauperism and crime. Relatively few non-British immigrants arrived in Boston until the 1840s, when the Irish permanently altered the city's social geography. In 1850 the Irish accounted for a quarter of the city's population (by contrast, less than 2 percent of the population was African-American and less than 2 percent German). The Irish concentrated in the lowest-skilled, most irregular, worst-paying jobs and nearly half of the Irish in the labor force worked simply as day laborers. As a result, the Irish filled the workhouse, the jails, and the morgue. In 1858, nearly two-thirds of those in the House of Industry and half in the House of Correction were of Irish birth, while the mortality rate in Irish sections of the city was double that of wealthier districts. Irish immigration fueled nativism and spurred new reform efforts. As early as 1835, after nativists burned the Ursuline Convent in Charlestown, Theodore Lyman warned in his mayoral address that the Irish would never be assimilated and that their children would grow up in idleness and ignorance. Despite the failure of the House of Reformation and the pessimism expressed by its officers, reformers remained determined to reach the children of the urban poor. In order to forestall the social catastrophe he feared was imminent, Lyman proposed a new version of cultural reform—taking delinquent children out of the city and training them in the values of a Protestant culture. The offspring of the poor would not simply be trained to work as they had been in the House of Reformation, but would be transformed culturally and religiously.[35]

Lyman, heir to a China trade fortune, made the state reform school a reality when he donated ten thousand dollars for its creation. The legislature established a commission to investigate the treatment of juvenile delinquents, and Lyman's second gift of ten thousand dollars in 1848 and his fifty thousand dollar bequest a year later enabled the state commissioners to purchase a rural site in Westborough, Massachusetts, and construct an institution for 150 inmates.[36]

The state had learned some lessons from the failure of the House of Reformation. The commissioners built the reformatory in the countryside, far from other institutions for the deviant, and designed it to maximize security while minimizing the appearance of restraint. The buildings formed a natural enclosure, making an exterior wall unnecessary, and only trusted boys worked in the fields outside. The reform school thus escaped the fortresslike appearance of the urban reformatory. In addition, the reform school was to provide moral as well as manual training. Because so many inmates would come from urban, Irish Catholic families, farming and religious instruction became essential ingredients in the reform plan. First- and second-generation Irish Catholics, living in Boston or the Massachusetts mill towns, would learn the agrarian republicanism and Protestantism that formed the core of American culture.[37]

Boys were committed to Westborough not because they were criminals, but because they were poor and without adult supervision. Of the boys committed between 1848 and 1859, 43 percent were sent for "stubbornness" and 40 percent for larceny and other property offenses.[38] Stubbornness generally meant vagrancy or homelessness, while petty theft accounted for the property offenses. These were the crimes of the urban poor, forced to live on the streets because of family tragedy. Over half the inmates had lost one parent, while another 9 percent were orphaned.[39] For the working poor, even in the best of times, employment was episodic and the loss of the male household head (true for a quarter of the boys) forced families upon the kindness of relatives, the stinginess of relief, begging or petty theft, and institutions. Apparently Protestant families sometimes brought complaints against their children so they could be sent to the reformatory. For them, incarceration was part of a family strategy to have children educated and housed temporarily until their economic circumstances improved. However, Catholic families "endeavor[ed] by various expedients to keep their children away from this discipline and influence when complaint has been made against them by the officers of the law." For them, incarceration was another stroke of misfortune, an intervention by an oppressive state interested in stealing their children. Thus the children about whom reformers were most concerned entered the reform school least willingly and in smaller numbers than anticipated, and were likely to resist its authority.[40]

Irish Catholics formed a significant minority among the inmates. Of the 1,627 inmates sent between 1848 and 1855, 12 percent (194) had been born in Ireland, while another 20 percent (334) had one Irish-born parent.[41] Officials emphasized religious exercises to these boys. Morning and evening prayers, religious observances on Sunday, Sunday school lessons, and memorization of Biblical verses were all integral to the reform program.[42] A letter from a former inmate, published by the institution, indicates the image the administration wished to project. At a time when forcing Catholic children to read the King James version of the Bible in the public schools was becoming a matter of political controversy, the boy noted that he read all the books the superintendent had given him and he asked, "will you please send me the song 'We Won't Give Up the Bible,' as I should be glad to have it." Moral reform was as important as manual labor in remaking the children of the poor.[43]

However, the reformatory was from the beginning a miniworkhouse shaped by the dictates of less eligibility, and it avoided the academic "frills" that E. M. P. Wells had introduced into the House of Reformation. Although farming was the primary occupation at Westborough, it was not the only one. Local manufacturers contracted for the boys' labor, and the inmates spent six hours per day shoemaking or caning chairs during the slack season on the farm. Contract labor provided income as well as sources of placements after release. While no single employer received more than a handful of boys, the largest number of placements (232 by 1855) were with boot and shoe manufacturers, which reflected the industry's importance in the state's economy. However important the rhetoric about country life—and farmers received the second largest number of boys (218)—most boys were destined for the factory, not the farm. Boys were released to carpenters, tailors, masons, machinists, and tanners in the hope that they had acquired the discipline needed to fill working-class jobs.[44]

Boys found the reformatory strictly regimented. They arose at five or five-thirty, depending on the season, washed, and went to the schoolroom for prayers. Breakfast was at six or six-thirty and the boys worked from seven until ten. The inmates attended school from ten to noon, which was followed by a period of recreation and dinner. At one they returned to work until four, when they had another hour for recreation and supper. Between five and seven they had evening lessons followed by moral instruction, prayer, and bedtime. The institution was designed eventually to accommodate three hundred, but it incarcerated as many as six hundred boys by the late 1850s. In order to maintain discipline, boys were marched in lock step from one building to the next. They were required to work in silence and to request permission before addressing an officer.[45]

In the face of severe regimentation and authority, the boys developed their own subculture and resisted the discipline of the institution. Officials noted in 1852 that a boy who tried to reform was ostracized; his companions circulated reports "which have a tendency to make him an object of suspicion," or they taunted him "with some unfortunate occurrence in his past life, of which they have knowledge." Sometimes other inmates called him a hypocrite or accused him of forsaking his religion, a charge the administration found baffling, but which makes sense considering the large number of Catholic boys among the inmates. Boys shouted obscenities or sang at inappropriate times—such as during the Protestant services they were required to attend. Resistance also took the form of running away or refusing to inform on others. Perhaps the most serious signs of disaffection were the fourteen arson attempts between 1848 and 1859.[46]

On Saturday, August 13, 1859, shortly before six in the morning, cries of fire spread through the reformatory. A fifteen-year-old inmate from Salem, Massachusetts, Daniel Creadan, who had been sentenced for a minor larceny, took straw from his mattress, stuffed it into the ventilation system, and set fire to it. Although the structure was built of brick, with a stone foundation and a slate roof, the ventilation channels were made of wood and carried the burning straw throughout the building and up into the attic. The institution's rural isolation, a selling point when state commissioners had surveyed the site in 1847, now proved to be a severe liability. The fire company from the town of Westborough had to travel two and a half miles to the reformatory, while those from other towns had to go even farther. By the time firemen brought the blaze under control that afternoon, about two-thirds of the building had been destroyed.[47]

The investigation following the fire revealed terrible conditions in the institution. Inmates had been kept in solitary confinement, manacled to the floor in dark, poorly ventilated cells. At the time of the investigation, three boys had been incarcerated there for several months. Philip Breason, confined for twelve weeks for running away, had been served only bread and water for four weeks of his sentence. George Nourse had spent thirteen weeks in solitary for assaulting an officer, while Edmund Roach had been imprisoned for two months for attempted arson. Roach's case was particularly interesting, for another inmate, an informant for the administration, had suggested the arson plan, procured the matches, helped hide them, and then turned Roach in. Discipline had deteriorated to the point that officers constantly feared an assault by inmates and used brutal force to maintain a semblance of order. At least one teacher carried a revolver with him to class. The committee concluded that the reform school only served to "darken, harden and embitter" those imprisoned. The reformatory, once again, had become little better than a juvenile version of a work-house/prison.[48]

Acts of rebellion—understandable reactions to brutality—were also quite pragmatic. Boys in the reformatory were committed to the state for their minority (age twenty-one) and given an alternative sentence to the jail or a house of correction. Since the alternative sentence was generally shorter, a premium was placed on disruptive behavior since boys transferred from the reform school served their alternative sentence. Resistance to Yankee Protestantism was a second source of rebellious behavior. While piety cannot be dismissed entirely, it seems more likely that resistance to proselytism stemmed from cultural sources. First- and second-generation Irish-Americans had undoubtedly heard tales of rebellion against English authority. These boys experienced moral reform not as an invitation to adopt new values but as a familiar exhortation to abandon their faith and their culture.

The immediate causes for the decline of the state reform school were that planners had underestimated the number of delinquent children who would be committed to it, and legislators seriously miscalculated the impact of the alternative sentence. But these causes are not sufficient to account for what happened at the Westborough reform school, since its history is so similar to that of the House of Reformation and other reformatories. The whole reform program—removing poor children from the streets to prevent them from becoming paupers and criminals and providing vocational and moral training—rested on the erroneous assumption that poor children were more malleable than their elders. In fact, instead of being grateful to their "rescuers," adolescents brought their culture and religion, the undisciplined habits of street life, the burdens of poverty, and their family tragedies with them, and the institution became embroiled in the same conflicts that disrupted American society. Cultural reform was undermined by the determination to prevent pauperism and turn street children into productive laborers at the lowest possible cost.

The scandalous conditions revealed in the investigation following the 1859 fire forced public authorities again to rethink their juvenile corrections program. By midcentury the hegemony of the congregate institution was over, and reformers advanced new methods, more in keeping with the emphasis on family and domesticity in bourgeois culture, to attempt the remaking of working-class children.

PART II

Domestic Reform

D<small>OMESTIC</small> reform was a combination of traditional moral reform, a pastoral ideal that associated independence and virtue with rural life, and an emphasis on family and maternal training, which formed the core of the Victorian approach to children. The term "domestic reform" better expresses the intentions of reformers than "romantic reform," which is associated with anti-institutionalism and perfectionism, and which is usually thought to have disappeared by the end of the Civil War. Domestic reform continued to shape institutions for delinquents, particularly private ones, until the 1880s. These institutions rejected the discipline of the congregate asylum and demanded that delinquents internalize bourgeois values rather than follow an externally imposed order. Institutions stressed different aspects of domestic reform depending on their clientele: those for girls and young children emphasized feminine influences and a domestic routine more than farming, while those for boys placed a higher value on rural living and farm labor.[1]

Charles Loring Brace was the most eloquent exponent of the influence of the pastoral on delinquents. Watching plants grow, harvesting fruits and vegetables, and working with animals were all considered of natural interest to urban children. On farms boys learned "the best occupation which a laboring man can have," and they were assured of finding jobs at good wages where they would be "less exposed to temptations than if engaged in city trades." Brace argued further that

51

labor in the soil was "more medicinal" to diseased minds than work in shops. For Brace and other domestic reformers, rural life was a therapeutic response to deviance.[2]

Brace championed family influences as well as the value of rural life, and as such is an architect of domestic reform. Brace was not interested in simply turning out versions of Jeffersonian yeomen. Familiar with ideas about Christian nurture advocated by Horace Bushnell, whose parish he had attended in Hartford, Connecticut, Brace believed that family life shaped the child for good or ill. Parents were God's gardeners and the cure for delinquency was placement in a family—"God's reformatory"—where substitute parents could graft new values onto the transplanted urban child. While Brace promoted the immediate placement of children in families, the majority position among domestic reformers was to create "family style" institutions. These housed a small number of delinquents tended by "parents" who prepared children for eventual placement into families.[3]

Parents, especially mothers, were charged with the transmission of cultural values. As the workplace and the sources of economic productivity were stripped from the home, it became the locus of motherhood, child nurturance, and cultural reproduction. Temperance, thrift, industry, self-restraint, and future orientation remained core values of bourgeois culture but they were taught by mother at the hearth rather than through a network of voluntary associations. Institutions established around midcentury attempted to reproduce the forms of home and family in the hope of creating a better environment for the cultural transformation of poor children.[4]

The pastoral ideal and the nurturing home found their material expression in the Victorian suburb. The suburban home embodied the separation of male and female spheres found in Victorian culture, and it became a moral counterpoint to the greed and corruption of the urban world, even as it was supposed to help prepare the young to enter that world. The suburb also provided a sentimentalized version of rural life, with the garden providing contact with the soil without the drudgery of real farm labor. With home, family, and the pastoral ideal becoming so central to the transmission of bourgeois culture, it is not surprising that when reformers began to search for new models for their institutions, they found one in their own backyards.[5]

CHAPTER 3

Private Alternatives to the Asylum

A short story, "The Young Forgers; or, Homes and Prisons," published in 1859, contrasted the fates of four boys who had been arrested. Two, Frank and Mayhew, were saved from the juvenile reformatory by the intervention of a city missionary, who placed them in country homes. Eventually they returned to the city fortified by country virtue and earned their fortunes in business. The other two, A. Q. and Roland, were sentenced to the House of Reformation, where the other inmates further schooled them in crime. Upon their release they continued their criminal careers and A. Q. landed in prison for being a highwayman, while Roland, a murderer, committed suicide to escape the gallows.[1]

"The Young Forgers" echoed the beliefs of increasing numbers of midcentury reformers who thought that hope for delinquents lay in domestic reform and not in the congregate reformatory or with public authorities. Starting as early as the 1830s, voluntary societies created two alternatives for delinquent children: small, family-style farm schools that emphasized short periods of training before placement, and "immediate placement," which took wayward and delinquent youths from city streets and put them directly into families. While these two forms of domestic reform appeared together, first the family-style institution and then the immediate-placement model predominated. In each, the values of a bourgeois culture were learned not through discipline, regimentation, and a protoindustrial order, but in a model home.[2]

The most important of Boston's private child-saving agencies was the Boston Children's Aid Society (1863). Although it was not the first agency in Boston to practice domestic reform, it became a model for child-saving agencies both in Boston and nationally. Its history illustrates the evolution of domestic reform as a rival to the congregate institution as well as the eventual triumph of immediate placement within domestic reform.

The Emergence of Domestic Reform

The transition to domestic reform programs began with the founding of the Boston Farm School in 1833. E. M. P. Wells became its first superintendent after resigning from the House of Reformation, and the Farm School gave him the opportunity to implement his educational philosophy. The institution siphoned off the least delinquent boys from the municipal reformatory and offered them a program combining formal education, which included botany and husbandry, with extensive work on the garden plots given each boy. The school's location on an island in Boston harbor made a wall unnecessary, while its 140 acres allowed ample space for recreation and farming. The Farm School took some boys as young as seven and usually apprenticed them to farmers by age fourteen for the remaining years of their minority.[3]

As a private institution, the Farm School had significant advantages over the municipal reformatory. Perhaps most importantly, it was freed from the constraints of less eligibility. As a small institution with wealthy backers, the Farm School could experiment with any educational program it chose without raising the ire of taxpayers who thought that they were subsidizing the children of the "vicious poor." Secondly, it controlled its admissions, and, since parents/guardians surrendered custody to the institution, it had the option of expelling troublemakers or having them committed to the reformatory. Thus the municipal reformatory retained the most difficult cases while the Farm School tried to take children who offered the best possibility of success.

The choice of the controversial Wells as superintendent, the hours spent in school, and the emphasis on gardening make it clear that the founders were developing an alternative to the House of Reformation. Boys performed whatever agricultural tasks needed to be done rather than laboring continuously in shops under the supervision of manufacturers seeking to extract a profit from their labor. As a result, boys (ideally) internalized "habits of industry and order" and did not simply obey orders. The Farm School did not incorporate all the characteristics of domestic reform, lacking female instructors or matrons in its early years and failing to employ the language and symbols of family and home, but it provided a significantly different model of reform.[4]

The Children's Mission to the Children of the Destitute (1849) adopted the other variant of domestic reform: immediate placement. The Children's Mission acquired its name by raising funds among children in the city's elite Unitarian parishes. The Mission employed two agents, a city missionary who scoured the city's wharves and dumps looking for homeless youths to counsel, and an agent who took children with no prior arrest record from the city "lock-up" and acted as their probation officer. Both men sought to gain children's confidence and persuade them to go to homes in the country, and, in the 1850s, between 175 and two hundred children made the trip annually.[5]

Reformers never doubted that immigrant and working-class children would be remade as "real" Americans. By living in farm families, attending Protestant services, seeing the results of hard work in the annual harvest, and imbibing new cultural values, youthful delinquents and loiterers, like the fictional Frank and Mayhew, would be prepared for productive lives. The superiority of rural life was such an ingrained assumption that no thought was given to investigating rural families to ensure their suitability or to see that children and families were getting along. The idea that Yankee Protestant farm families could abuse or overwork children never crossed anyone's mind — placement in a rural family was de facto an improvement over what reformers thought passed for family life in working-class neighborhoods. Immediate placement, although adopted by a number of child-saving agencies, remained a minority position not because of concerns about abuse but because of fears about the effects of scattering delinquent children across the countryside.[6]

Both the farm/family model employed at the Boston Farm School and the placement policy used by the Children's Mission were modified by later agencies. The farm/family model eventually emphasized family values at least as much as rural ones, stressing the role of "parents" (superintendents) in molding the delinquent child's character. Placement became acceptable once it was done carefully and included more supervision of both children and families. Although domestic reform continued to evolve, by midcentury it commanded considerable attention.[7]

Advocates of domestic reform provoked a lively debate about the methods for handling dependent and delinquent children. They challenged the defenders of congregate asylums at the conventions of institution managers in 1857 and again in 1859, and the debate continued at the National Conference on Charities and Corrections meetings for the rest of the century. The split initially reflected that between public and private reform: all but two public asylums were congregate in the 1850s, while farm schools and placement programs generally were run by private agencies.[8]

The meaning of domestic reform is revealed in the language domestic reformers used to criticize the congregate asylum. They called it "artificial" and mechanical and charged that its management of children was "technical." It regulated behavior by establishing "outward obedience and general order," and it treated children as little machines. The problem of the congregate asylum was that it failed to reach the heart of the delinquent and create "true" reform. The congregate asylum may have regulated behavior and perhaps deterred crime, but it failed to convert delinquents to a new culture. Like the moral entrepreneurs before them, who used religion with the same intent, this group of reformers saw the cultural conversion of delinquents as central to their mission.[9]

The most radical critics of the congregate asylum advocated immediate placement. Placing dependent children in local families had been a common practice in colonial American towns, but Charles Loring Brace and other advocates of immediate placement proposed sending whole trainloads of children to the West. This position won no endorsements at the reform conventions, and eventually western states accused Brace and his imitators of alleviating the crime problems of eastern cities by dumping future criminals at their doorsteps. To gain acceptance, immediate placement had to conform to a domestic model, with the emphasis more on the family environment than on letting nature take its course with children deposited in the countryside.[10]

The farm/family school emerged as the perfect compromise between immediate placement and the congregate asylum. While the family was the "divine institution" for training children, the farm/family school was the next best thing. Charles Loring Brace conceded that some children needed training before placement, and called the farm/family school "something like a genuine family," in which each child had the opportunity to develop "an affection for the superintendent." Even the superintendents of the congregate asylums agreed that the farm/family school was worth a try. They endorsed it as "the proper system for certain classes of delinquents," and the convention voted that it was "glad that experiments were being made to test its applicability in the U.S." The most prominent experiment occurred in Boston.[11]

The Boston Children's Aid Society

The Boston Children's Aid Society (CAS) illustrates the history of domestic reform. It operated a probation service, two farm schools for boys (Pine Farm and Rock Lawn), and a home for girls, but it eventually closed all of its institutions and adopted an immediate-placement policy. The CAS also pioneered the use of social-work techniques and was widely acknowledged as one of the nation's leading child-saving agencies.

The Society's public image suggests that it formed a bulwark against working-class radicalism. Boys at Pine Farm did not have access to newspapers, but the news "they ought to know is read to them." In class they learned patriotism and good citizenship, and "simple political economy, especially in regard to labor problems." Such lessons protected society from "demagogues and labor agitators." The Children's Aid Society proposed to civilize the "young creatures" with a "distaste for work and sober ways" and "growing aptitude for marauding." Support for the CAS stemmed from "enlightened self-interest" and "Christian sympathies," since bad boys grew up to be worse men.

The ends of the Society "in these days of the tramp and of the illiterate voter" did not involve charity, but offered a "means of protection against a danger to society."[12]

Despite the rhetoric, the Children's Aid Society's records reveal many "Christian sympathies." The discovery of boys locked in solitary confinement in the city jail led a group of women to organize a society to instruct them. They found the boys

shut up by themselves, without society or occupation. They stand by their grated door, clinging to its bars, as birds cling to the bars of their cage, watching hour after hour in hopes of seeing the face of a passing visitor or officer; or they sit on the bed crying, refusing to sleep or eat.[13]

The ladies' benevolent intentions were thwarted, however, when the sheriff refused to allow more than two or three visitors at a time, and declined to let them teach the boys in groups.

Rejection at the jailhouse, along with the obvious need for preventive work, pushed the Society into an experiment with probation. Boys were taken directly from police court and released to the Society's agent, Rufus Cook, who was also the Suffolk County Jail chaplain. The efforts were apparently quite successful: the Society reported that of eighty-eight boys taken from police court and thirty-five from superior court, only seven had to be returned from probation.[14]

Despite its success with probation, the Society decided to establish group homes for delinquent children as alternatives to the public reformatories. Institutions afforded a better opportunity to shape delinquents than occasional visits from an agent. Moreover, the homes were located outside of the city and boys were able to participate in farm labor and to experience the affectionate discipline offered by the superintendent and his wife, who provided a surrogate family for them. The CAS opened its first home, Pine Farm, in Newton, Massachusetts, in 1864. The farm school, where boys stayed an average of sixteen months, provided a proper domestic environment as well as a rudimentary education. Upon leaving they were placed in farm families or returned to their parents. The girls' home, also in Newton, opened in 1866 and trained girls in sewing, cleaning, and general housekeeping before placement.[15]

The Society's Pine Farm epitomized domestic reform. A gentle "father" stressed reason rather than force in keeping order, while the "mother" taught civility and culture, and both sought the child's trust and affection. Imposing order and regulating the behavior of delinquent boys was the function of the public reformatory; domestic reform sought more. By applying affectionate methods of child rearing —sparing the rod and substituting the withdrawal of affection as punishment, appealing to reason, relying on guilt and the development of conscience—to delinquent youngsters, the Society hoped to have them learn the self-regulation from which the other bourgeois virtues stemmed.[16]

At Pine Farm a farmer and his wife, assisted by a teacher, presided over a "family" of about thirty boys, who helped with the chores as they would have in a real farm family. In addition to two daily sessions in the schoolroom, the boys made their beds, swept the floors, washed dishes, assisted in the kitchen, and helped with the ironing. All the boys planted, weeded, and cared for the fields. When work was slow, some boys shingled the barn while others mended shoes. Formal punishment at the farm consisted of confinement in bed or forfeiting dessert after dinner, but the more serious loss was temporary exclusion from the family.[17]

A monthly visiting committee from the board of directors soon recorded its approval of the experiment. The boys' recitations in school were "correct & ready," their bearing "quiet & orderly," and their expressions "frank" and "open." Visitors compared Pine Farm favorably to the House of Reformation, noting that the boys came from similar backgrounds, but those at Pine Farm seemed much more content. "We have not anything like as good opportunity & means as the city has. Why should we be allowed to beat the City so wholly out of sight, by our methods?"[18]

The methods of domestic reform contributed to the Society's success. Visitors described both Pine Farm and a second home for boys, Rock Lawn (1885), as "homes," with all that the word implied in sentimental Victorian culture. A visiting committee thought the presence of a staff member's small daughter at Pine Farm would help reform the boys. They would meet a "neatly dressed & pure-minded" girl "so unlike those whom they have been accustomed to see" and through her discover the "loveliness of womanhood," which was "second only to the influences of religion" in its "refining and elevating power." In a small institution, the caretakers could develop an intimate acquaintance with each boy, and realistically hope to have him internalize their values, much as parents might try to influence their children. Patrick Narcone, for example, was returned from a placement after having stolen some money. The superintendent hoped to have the boy acknowledge the theft, which he eventually did. "[H]e has written a letter to the man he stole it from confessing his sin and offering to make restitution & asking his forgiveness. It was very hard for him to do all this—the tears fell like rain."[19]

The private status of the CAS was a second reason for its success. The directors decided on the number and type of inmates each institution accepted. Thus the schools took only the more promising cases and they never confronted the problem of overcrowding that hobbled the public reformatory. Commitments to Pine Farm or Rock Lawn were voluntary and a parent or guardian surrendered a boy to the Society in order to avoid the reform school or to obtain shelter until a family crisis passed. It is likely that parents as well as boys thought commitment to CAS less punitive and superior to its alternative. In addition, the problem of less eligibility never arose. Some of Boston's wealthiest and most prestigious families supported the Society, so the expense and potential advantage given delinquent children by the education they received never became an issue as it did with the public reformatory.[20]

Yet the Society depended on the public reformatory for its success in a way that was never intended by its founders. Pine Farm and Rock Lawn kept order and yet maintained their gentle, familial discipline because they could commit troublesome youngsters to the reform school.[21] Boys tested the boundaries established by the institution and the commitment of the worst offenders reinforced not only those boundaries but also the lesson of self-regulation.

The Society tolerated some disorder but did not hesitate to have difficult boys committed. On a working farm, boys sometimes had to perform their tasks without immediate adult supervision and runaways were a constant problem. The directors recognized that escapes were unavoidable and commented that if they added "bolts and bars" they would "no longer have a home but a prison." Sometimes the Society gave up on a boy rather than risk changing the atmosphere of the institution. The agent allowed George Meade to remain at home in Boston as long as he agreed that he could be brought back to Pine Farm at any time to show that he had been caught. When resistance went beyond escaping, the Society took boys to court as an object lesson to the other inmates. Alfred Mingel had a temper tantrum at the breakfast table, swearing and fighting with the superintendent, after having been warned on several earlier occasions to control his temper. The CAS had him examined by a physician, who found no signs of insanity, and then had him committed to the reform school. After an arson attempt, the Society took James McDowell to court, where he was sentenced to prison. Giving boys the opportunity to fail allowed Pine Farm to see whether it was succeeding, while the threat of the reformatory and the prison kept resistance within limits.[22]

Most of the boys who remained at Pine Farm found a home there. The Society recorded with pleasure the comments of boys like Alan Austin, who had tried to run away two or three times in his early days at the farm, but who exclaimed when he was about to return to his parents in Boston, " 'I shall be homesick in the city.' " Alumni often appeared at Thanksgiving or at Christmas to share dinner with the boys and to express their gratitude to the superintendent. Charles English visited in 1879, eight years after he had been placed with a farmer in New Hampshire, and reported that he had found religion and was living a life of "usefulness and honor." Perhaps most appealing to Victorian sentiment was the dying wish of one boy: " 'Tell Mr. Washburn [the Pine Farm superintendent and "father"] that he was the truest friend I ever had.' " Indeed, some believed that the boys became too attached to Pine Farm, one visitor commenting that some boys saw family placement after Pine Farm as a form of punishment and were eager to "return to the sheltering care of the Farm."[23]

Shared religion and ethnicity provided parents, inmates, and the superintendents with a common bond, and help explain Pine Farm's ability to create a homelike environment. Nearly three-quarters of those in a sample of 354 Pine Farm boys were of either American, Canadian, Scotch-Irish, Scottish, or English origins and only 14 percent were Irish. (Undoubtedly birthplace masks some youths of Irish ancestry, but not many. Only 18 percent of the boys were Catholic.)

It is apparent that many parents of Protestant origin used the CAS to keep their children out of trouble or as a resource after the death or desertion of a spouse: nearly half of the boys were "half-orphans" while another 12 percent had parents who were separated or had remarried. Some of these families used the institution to shelter and train their sons until they could reassert their parental claims. For boys without families, Pine Farm provided the closest thing to a family that they had experienced. Mr. and Mrs. Washburn provided these boys with family life and they in turn became quite attached to the Washburns.[24]

Placement with Yankee farm families capped the CAS reform program for a majority of the boys and it was the logical outcome of domestic reform. Half the boys leaving Pine Farm were placed with farmers, only a quarter returned home, and 2 percent received urban placements, with the remainder going to relatives (4 percent), running away (14 percent), or being removed or receiving commitments to other institutions (4 percent). It is impossible to evaluate the long-term effect of the CAS program since nearly 60 percent of the boys simply disappeared from the records after placement. The remainder wrote or visited occasionally, or the Society heard from one alumnus how another was faring, but the successful tended to self-report.[25]

The absence of information indicates the haphazard nature of the CAS placement program, which was similar to that of other agencies. The CAS ran advertisements in newspapers and placed boys on the basis of letters sent by prospective families. Follow-up visits began in 1883, almost twenty years after the CAS started placing children, but even after that date no steps were taken to investigate homes prior to placement. Occasionally boys returned to Pine Farm complaining of ill treatment, but a boy's ability to run away or to move to another farm and make his own arrangements kept the volume of complaints low. Nonetheless, the Society began to reassess its program.[26]

Domestic reform did not work with all boys. Catholic boys had a difficult time in a Protestant agency, and although their number was small, they posed a constant problem. Until 1892, no Catholic priest tended to the spiritual needs of the Catholic boys, and thereafter they still had to attend Protestant services so as not to disrupt the "family unity." Not surprisingly, the CAS encountered charges of proselytism. Catholic boys (seventy-three in a combined Pine Farm and Rock Lawn sample of 437) were more likely to be orphaned than Protestant ones (16 percent vs. 5 percent), and had a slightly higher rate of placement in the country (60 percent vs. 55 percent). The mother of Francis Healy, accompanied by a priest, sought to rescue her son from a farm in Marlboro, Massachusetts, where he had been placed. The farmer resisted the rescue attempt, in which the mother used "force," but returned Francis to Pine Farm "thinking that the boy was not safe with him," and the Society placed him elsewhere. Such disputes continued until 1896, when the CAS agreed not to place a Catholic boy in a home until consulting with the local parish priest about its suitability.[27]

Prejudice against African-American youths caused difficulties in obtaining placements. In December 1892, Lawrence Gile, who had been rejected by two families, asked the Society to find out the political affiliation of the new family to which he was being sent, vowing that he would not go if they were Democrats. Fortunately, as he wrote his brother, who was awaiting placement, "they are full-blooded Republicans, and it is all right." The Giles had a black father and an Irish mother and their light color allowed the CAS to place them more easily than other blacks. John Rice was more typical: he was "a good steady boy" who could have been placed "a year ago but for his extreme blackness."[28]

The presence of blacks within the CAS institutions is a reflection of African-American poverty and vulnerability to family disruption. African-Americans were largely employed in unskilled jobs, possessed little wealth, and had a higher proportion of female-headed households than did the next-poorest group, the Irish. This economic marginality forced blacks onto the charity rolls but blacks, whenever possible, took care of their own. Orphans or deserted children were frequently taken in by other black families in an informal adoption process. Still, blacks were overrepresented in social welfare institutions and accounted for 3.6 percent of the sampled inmates at the CAS farm schools, which was about double their proportion in the population.[29]

Domestic reform faced its severest test with Catholic and African-American youngsters. Domestic reform relied on families taking delinquents into their homes and treating them like their own children.

Blacks and Catholics were unable or uninterested in becoming members of rural, Protestant families, and they challenged the notion that the poor could be made over by transforming them culturally. The problems with Catholics and blacks were a sign of difficulties to come.

Parents also proved difficult as they tried to manipulate the Society for their own ends. About one out of ten sought to break their agreement with the Society, which was interpreted as obvious evidence of their unfitness to care for their children. The parents of one boy, Sylvester Summer, wanted to have him sent home since the mother planned to move to New York City. The Society refused to relinquish him, arguing that he would not do well in such an environment under such "slight control." After some angry correspondence, Mr. Summer agreed with the decision. Mrs. Summer went to visit the boy before the family left, and while the superintendent was occupied elsewhere, spirited him away, and later claimed to have sent him to North Dakota. The CAS contacted the Associated Charities, "hoping that an outside visitor can find out what we cannot." The Associated Charities was unsuccessful, and apparently Sylvester remained in Boston, for in 1899 he was reported doing well working on a towboat. It is likely that the move to New York was a ruse designed by the parents to have their son returned once their family situation had stabilized. The case illustrates parents' ability to use the institution for their own ends and the limits of reformers' power even when they cooperated with other agencies.[30]

Gradually Pine Farm changed to meet the challenges posed by difficult youngsters and their parents, but each decision shaped the next and they were unplanned as to their cumulative effect. In 1884 the Society began placing young children who had not been charged with criminal offenses directly into families. This shift in policy, discussed more extensively below, expanded the number of children the Society could handle, but it had the added effect of drawing off a younger, more plastic population from the institution. A second decision the following year had a similar effect. Older boys remained at Pine Farm while the younger ones were placed in a second farm school at Rock Lawn. While there was no strict age limit and the ages of boys at the two institutions overlapped, boys at Rock Lawn were on the average two years younger (ten vs. twelve) than at Pine Farm. Perhaps because the boys at Pine Farm were progressively growing older and more difficult, the directors concluded that too much emphasis had been placed on training delinquent boys and not enough on wayward or vagrant ones. Even though the Society continued to take older boys at Pine Farm, it screened them more closely and declined those charged with crimes.[31]

The number of runaways increased over time, paralleling the increasing age of the inmates. At Pine Farm the mean age at entry increased from ten years of age in the 1860s to over twelve in the 1880s, and the number of boys who ran away increased by over 50 percent in the same period. One visitor wrote, "Rudd, Bigelow and White started to run away, but were caught before they got away. Hart and Berman ran away on July 28th but were followed at once . . . & brought back. . . . Hart has now run away some half dozen times." A few boys accounted for much of the problem and talked others into joining their escapades. A boy like John O'Brien, who ran away four times, had to be tied to his bed and fed bread and water for two days in order to impress other boys with the gravity of the offense.[32]

The Society also realized that farming was not an appropriate vocation for everyone. Sam Billings, for example, left his first placement after the farmer complained that he was lazy and had to be whipped four or five times. At a second farm, he also had problems. "Mr. Wilson could cover three hills of potatoes while Sam dropped one and became so vexed that he told Sam to leave which he did and went home." The Society decided to let Sam remain in Boston, where he found a job as a paper hanger and, according to his supervisor, worked well.[33] Recognizing that domestic training, farm families, and country virtue were not enough to prepare boys for an industrial economy, the CAS introduced carpentry lessons and printing classes at Pine Farm. The accumulation of difficult cases—older boys, those who could not be placed, and those who rejected country life—forced the Society to adopt measures that made it seem less like a family and more like a juvenile reformatory.[34]

Descriptions of Pine Farm in the late 1880s show how profoundly it had changed from the domestic environment of the 1860s. As in the reformatory, boys were segregated and classified, and their day was

Pine farm, n.d. Boston Children's Services.

Pine Farm looked like a farmhouse, not a reformatory. But in the 1880s, manual training, military drill, and a more regimented schedule were introduced, signaling the rise of a more industrial and less domestic model of reform.

regimented by the ringing of bells. Honor roll boys received special privileges, while troublemakers sat at a segregated "table of disgrace" in the dining hall. Boys arose at 6:30 and had fifteen minutes to prepare for breakfast, and another fifteen minutes to learn scriptural verses for the service that followed. They then worked until 9:15, when the bell rang, warning that they had fifteen minutes to finish their chores before appearing in the schoolroom. School lasted until noon, followed by thirty minutes of "physical culture" and dinner. At one the boys returned to work until five, when they ate supper. In the evening, boys drilled in military formation or played field sports until time for services. Bedtime was at 8 P.M. The informality of home and family, the gentility introduced by feminine influence, the whole substance of domestic reform had been abandoned.[35]

As domestic reformers tried to place more children into families, they undermined the basis for the family-style institution. The farm school had worked well with younger boys, but these were precisely the boys who needed institutional training least and who could be placed directly into families. Older boys were less susceptible to domestic reform, more rebellious, and more grounded in their cultures. Pine Farm's problems were not solved by rejecting boys with criminal records. Wayward or vagrant boys ran away and resisted the staff as frequently as had their delinquent peers. They had the same life experiences as did delinquent boys: they came from the same neighborhoods, the same family structures, and the same class. They seemed like the worthy poor, but they acted just like the unworthy poor did.

Thirty years after being created as an alternative to the public reformatory, Pine Farm had become a remarkably similar institution. Manual training (especially carpentry), physical culture, the classification and segregation of inmates according to offense, and military drill swept through the reformatories in the 1880s, and marked the arrival of a narrower conception of reform that emphasized training for an industrial economy, not membership in a rural family. The Children's Aid Society realized what its farm/family school had become and it searched for a way to revive domestic reform.

The CAS's experiment with delinquent girls pointed the way for the Society to go. The home for girls existed only from 1866 to 1872, and then, after seven years without a program, the CAS began placing girls out. The immediate-placement policy proved successful with delinquent girls, and it was adopted for the boys as well.

While no inmate records exist, the institutional records show that the girls' home struggled with the same issue of moral contagion as had the House of Reformation. Twenty girls lived under the supervision of a matron who taught them sewing, cleaning, and general housekeeping before they were placed in families. However, the family setting did not permit the segregation of inmates, and the problem of moral contagion soon arose.

Less than a year after the home opened, the directors voted to expel Fanny O'Reilly because of her influence on the younger girls. Soon another girl, Lizzie Hogan, a "fountain of corruption" who had been guilty of "almost every form of wickedness," was accused of "contaminating" the other girls. Before the directors decided whether or not to expel her, she ran away. In June 1868 an inmate burned the house down, and although the CAS had it rebuilt, the Society complained that it could not find "proper subjects" for the home and closed it in 1872.[36]

Placement provided the solution to the contagion problem. When a patron left the Society a bequest for the care of girls, it was so reluctant to undertake the project that the directors discussed going to court to see if the provision could be broken. When a group of women members blocked the move, the directors agreed to invest the bequest and use the interest to fund a placement program for delinquent girls. The "ladies' committee," probably hampered by lack of funds, placed only twelve girls between 1879 and 1884, but they took girls difficult to house even in the State Industrial School for Girls because "it was feared their influence would be bad on those around them." The ladies' committee moved boldly into placement and the rest of the CAS soon followed.[37]

By the end of the century child-savers had become leery of institutions. They argued that even the best of them were flawed and failed to maintain the family model. Instead of keeping children in these ersatz families, domestic reformers maintained that true domestic reform had to occur in a truly domestic setting. Only placement could promise this and therefore the CAS closed Pine Farm in 1896 and Rock Lawn in 1899. Because it was a private agency, the Society was able to close its institutions, reorient itself, and maintain its position as a flagship of American child welfare reform.[38]

The Triumph of Immediate Placement

The movement toward domestic reform begun at midcentury triumphed in the 1880s and 1890s among members of the social welfare community. The superiority of domestic reform was so self-evident that there ceased to be a viable debate. In practice, institutions for children continued to be founded—247 in the 1890s alone—as the South, West, and Midwest discovered problems of delinquency and dependency, and as immigrant Catholics and Jews established institutions for sectarian purposes. But the consensus in the reform community favored placement. The triumph of placement can be accounted for by the internal logic of domestic reform, problems with institutions, and the rise of professional social work.[39]

The Children's Aid Society embraced placement in 1879 and gradually expanded and systematized the program. After seeing the success of the ladies' committee in placing delinquent girls, the CAS decided to place younger children, for whom placement had always been difficult since they were too young to work. The Society paid families to board these children and hired Charles Birtwell as its general agent in 1886 to monitor their treatment. The Society also began to pay closer attention to the children placed out from Pine Farm, and hired an agent to correspond with and visit the farm families in which boys were living. Birtwell, who emerged as one of the nation's preeminent child welfare professionals while employed by the CAS, professionalized visiting and argued that all children should be placed. Birtwell constantly posed the need for family life and a "natural" home for children against the "artificial" life of the institution.[40]

The criticism that reformers had once made of the congregate asylum was now being used against the farm/family school. For Birtwell and other reformers of his generation, the artificiality of the institution was more important than the model on which it was based. Birtwell charged that some of the most important words in the English language were being robbed of their meaning. "That is not a 'family' plan' which means groups of twenty or thirty or fifty children under one roof. We misuse terms with the best of motives; we want to have everything seem as good as it can. But let us be truthful." In the name of the "natural," which by the 1890s had more of a domestic than a pastoral meaning, Birtwell pushed the CAS toward immediate placement.[41]

Domestic reformers maintained that institutions—even the farm/family school—did not turn out self-regulated individuals. Institutionalized children lacked independence and the ability to cope with life outside of an asylum. Just as welfare created paupers, institutions seemed to sap will and create dependents. One commentator feared that former inmates might as adults expect the government to support them. Only in a real family, these reformers believed, could a child see the results of individual labor and learn to make the transition to productive adulthood in the marketplace.[42]

Placement left farm/family schools almost indistinguishable from public reformatories. Pine Farm's history showed that as intractable cases accumulated, it became indefensible to house less delinquent children with them, and the entire rationale for group care eroded. With the decline of the institution, placement beckoned to reformers even more, and the rise of social work answered the main objection to placement, namely that it was haphazard.[43]

Charles Birtwell exemplified the shift toward professional social welfare. Birtwell lectured at Harvard, employed college-educated young men and women, encouraged other social welfare agencies to hire members of his staff, wrote articles about trends in social welfare, and became a spokesman for the CAS and child placement at professional meetings. He divided the CAS into bureaus, each headed by a paid agent and he expanded the number of children placed out from 133 in 1890 to 208 in 1891 to 300 in 1892. While each staff member supervised a large number of children and the degree of attention paid to each child can be questioned, the Children's Aid Society had moved a long way toward a modern, bureaucratic approach to child welfare. Social work made immediate placement acceptable.[44]

Placement offered social workers the opportunity to define professional skills, but its accomplishments for children were more limited. Boys had always found places as farm hands and girls as domestic laborers but few had become family members.[45] Over time, even the utilitarian motives for taking adolescents faded. While placement appears at first to be the perfect late Victorian reform—stressing the role of family and domesticity in the socialization of poor children—in fact it ran counter to the currents of family history in the nineteenth century.

Placement depended on families taking a youthful stranger—and a potentially troublesome one—into the family circle at a time when families were becoming smaller and more intimate. Bourgeois households had shed excess members, such as apprentices or boarders, along with the household's economic functions, and families lavished attention on their own children, whose period of dependency lengthened. Farm families as well as urban ones were reducing their birth rate and creating smaller, more tightly knit families. Placement eventually succeeded as a way of delivering children under three—most commonly female infants—into urban bourgeois homes. But placement of adolescents was becoming an anachronism even as it triumphed as policy.[46]

Domestic reform enjoyed a modicum of success. Family-style institutions operated under carefully controlled circumstances, insulated from the demand of less eligibility because of their private status, with a small number of children who were treated humanely. Placement policies promised an even better method of having children internalize the values of bourgeois culture because, ideally, children became members of the families in which they were placed while social workers monitored the match. In reality, placement did not work as reformers expected; it was not possible to accommodate all the children needing care, and families became more reluctant to take older, more difficult children. Moreover, placement did not work for children such as blacks and Catholics, who were too alien or troublesome for the Protestant families who remained the ideal sources of placements. Domestic reform succeeded—but only with a select clientele. The others were left to the public reformatory.

CHAPTER 4

Domestic Reform and the Delinquent Girl

Domestic reform provided a solution to the problem of moral contagion. Immediate placement promised to avoid it altogether by isolating a delinquent girl in a family under the eye of a mother/matron, who instructed her in domesticity and supervised her moral reclamation. But placement was not an accepted policy at mid-century and in 1856 reformers created instead a family-style institution, the State Industrial School for Girls (Lancaster), that trained girls prior to placement. The family-style reformatory, with its separate cottages, limited contagion by allowing reformers to classify inmates by offense, thus separating older, more delinquent girls from younger ones. Eventually reformers moved to immediate placement for younger girls, and by the 1880s, Lancaster housed only older, more delinquent inmates.

Domesticity provided the program for the girls' reformatory. Girls learned domestic skills and the cultural meaning of domesticity, and then were placed in families in order to finish their moral apprenticeships. Reformers hoped that delinquent girls would eventually be able to reproduce cultural lessons in their own families. This domestic reform plan was undermined by two things: the demands of less eligibility, which dictated that girls in a public reformatory be given narrow vocational training; and the actions of the families in which girls were placed, who treated them as domestic servants rather than as moral apprentices.

The Movement to Reform Girls

The advance of domesticity, a "sphere" within bourgeois culture that idealized the family as the locus of women's activity, highlighted the presence of unsupervised or disorderly working-class women on the city streets. Prosecutions for offenses against public order and public chastity (the latter involving female offenders nearly exclusively) surged in the nineteenth century as the streets, particularly the downtown business district, became the preserve of bourgeois decorum.[1]

At the same time that male officials became more aware of the presence of women on the streets, women reformers raised the possibility of reforming "fallen women." They questioned whether these women were morally responsible for their wrongdoing, and shifted the blame to the male seducers who had led them astray. In the 1830s women evangelicals organized missions to redeem prostitutes as an extension of their efforts to educate men to follow a single standard of morality. Such feminist efforts, which were more radical than those of women's benevolence generally, raised awareness of and sympathy for the "fallen" and made possible the creation of the state reform school for girls at midcentury. The reform school was not a feminist reform, however, since it in no way challenged male authority; rather, the founding of the reform school signaled the first step in what would become a separate incarceral system for women.[2]

Rescuing girls from the streets was key to the moral transformation of the poor. Street hawking, begging, and foraging, reformers believed, might make boys independent, but they always exposed girls to sexual exploitation or casual prostitution. Moral corruption threatened not only the girls but also the men with whom they came in contact and girls' future families, and thus their rescue was even more imperative. According to the act establishing Lancaster, the state had to prove only that a girl was leading an "idle, vagrant or vicious life" or was in the public streets in a condition of want in order to secure her incarceration. Girls could be sent to Lancaster because they had lost their families, escaped their families' control, or lived in families disrupted by alcoholism and poverty and were therefore in moral danger.[3]

Moral danger was particularly acute for prepubescent girls. Puberty loomed as a potential crisis in a girl's physical and moral development: physicians argued that physical or mental overstimulation marred reproductive capability and weakened the capacity for moral self-restraint. Working-class street girls were in obvious danger of overstimulation since the successful ones exhibited shrewdness in business dealings, engaged in sexual banter, and learned to handle male attention, while the unsuccessful ones were exploited. In both cases disaster resulted. Since their families did not provide them with the proper channels for female experience, reformers created Lancaster as a substitute family. The reformatory's domestic routine and its placement policy were both predicated on the belief that most wayward and delinquent girls could be retrained for motherhood and marriage, their sexuality properly redirected, and their cultural values refashioned.[4]

Saving girls, according to several reformers, was "sublime work" — at least in part because of the efficiency it promised in cultural reform. Rufus Cook, the chaplain of the Suffolk County Jail and an agent for the Children's Aid Society, argued that saving one girl was the equivalent of saving ten boys. Just as "bad" women furthered moral dissipation, "good" ones uplifted those around them. The trustees of the Lancaster School agreed that it was important to save a woman since "in her bosom generations are embodied, and in her hands, if perverted, the fate of innumerable men is held." Women made the "characters of the young and so of a race," and reform promised to ripple through generations.[5]

Domestic reform provided a new opportunity to reform delinquent girls. The House of Reformation, designed principally for boys, had no program for female inmates. Girls performed domestic tasks but this reflected a division of labor in the institution and was not rationalized as reform. Domesticity not only defined a problem, but it also suggested a theory for reforming delinquent girls.[6]

The Origins of the Lancaster School

Ideally, Lancaster resembled the Victorian family. The male superintendent was the somewhat distant head of the family, while the "mother" in the cottage supplied girls with emotional support, training, and discipline. Lancaster acquired its first female superintendent in 1885, but this did not represent a major change in the organization, function, or philosophy of the institution. Lancaster did not show traces of the radicalism of female moral reform of the 1830s, nor did it anticipate the separatism of female prison reform of the 1880s, with its emphasis on saving women from male exploitation in the prisons. Domestic reform shaped Lancaster from the beginning.[7]

The emphasis on domestic rather than feminist reform reflected the influence of the institution's enlightened but solidly bourgeois supporters. A group of Boston women in 1849 originated the drive to have the state establish a girls' reformatory. Mary May, probably the wife of Unitarian minister Samuel May, initiated the first of twenty-five petitions requesting that the state legislature, which had just created a state reformatory for boys, investigate the possibility of establishing one for girls. Women accounted for over 40 percent of the signatures on the petitions, and four petitions were signed only by women. However, if women were the driving force in this campaign, circulating petitions through the state's Unitarian and Congregationalist churches, they were not the only advocates of a female reformatory. Among the nearly thirteen hundred names on the petitions were those of wealthy merchants and manufacturers, constables and politicians, clergymen, and such well-known reformers as Theodore Parker, the Unitarian minister, James Savage, president of Boston Lying-in Hospital, Simon Greenleaf, president of the Massachusetts Bible Society, Moses Grant, president of the Boston Society for the Prevention of Pauperism and a director of the House of Reformation, and Francis Fay, president of the Prisoners' Friend Society. On one petition from Boston, eighteen of the forty-three signers were listed in Abner Forbes's *The Rich Men of Massachusetts*. This was neither a radical nor a feminist effort, but one by members of an established class.[8]

The state legislature equivocated despite the prominence of the petitioners. It delayed appointing a commission to study the matter, and when the commission finally reported, it concluded that delinquent girls required family care rather than institutionalization and that any state provisions for girls should be limited to housing them temporarily until placement. With this less than ringing endorsement of a reformatory, the legislature did not appropriate any funds.[9]

Samuel Gridley Howe influenced the commission's recommendations. Howe, a career reformer who fought for Greek independence, founded the Perkins Institute for the Blind, supported John Brown, and eventually became chairman of the Board of State Charities, feared that the commission would suggest a congregate reformatory, like the recently opened state reform school for boys. Drawing on his experience as a trustee of the Boston House of Reformation, Howe argued that a congregate institution would spread moral contagion. Only placement in a home ensured strict isolation and offered the individual maternal attention needed to reform a girl's character. Howe believed that incarceration would haunt a girl for the rest of her life, noting that he knew of adult women who were still referred to as " 'House of Reformation girls.' " Howe proposed that the state purchase a small farmhouse to keep girls for a few days until places could be found for them in New England families, which were reform schools "built up by God himself." [10]

Howe's victory over proponents of a reformatory was temporary. The reform school proposal enjoyed significant support around the state and the election of Emory Washburn as governor in 1854 provided an immediate impetus for change. Washburn, a Whig advocate of active government and a supporter of the boys' reformatory, urged in his inaugural address that the state build a reformatory for girls. The legislature, claiming that city streets were full of lewd, obscene, and profane vagrant girls, agreed that an institution was necessary. The legislature did not discuss the possibility of placing girls directly into families, which indicates that placement was too radical a solution to delinquency. Francis Fay, one of the original petitioners favoring a reformatory, became chair of a new investigatory commission that examined both European and American institutions before recommending that a family-style reformatory be built in the rural community of Lancaster. [11]

The Lancaster School was the first public family-style reformatory built in the United States, and the organization and architecture are significant. The Fay Commission specifically rejected the European family-style reformatories as inadequate: the French agricultural school Mettray was too militaristic, the German Rauhe Haus was too closely tied to German Protestantism, and the English Redhill required that inmates accused of criminal offenses be imprisoned before being sent there. Rather, they selected the model of the family as idealized in Victorian bourgeois culture for their institution. Lancaster, like the ideal Victorian home, was situated in a pastoral setting, was supervised by women who worked under the general authority of a pater familias, was dedicated to a secularized Protestantism, and emphasized home-craft. The institution was the perfect expression of domestic reform.[12]

Reformers, Families, and Delinquents

Both reformers and parents saw Lancaster as a way to preserve family, even though family preservation meant something different to each. For parents, Lancaster provided daughters with skills, some education, a job, and hard-earned respectability, while for reformers it offered an opportunity to reconstruct working-class families through domesticity and bourgeois values that could be communicated to others. For both it saved a girl from the streets or the brothel. For the girls themselves, Lancaster reinforced the limits of class and gender.

Mary O'Connell typifies the first girls sent to Lancaster. In late July 1862, O'Connell's father and stepmother brought her before the Roxbury probate court to complain that their daughter was beyond their control. The thirteen-year-old girl left home for days on end, "sleeping in the woods, barns and outhouses, [and] associating with both boys and girls." Her father feared that Mary would soon become a "bad girl"—probably a reference to sexual activity. The parents' testimony led the court to commit Mary to Lancaster for her minority. After thirty-nine months of training, Mary was indentured as a domestic servant. Mary received her discharge from state oversight on her twenty-first birthday, having spent over three years in an institution and five additional years under supervision, and having never committed a crime.

Mary was not displeased with her sentence to Lancaster. The matron who bathed her and cut her hair upon entrance to the reformatory reported that she was badly bruised, the result of beatings given by her parents, who punished her for not bringing home sufficient money when she went out begging. Her father, an alcoholic with six children, had married a woman with seven children of her own, and Mary's forays into the streets helped support the family. The officer who brought the girl to Lancaster called her "more sinned against than sinning." As for Mary, she declared that she would willingly go to Lancaster or "*anywhere*, save to her own home."[13]

Mary's case suggests three possible interpretations of Lancaster's role. For the founders and supporters of Lancaster, Mary was the perfect candidate for reform. The institution rescued her from the streets, from possible sexual exploitation, and from unfit parents, and restored her to the domesticity they sincerely thought best for all women. From this perspective, the institution culturally remade working-class girls and provided the moral training their families did not. For the parents, the institution offered the last hope of controlling their daughter. Mary was becoming increasingly resistant to contributing to the family economy and they feared the hope of freedom she saw in the streets. When beatings no longer kept her obedient, the family decided to forgo her earnings and deposit an impossible burden with the state. The streets had transformed their daughter from an asset to a liability and the reformatory would prevent her permanent ruin. For Mary, Lancaster offered a refuge from her drunken and abusive father, from a stepmother's usurpation of authority, from the mirage of independence offered by men in barns and outhouses. It did not open any new avenues for her; it simply pointed her toward the narrow road of hard work and respectability.

Lancaster, according to reformers, provided a family for girls like Mary O'Connell. Small cottages housed the girls under the supervision of a matron, referred to as the "mother" of the "family," an assistant matron, who doubled as a teacher, and a housekeeper. Each cottage provided a separate environment with its own kitchen, washroom, parlor, schoolroom, workroom, and the girls' bedrooms. The cottage was large enough that each girl could have a single room if necessary, and there was a basement room for solitary confinement. As befit the family image, cottage windows were not barred and the reformatory did not have an exterior wall. The girls learned to cook, sew, knit, and perform other domestic tasks in addition to their school work. The reformatory sought to teach girls "industry, economy, self-reliance, morality and religion" and to maintain order with "*the cords of love*." Indeed, annual reports maintained, the "mother" (matron) welcomed back runaways with open arms, expressing her pleasure that her children had returned. Officials hoped that each girl would learn "a home interest, a home feeling and attachment" at the school.[14]

Life at Lancaster was marked by ritual and routine. Newly admitted girls underwent a rite of purification: their old clothing was burned, and the girls were bathed, groomed, and given physical examinations before being issued a new set of clothes. The girls all followed the same schedule and domestic chores dominated the day. They arose at six to straighten up the rooms and to prepare breakfast, which they ate at seven. Household chores were done until 9 A.M., when chapel services began. After services they worked at household tasks again until dinner at noon, and they began school at 1:30 P.M. At four-thirty they quit school and got ready for supper at 5 P.M. After supper, they sewed, knit, or read until eight, when prayers were followed by bed. The schedule left approximately an hour free, which the girls presumably used for recreation. Unlike private asylums for poor orphan girls, Lancaster provided a limited education. Despite the claims of domestic reform that girls would acquire the values of a new, bourgeois culture, in practice less eligibility restricted training to learning household tasks and the rudiments of reading and writing.[15]

Initially, the "families" held girls of all ages without regard to offense, an approach the trustees considered natural and conducive to reform. Mixing the girls had the advantage of dividing the more "intractable" among the different cottages, and thus preventing them from forming "combinations to resist authority." Meanwhile the younger girls, less independent and more in need of kindness and affection, formed close bonds with the matron and the assistants. They became "a kind of unconscious police" who reported "vicious habits, conversation, or plans of insubordination" to the matron.[16]

While useful for maintaining order, mixing girls raised the issue of moral contagion. Sexually active girls, not girls like Mary O'Connell, posed the greatest difficulty for the institution. In a survey of asylum superintendents and reformers conducted prior to Lancaster's opening, the consensus was that girls who had lost their chastity could be admitted only if they were kept strictly segregated from the other girls. The administration preferred to exclude the sexually experienced, but this was not easily accomplished.[17]

Bradford Peirce, the superintendent and chaplain of Lancaster, had the difficult job of determining the nature of girls' sexual experience. He drew the line at girls involved in commercialized vice, arguing that keeping such girls under constant surveillance would disrupt the family environment. Peirce admitted some sexually active girls and soon took advantage of the family-style reformatory's ability to isolate particular offenders. He requested two additional cottages so that the younger girls could be housed apart from other inmates. He noted in his second report that forty-five of one hundred inmates had committed offenses against purity, although he added that in most cases the offense was "personal" rather than "social." Despite precautions, the problem of moral contagion arose. Some girls pitched "their tents toward Sodom" and had to be released. Still, the family system meant that "contagion" was limited.[18]

The girls in Lancaster had learned about vice because their family situations had left them vulnerable. In many ways, the girls could have been (and in the first year one-fifth of the girls were) the sisters of the boys at the state reform school. They came from working-class families broken by poverty and the death of a parent. Of the inmates received between 1856 and 1860, only 21 percent came from two-parent households. Lancaster girls were the children of the foreign born—nearly three-quarters of the parents were born in Ireland—and their parents held jobs in the least-skilled and most capricious sectors of the labor market, as laborers, unskilled mill hands, and domestics. The children of the unworthy poor, these girls begged, peddled matches and apples, and stole to contribute to the family economy, and the streets supplied their education. Only in one respect did the girls at Lancaster differ from the boys in the reform school. For the first year's inmates, over 40 percent of the complainants were family members.[19]

It is a telling fact that Irish Catholic parents took their daughters to probate court and had them committed to a public institution in which Protestantism was central to the definition of reform. Parents shrank from a daughter's prospective prostitution. For them, prostitution was not considered simply one of several bad bargains working-class women had to choose among. To preserve a daughter from "ruin" they were willing to forgo her earnings and risk the possibility of her religious conversion.[20] Parents did not have to accept bourgeois values to come to this conclusion. Rather, traditional Irish culture proscribed women's roles in a way that fit well with bourgeois domesticity in the United States, and parents saw in Lancaster the opportunity to defend their daughters according to the values of their culture. Traditions of gender segregation, late marriage, celibacy, and low rates of illegitimacy in Ireland suggest why parents were willing to cloister their daughters in a state institution. To preserve them from the casual interaction with men and precocious sexual experience that characterized street life in American cities, they were willing to take extraordinary steps. Despite differences in class and religion, parents and reformers shared similar cultural proscriptions about the proper expression of female sexuality.[21]

Placement

Parents and reformers expected that placement in a family would continue the reform program once girls left Lancaster. Parents, especially the Irish, saw placement as a familiar form of domestic service, a difficult but honorable way of earning a living and one that kept their daughters confined to a proper domestic sphere. Reformers saw placement as an apprenticeship in which, under the care and loving attention of a kindly matron, girls were supposed to learn how to manage a household, provide children with a moral education, set the "tone" of the family—in short, to shed their immigrant and working-class heritage and model themselves on New England matrons. In the first report, the superintendent, perhaps expressing as much hope as reality, announced that already there were requests to take the girls into families as "children." His optimism was unfounded.[22]

The trustees soon recorded their disappointment at families' reasons for taking girls. "Too many apply for girls from sordid or selfish motives, to make menials of them" rather than regarding the placement of a girl as a "sacred trust." Trustees chided families for taking fourteen- or fifteen-year-old girls and expecting them to be perfectly reliable, "to know their place and keep it; to do exactly as they are told; not to be impertinent or bold, or careless," and to be better than the hired help available. Women, who managed the household, did not extend to these girls the maternal "sympathy, kindness and affection" that was the only way to secure their "attachment and cheerful obedience and fidelity." Rather, they complained that girls were saucy or too interested in boys, or stole or wasted the family's resources. One woman wrote that the girl placed in her home had to be returned to Lancaster because she was "slack and childish." She would "leave work and play with children all day long." Another complained that her girl "wants all the privileges the children have," while a Mrs. Hazelton noted simply that her girl "does not keep her place." Girls acted like the adolescents they were rather than like the servants their mistresses wanted.[23]

Another problem was that over time fewer girls wished to go into domestic service. Women in the late nineteenth century had more employment opportunities than earlier, which made domestic work less desirable. Labor statistician Carroll Wright surveyed women's employment in Boston in 1880 and found that 41 percent of Boston's working women were employed as domestics, with another 25 percent working in clothing manufacturing. Occupations reflected ethnicity; Irish women dominated domestic service, accounting for 43 percent of the total, while American-born women accounted for 68 percent of those in clothing manufacturing and 70 percent of those in all manufacturing.[24] While a market for domestics certainly existed, it was starting to attract fewer American-born white women, suggesting that Lancaster girls, three-quarters of whom were American born, would have been less likely to choose domestic work if left on their own. Moreover, other ethnic groups—such as Italians—gradually appeared in Lancaster's ethnic profile and they too were loath to go into domestic service. Nonetheless, in a sample of 417 inmate records taken between 1870 and 1939, 60 percent were indentured into families immediately after training. When stratified by decades, the sample reveals that not until 1920s were fewer than half of the girls placed in domestic service. More than the marketplace and the chronic shortage of domestics were at work here. Lancaster officials endorsed domestic work, commenting that "families of the middle class" provided the "safest places and best homes there are" for working-class girls. Experience proved them wrong on these counts too.[25]

Sexual exploitation, although rarely discussed, confronted Lancaster's parolees. A sample of case records did not reveal instances of sexual abuse in employers' families, but these occurrences may not have been recorded in order to save families from embarrassment. The trustees admitted that girls "too often meet passion and lust" in their families and had to be returned to Lancaster. On another occasion they wrote that the girls provided temptations that "we have known the respected heads of some families to fall before." Lancaster officials were not responsible for the lechery of some men, but one can imagine the impact on a young woman "saved" from the streets only to be placed in a position of being sexually exploited by her foster "father." There is a certain irony, as well, to placing girls into domestic service, since that was the major occupation cited by prostitutes as their previous employment. Working-class women had a narrow range of choices— marriage, domestic labor, prostitution, and, increasingly, factory work —but reformers continued to see their problems as moral and cultural rather than economic and political. Even as evidence mounted that Lancaster girls were treated more as servants than as moral apprentices, and occasionally were subject to sexual exploitation, Lancaster officials adhered to their policies. Reformatory officials, both male and female, remained convinced that domesticity offered the best solution to female delinquency.[26]

To the usual complaints of servants—poor quarters, exhausting work, long hours, little or no privacy, and the possibility of sexual harassment—were added the tribulations of being a "state girl." Mistresses may have felt it necessary to supervise free time carefully in order to prevent any moral relapses. A state agent, who visited placed girls, checked the postmarks on all mail and sometimes read their letters in order to prevent improper correspondence. Girls were forbidden to go home and all visitors had to be screened. The trustees also worried that a girl's past (or imagined past, since the actual record was private) was thrown back at her by the family or others. As one girl complained, attending church with her family was more humiliating than uplifting, since "the people all stare at her, and the boys call her names outside the church."[27]

It is impossible to delve into the motives of those families who took delinquent girls into their homes except to say that altruism is rarely an unalloyed virtue. Lancaster solved the servant problem by providing families with girls trained to be domestics. However, the trouble girls caused undoubtedly made up for the inexpensiveness of their labor. As the comments cited above show, they stole, ran away, and were insolent in a way that few domestic servants could afford to be. Lancaster girls brought their troubled pasts with them as well as possible expectations of being welcomed into a family. Families apparently expected the girls to behave like servants or at least like obedient daughters. Both experienced rude shocks.

Evidence of discontent by both parties is found in turnover statistics. Families had the option of returning unsatisfactory girls and increasing numbers did so. In the early years, girls and families weathered the trials of placement. According to one study, the percentage of girls who stayed in their original family declined from 38 percent in 1856 to 21 percent in 1880, while girls requiring three or more placements increased dramatically, from 3 percent in 1856 to 40 percent in 1880. A relationship fraught with difficulty became even more so as older and more delinquent girls began arriving at Lancaster.[28]

New Candidates for the Reform School

Sometime in late 1876 sixteen-year-old Josephine Barnett, daughter of a respectable harness maker, spent the night with a married man. When she arrived home the next morning, her mother barred the door, telling her daughter to "go with those she was with the night before." It is unlikely that this was the first dispute between mother and daughter, but this time the quarrel ended Josephine's ties to her family. She moved into the Rutland House, a well-known Boston brothel, where she was found by police looking for underaged girls. In January 1877, she was committed to Lancaster for being "stubborn and disobedient."[29]

While Josephine was certainly stubborn and disobedient, that was the least of it. Here was a girl very different from Mary O'Connell, one that Bradford Peirce would have kept out of the institution in 1856 —she had voluntarily engaged in sexual activity, including adultery, and had resided in a brothel. But Josephine was neither rejected nor released, a signal that reformers' notions of who could be reformed had broadened to include sexually active girls, even those who had participated in commercial vice.

The official charges levied against girls give no indication of what their offenses were. Josephine had been found guilty of stubbornness, as had over 50 percent of a sample of Lancaster's inmates, and someone examining published institutional data would have no inkling as to what the offense entailed. For example, Bridget Donnolly frequently stayed out all night with young men and was arrested for nightwalking. But a complaint of stubborn and disobedient was entered "at mother's request." Margaret Smith, also committed for stubbornness and disobedience, attended "North St. dance halls" in Boston's brothel district, and associated with "persons who frequent such resorts." Officials admitted that even charges of larceny hid "a short life's experience in waywardness and vice." In fact, the original commissioners intended that charges and testimony be hidden from the community. Officials masked a girl's deviance by listing a relatively innocuous offense as a way of protecting the reputations of both the girl and the reformatory.[30]

Case records reveal what the charges against a girl do not, namely, that for an increasing number of girls, deviance was defined in terms of sexual activity. Mary Blaine, arrested for drunkenness and living an idle, vagrant, and vicious life, was an orphan who lived in a brothel run by a Mrs. Fisk. "On the night of March 16, 1875, she rode about the city with a daughter of Mrs. Fisk, in a drunken debauch, calling at different saloons and drinking large quantities of intoxicating liquors." The two girls passed out in the carriage and the hack driver took them back to the stable and left them to sleep off their binge. "When they were discovered the next morning at about 5 o'clock, the Fisk girl was dead." Mary Blaine was drunk and idle, as her official record indicated, but she was also a prostitute.[31] Mary Trotter, sentenced to Lancaster for larceny, had stolen a five-dollar skirt from another girl in the brothel where they both worked.[32] Although the charges listed for these girls were technically accurate, they obscured the real offense—sexual deviance.

Most girls lacked the commercial experience of Josephine Barnett, Mary Blaine, and Mary Trotter. The more usual inmates, like Margaret Smith and Bridget Donnelly, traded sex for treats and attention or frequented locations where their eventual prostitution was likely. By the 1870s these girls, rather than the Mary O'Connells, became Lancaster's true subjects.[33]

The increase in sexually active girls, including prostitutes, incarcerated at Lancaster reflects changes in the larger culture as well as new policy in Massachusetts that emphasized immediate placement. In the 1870s, reformers in several states defeated proposals to legalize and regulate sexual trade and reinvigorated efforts to eliminate prostitution. Besides battling prostitution, the "purity crusaders" created institutions, such as the YWCA, to protect single women, helped establish separate prisons for women, and tried to educate young men as to proper standards of morality. From this purity crusade came a more sympathetic view of adolescent girls who had committed moral offenses. For example, attempts to raise the age of consent to twenty-one suggested that women under that age were not considered fully responsible for their deeds. Age-of-consent campaigns were only modestly successful, but they created a climate in which the reform of sexual delinquents could be undertaken and proposals to place delinquent girls directly into families could be considered.[34]

The purity crusaders, like the female members of antebellum benevolent societies, were not radicals and feminists. They were extending domesticity into the public realm, not challenging the gender and class distinctions of their society. They created bureaucracies and organizations, including a separate female incarceral system, that paralleled institutions established by males. The effect on Lancaster was that it became one of a series of institutions that incarcerated women at the same time that the adoption of an immediate placement policy brought a larger population of delinquents under state supervision.[35]

The architects of placement in Massachusetts were Samuel Gridley Howe and Franklin Sanborn. Howe and Sanborn were the leaders of the Board of State Charities, established in 1865 to bring organization and efficiency to charity. Howe and Sanborn proposed an immediate-placement policy for economic and ideological reasons. Placement promised cheaper reform than juvenile institutions, which would become only temporary waystations. Placement met the demand of less eligibility: delinquents would be trained in families for their future work roles while the state could avoid spending so much on educating the children of the unworthy poor. Besides, placement in families was the essential expression of domestic reform, for it provided delinquents with individualized tutoring in domesticity. Placement promised to be the model of cost effectiveness, while reformatories were costly failures.

Howe and Sanborn also warned that institutions bred vice. The reports of the state board echo the language Samuel Gridley Howe used in his letters opposing the creation of Lancaster. The reports argued that "vice" had to be separated and diffused, while institutions gathered it together to fester and spread. Institutional attempts to imitate the family were "counterfeit" at best and at worst were "dangerous and pernicious." Single-sex institutions were unnatural, as were those that segregated individuals by age. The true reforming influence of women upon the young could not be exerted in "mimic families," only in real ones, which were the root of "individual virtue and happiness, and of national strength and prosperity." To the extent that institutions were necessary, they should only house children briefly before placement. In the name of domestic reform, the language of family was turned against the "family" institution.[36]

Placement reflected Howe and Sanborn's relative optimism about reforming delinquent children. Howe and Sanborn's second report of the State Board of Charities has often been cited as evidence of the shift in reform thought toward hereditarianism.[37] Certainly there is ample evidence of hereditarian thought in the report, but historians have overlooked the more hopeful comments about reforming children. To be sure, Howe and Sanborn attributed delinquency to the lack of "vital force" due to poor nutrition and the use of stimulants and to inherited tendencies that lessened ability for "self-guidance." But the context in which these remarks were made show a Lamarckian view that heredity was quite malleable. They noted that while the children of the "intemperate and vicious classes" tend to "point in the wrong direction," the "tendency is not yet so established that they point spontaneously. They are still susceptible to the influences of education, and of moral and religious training." Howe and Sanborn believed that education and moral training could only occur in a family while institutional care reinforced inherited predispositions. Placement was not predicted on hopelessness. Theirs was still domestic reform and they still believed that an immigrant working class could be leavened with bourgeois virtue through the cultural transformation of their children.[38]

Despite the rhetoric, the state board implemented its placement policy gradually. The state's visiting agent, hired in 1866 to supervise children placed out of the state's almshouse, began supervising delinquents placed out of the reformatories as well. When this expansion of duties proved too much for a single individual, the state established the Visiting Agency in 1869. Far more significant than the creation of the new agency and the hiring of several assistants was the provision requiring that the courts notify the agency of all trials involving juveniles. The state agents, who attended seventeen thousand trials in the first ten years of the agency's existence, advised judges on the disposition of cases and encouraged them to remand younger children to their custody until they could be placed into families. With the full implementation of this policy in the 1870s, younger boys and girls avoided reformatories altogether and the number of children placed out directly surpassed the number in institutions.[39]

In spite of the apparent success of placement, Howe seriously miscalculated its impact. As we have already seen, placement was no panacea for delinquent girls. Girls found places because their labor as servants was highly valued. But more difficult girls could not be placed easily and they, together with those who failed in their placements, were housed at Lancaster, which never turned into the temporary home Howe had envisioned. Instead Lancaster adopted a new role: it housed girls who would have been rejected earlier and, in the name of economy and less eligibility, it provided them with straightforward vocational training unadorned by the language of family and home. Girls who were compliant remained until placed out as domestics; the others were transferred into the adult prison system.

The Lancaster administration, realizing the implications of the new placement policy, staunchly defended their institutional interests. They anticipated that Lancaster would fill up with incorrigibles if the placement plan succeeded, and they argued that many girls were unprepared to be placed into families immediately after being taken from the streets and warned that they could exert a bad influence over other children and family members. The women's advisory board took a more aggressive stance, arguing that "so good an institution is better than any family" for many girls. The protests were in vain, and in 1873 the trustees glumly concluded that recent inmates had "wandered farther from home, and have been more prodigal in the waste of life, than those formerly sent." Marcus Ames, superintendent since 1861, charged that Lancaster was being turned into a house of detention, and he and a majority of the matrons and assistants resigned in 1875.[40]

The effect of the placement policy was soon apparent. The mean age at entry increased from twelve years, nine months in 1856 to nearly fifteen by 1874, and the age limit for entry into Lancaster was increased from sixteen to seventeen in 1870. At the same time, the average length of stay dropped from twenty-eight months in the 1870s to eleven months in the 1880s. Younger girls were drawn away from Lancaster while the older ones remained for a shorter time before being placed in families or, more importantly, before they were transferred to an institution for adults.[41]

Lancaster, in the words of the trustees, was becoming a "middle place" in an emerging system of incarceral institutions for deviant females. Lancaster began to serve as a disciplinary backup to other institutions. The reformatory received the difficult cases from the state almshouses and primary schools for young orphaned or destitute children. Lancaster also began to transfer its difficult cases to the state almshouses at Tewksbury (for the chronically insane) and Bridgewater (the workhouse), and to the Sherborn Women's Reformatory and the Massachusetts Home for the Feeble-Minded.[42]

Reformers created this institutional system to handle the unreformable. As hereditarian theories of deviance captured more attention in the 1870s and 1880s, "feeble-minded" women aroused particular concern. Lacking mental and moral capacity, they were a Malthusian nightmare, threatening to propagate generations of paupers and criminals. Reformers maintained that "moral imbeciles" could not learn self-restraint, and therefore had to be restrained. Lancaster was the first step in identifying those who required permanent incarceration.[43]

Administrators refined Lancaster's classification scheme to control the new mix of inmates. House number 5 held the minor offenders and the administration requested construction of a disciplinary cottage for "hardened" offenders and for girls returned from placement. The necessity for such a cottage was reinforced when, in an unprecedented act of rebellion, two girls burned down house number 3.[44] The cottage system allowed Lancaster to segregate its inmates and therefore to attempt to train more serious offenders. Domestic reform had turned into a bureaucratic system that measured, classified, labeled, and segregated female deviants.

Lancaster officials narrowed their vision to fit the reform school's new role. They argued that Lancaster was a training school for those who could become self-supporting as domestics and they accepted that girls' positions in families would be as servants rather than daughters. Trustees commented that the most profitable work for girls was as servants, and that domestic service was probably best for all "*poor* American girls." In addition to learning how to do housework properly, girls received instruction in knitting, sewing, cooking, bread making, laundry work, and pastry making. In rhetoric as well as reality, domesticity had become domestic work.[45]

Domestic reform concluded with the creation of a state welfare bureaucracy and an elaborate system of institutions. The state employed social workers to investigate and supervise the families that accepted children, while a host of specialized public institutions isolated and labeled the deviant. In the name of transforming the cultures of the poor, domestic reformers extended the reach of reform, intervened in the lives of more girls, and thereby expanded the functions of the state and laid the groundwork for the reforms of the Progressive era.

Between the 1850s and the 1880s, reform for girls had changed in two ways. The definition of the reformable expanded to include the sexually experienced and along with this came an increasingly intricate network of placement and institutional programs. During this same period, the meaning of "reform" for those in the reformatory narrowed. In the name of economy and less eligibility, Lancaster became a training school for domestic servants.

CHAPTER 5

Domestic Reform and the State Reform School for Boys

Domestic reform arrived at the State Reform School for Boys (Westborough) in 1861. A devastating fire in 1859 and ensuing charges of brutality and mismanagement forced the old administration and trustees to resign. The reformatory reorganized, adding cottages for the boys working on the farm, although the remnants of the old central building were still used to confine difficult boys and the institution still housed around three hundred inmates. The most significant change was the hiring of a new superintendent, Joseph Allen, who radically reordered the reformatory according to the tenets of domestic reform. Allen was a Unitarian teacher and the individuals who pressed for his appointment, Samuel Gridley Howe, George Emerson, and Samuel May, were all well-known liberal reformers. The state reform school began its new life under the best possible direction it could have had.[1]

Unfortunately, domestic reform was not long lived at Westborough. The policy of immediate placement doomed the reformatory to incarcerate older, more delinquent boys, while the demand of less eligibility narrowed the scope of reform activity in the institution. And at Westborough there was no cushion of domesticity to mitigate conflict between inmates and officials.

Domestic Reform

"*Fear* may restrain," Allen was fond of saying, "but *love* only can reform." Allen personified the constellation of values bourgeois Victorians associated with home and family. He was the gentle pater familias, who wore a suit made of the same cloth as the boys' clothes. He abolished military drill because he thought the boys were belligerent enough, and needed to learn reverence for life and respect for property, which could only be done under "refining influences." Therefore he set aside hours for singing practice, which he led on his violin. In keeping with the philosophy of domestic reform, Allen also hired a number of female employees, who, he thought, would uplift the boys by introducing a more spiritual element to the reform school. With the same intent, his wife and two young daughters participated in classes at the reformatory. Allen believed cultivating the soil would teach boys the dignity of labor, and he put older youngsters to work at heavy farm labor, while younger ones raised fruits and vegetables and the smallest tended garden plots. He taught enterprise by giving each boy a plot of ground, supplying fertilizer, and splitting the profits made from the sale of vegetables. Allen reduced the use of solitary confinement, commenting that he went a whole year without keeping a boy in the "lodge" overnight, and that on one occasion when he found it necessary to keep a small boy there, "I determined to occupy the next cell myself, to keep him company." He believed that all inmates could benefit from exposure to bourgeois values, but, unlike most of his contemporaries, he did not assume that bourgeois culture and Protestantism were the same. Allen offered the usual condemnations of drink and tobacco, but in his talks about great men, he included examples of Catholics such as Father Matthew, leader of the Catholic temperance movement, and Daniel O'Connell, the Irish patriot, and he allowed inmates to read the Boston *Pilot*, the local Catholic newspaper.[2]

Allen's relationships with inmates illustrate the methods of the domestic reformer. Instead of relying on bureaucracy and formal systems, Allen dealt with inmates on an ad hoc basis. He abolished merit badges, arguing that such external distinctions could not give a real indication of moral character. "A boy may be very troublesome," he wrote, "violating the rules constantly, and yet we know him to be a good boy at heart; while another may obey every regulation, and cause no trouble, and still we may not have the least confidence in him." Instead of punishing boys for running away, Allen argued they should be welcomed back and thus encouraged to return of their own accord. Showing confidence in boys encouraged them to develop the self-esteem and self-discipline upon which true reform rested. Allen ended the use of informers, noting that boys "tattled" for their own selfish reasons, while "the high-minded boy rarely reports a schoolmate even when he should."[3]

In essence, Allen aimed at an internal, moral transformation of his charges. Theirs would be a secular conversion experience, one that would leave them thinking and acting like the bourgeois reformers who were held up as their role models. Here, once again, was the essence of domestic reform as espoused by the Children's Aid Society and the Lancaster School for girls: working-class and immigrant children were culturally transformed and themselves became reformers who would transmit their new values to their families once they left the institution.

Allen's paternal sympathy for boys apparently made it easier for him to penetrate the inmate subculture. Allen relied on gaining a boy's confidence and getting him to realize and report his own faults. For example, Allen suspected that two boys were planning to spend some money that one had found but failed to turn in. He sent for the accomplice late one night, thinking that this would accentuate the personal and confidential nature of their discussion. He sat the boy under a bright light, so he would see the expression on his face, and he told "George" that he wanted to speak with him about something. He asked the boy if he knew what he wished to discuss with him, and after some hesitation, George admitted that it must be about the money. After telling Allen about it, George wished to turn the money over, but Allen suggested another plan instead. Saying that he thought the other boy was basically a good fellow, he asked George if he could persuade him to turn the money in and "acknowledge his fault" if he thought it "the proper thing to do." Needless to say the plan worked and the other boy turned himself in.[4]

Allen's account of his superintendency is, however, a little disingenous. Obviously he did not write about his failures. More importantly,

Allen did not discuss one underlying reason for his success. Although he claimed that he did not have any problems with older boys transferred to Westborough, one of the major reforms of 1861 was the creation of a nautical reformatory to which older boys could be sent, while the age limit at Westborough was lowered from sixteen to fourteen. Even though some ship boys were transferred to Allen's care, Allen could also send some of his more troublesome cases to the "school ships," which were intended to incarcerate the older as well as the more difficult cases. Domestic reform worked with younger boys in the public reformatory, but, like the Children's Aid Society's Pine Farm, it was an experiment that occurred under controlled conditions. And like the reform schools of the Children's Aid Society, Westborough relied on having a more repressive institution to reinforce it.[5]

The School Ships

The *Massachusetts* (1861–1870) and the *George M. Bernard* (1866–1872) were floating prisons. The ships trained boys between the ages of fourteen and eighteen to be seamen, and officials placed them on merchant vessels or whalers. Yet, except for brief summer training voyages, the ships remained moored in Boston or New Bedford harbors. The monotony and occasional danger of the sailor's life was probably made more irksome by lying at anchor for months at a time in the city harbor. The situation itself—a large number of urban delinquents with little desire to become seamen housed in the tight quarters of a sailing ship and subject to harsh nautical discipline—created the basis for confrontation. In 1861, just after the first ship opened, an officer wrote to the governor that he had been discharged from his post "because I would not flog a Boy tied up to the gangway by his two thumbs in which Cruel position he had been for three hours." Franklin Sanborn, of the Board of State Charities, wrote that order was maintained only because the boys knew that the officers would use revolvers should marlinpikes fail to cow them, while a trustee wrote to the governor that the administration lived in constant fear of mutiny.[6]

Boys in the school ships were children of the immigrant poor who had committed petty larcenies or status offenses. Approximately 90 percent came from urban areas, with nearly half of those incarcerated on the *Massachusetts* coming from Boston or the contiguous areas of Cambridge, Chelsea, Charlestown, and Roxbury. Fifty-four percent of the boys on both ships were either first- or second-generation Irish, and only 24 percent had parents born in the United States, while 60 percent were full or half orphans. Nearly 40 percent of the boys were incarcerated for minor or status offenses, including stubbornness, vagrancy, truancy, idleness, and drunkenness, and slightly more than 40 percent for larceny, with the remainder imprisoned for more serious crimes such as assault or breaking and entering. These boys, like the ones in Westborough, stole food, clothing, coal, or the means to gain these necessities. Their arrest records included fines for marble playing on Sunday and for throwing snowballs. Theirs for the most part were the "crimes" of the young, the homeless, and the poor.[7]

Urban delinquents showed little enthusiasm for the sea. Only about one-third of the 1,880 boys received at the ships went to sea, and the number who remained in maritime occupations is unknown. Boys shipped out with both merchantmen and whalers. Approximately 430 sailed on merchantmen, which carried on average only one or two boys. Another two hundred went on whalers, which generally took larger crews from the school ships. New Bedford was the center of the American whaling trade and over one hundred boys sailed on whalers out of New Bedford between 1866 and 1869. Financial interests were primary here since green hands were paid a pittance and few self-respecting sailors cared to be in a whaling crew. Delinquent boys with no families to be concerned about their safety were perfect fodder for a trade in which crews took tremendous risks. It is little wonder that so few went to sea despite pressure from officers and the hope of an early release.[8]

When the state established the school ships, it did not intend to oppress boys or to supply cheap labor for exploitation by whaling and merchant captains. The only alternative to domestic reform was a narrow form of manual or vocational training that did not violate less eligibility and that seemed more practical for older boys. On the school ships, nautical training was supposed to teach manliness and self-reliance and prepare boys for employment. Since the *Massachusetts* was launched during the Civil War, an enthusiasm for military discipline might be expected, and officials noted with pride the number of graduates who served the Union. Boys in the ships were divided into port and starboard watches and they alternated between six hour days in the classroom and six hour days swabbing decks, mending sails, and keeping the ships seaworthy. The boys attended Protestant services led by the superintendent or by local Protestant ministers and Sunday school lessons offered by volunteers from the YMCA.[9] Martin Eldridge, the superintendent, emphasized religious instruction, not because it produced more skilled sailors, but because it created Christian sailors who might be fitting representatives of American society. The school ships aimed to reform boys, but their methods were distinctly different from those of domestic reformers. The school ships were like the congregate asylums: they regulated behavior, emphasizing the external imposition of order and discipline rather than the internalization of bourgeois values. Despite the avowed goal of creating self-reliant, temperate, and industrious individuals, they prepared boys for unskilled jobs in which they would be supervised by others. Vocational training easily gave way to exploitation and it ultimately triumphed over domestic reform.

The school ships closed in 1872 for financial and ideological reasons. It was less expensive to incarcerate boys at Westborough than on the ships, and since relatively few of the boys actually went to sea, it was difficult to justify the cost of their nautical "training." Moreover, the whaling industry went into decline after its burst of expansion in the late 1860s, and with it went the prospects of placing boys on ships. The school ships also incorporated the worst abuses of the congregate reformatories at a time when Samuel Gridley Howe and Franklin Sanborn were urging the adoption of an immediate-placement policy. Nothing was more logical than recommending that the ships be closed and their inmates transferred to Westborough.[10]

One might predict that the arrival of older youths at Westborough would mean greater resistance to reform and trigger the adoption of sterner disciplinary measures. This happened in part; older boys seemed less amenable to affectionate discipline and feminine influences and required some form of practical training. But a decision to drop many of Joseph Allen's innovations at the reform school and to shift to a vocational training program actually preceded the arrival of the older boys and the adoption of immediate placement. Allen's experiment violated the demands of less eligibility, and officials had already decided to curtail it.

Less Eligibility and Manual Training

Howe and Sanborn charged that Allen's plan for reforming boys cost too much and left boys with exaggerated expectations. They noted that the average yearly income produced by each boy had fallen from $9.66 in 1857 to $3.71 in 1864 as the reform program shifted from chair caning to farming. They ignored the conditions the boys had worked under in 1857, when local manufacturers operated the reform school as a factory and reform took a back seat to the orderly maintenance of production. Howe and Sanborn argued that the reformatory's role was to teach boys industry and order, while Allen spent too much time on education, graduating inmates who entered the world with "notions too high, and habits of industry too little cultivated." Domestic reform, according to Howe and Sanborn, left boys unwilling to take the working-class jobs available to them upon their release. Allen resigned under pressure in 1867 and his resignation was a sign of impending change. Once again, conditions would prove to be less important than cost and humane treatment less important than the deterrence of pauperism.[11]

The reform school was also adapting to the industrial age. By 1880, 42 percent of the state's labor force was employed in manufacturing while three-quarters of its population lived in cities or towns, making Massachusetts the second most urbanized state in the country. Roughly three-quarters of the workforce was dependent on wages, owning neither farms, shops, nor factories, only their labor power.[12] This economic revolution could be ignored for a time in the private reform school, which answered only to its private benefactors, and in the girls' reformatory, where domesticity still dictated that girls be prepared for service, not industry. But the public boys' reformatory had to heed state officials' calls for utility. Placement in country families might work for younger children or girls, who could become members of their families and internalize their values, but the older boys who graduated from the reform school would enter either the proletariat or the prison.

Music lessons no longer seemed as important as in the past. Manual training or "industrial education" appeared both in urban school systems and in reform schools in the 1870s and 1880s. Urban educators promoted manual training as the way to teach moral values and discipline to working-class children and to respond to manufacturers' demands that the schools provide some basic industrial skills. "Hand learning," it was thought, held the attention of children poorly suited for book learning and was believed to be particularly appropriate for black, poor, and immigrant children. Training for specific trades and an emphasis on job placement and industrial efficiency replaced manual training after the turn of the century, but manual training marked the beginning of specialized educational tracks for specific groups of children.[13]

Reform school officials eagerly espoused the manual training philosophy, which provided them with an alternative program to domestic reform. Unlike the convict leasing program of the congregate asylum, whose sole virtue was that it kept boys employed, manual training was at least in part educational. Officials claimed that manual training, especially carpentry, involved work boys enjoyed and it placed inmates "under a constant mental and moral discipline." It taught "in a concrete form exactly the principles and habits which the reform school boy needs to be taught. Heedless, careless, slipshod ways invariably and necessarily bear immediate concrete fruit in poor or spoiled work, which he can readily see." Object teaching, clay modeling, drawing, gymnastics, and military drill were all introduced into the reformatory with the same purpose: to teach precision, order, attention, and discipline. The most widely adopted manual training program was the sloyd system of woodworking, in which students worked through a series of carefully designed exercises carving wooden models that became increasingly complex. Here too the lessons were largely ones of mental and moral discipline. The officers quoted the sloyd teacher that " 'again, a boy easily comprehends the comparison that the wrong way is a hard, rough way, whether he planes against the grain of the wood or whether he walks against the plans of God.' " While not quite the

Headed for Industry, October 1909. Lewis Hine Collection, Library of Congress.

Carpentry was introduced into the public schools (shown here), reformatories, and industrial schools in the 1880s. It taught the necessity for precision and following orders by training the mind through the hand. This type of manual training was thought to be the most effective way to teach black, immigrant, and working-class children.

same thing as teaching skills, manual training taught the work habits necessary for participation in an industrial workforce.[14]

Public reform school administrators had a limited ability to experiment with domestic reform. They were always vulnerable to the charge that their institutions cost too much and they could not provide institutionalized children with advantages unavailable to the children of the worthy poor. Once again, less eligibility undermined reform.

The Triumph of Immediate Placement

The other factor that reshaped the reform school was the creation of the State Visiting Agency in 1869 and the adoption of an immediate-placement policy. The State Board of Charities reported that in nearly 40 percent of the cases in which an agent appeared in court, the judge placed the child in a family rather than in a reformatory. Minor offenders received suspended sentences or fines, or were placed out, and only more serious offenders were committed.[15]

Samuel Gridley Howe and Franklin Sanborn acknowledged the effect of their policies upon the reformatory. The more successful the placement policy, "the worse will be the average character of the inmates left in the reformatory." Reformatories would become "what they are in reality, *houses of correction for juvenile criminals.*" According to this perspective, differences between the nautical school and the farm school were negligible. Those who could be reformed would be placed in families, while juvenile criminals would go to Westborough and live without the niceties Joseph Allen had introduced. For them, discipline and order were enough.[16]

Ironically, in many ways the boys in the reformatory in the late 1870s were not much different from those who had preceded them. While most (62 percent) of the boys admitted between 1879 and 1880 were born in Massachusetts, and nearly three-quarters were born in the United States, a more familiar picture emerges when one looks at the birthplaces of the parents. Nearly half the fathers and 52 percent of the mothers had been born in Ireland, while only a quarter of the parents had been born in the United States. Two-thirds of the parents were Catholic, and 30 percent of the fathers had died, as had percent of the mothers. Again the loss of the chief breadwinner caused children, either as a matter of family strategy or out of crisis, to become wards of the state. Of the sixty-six living fathers, two-thirds were laborers and four were factory operatives, with others working in trades ranging from blacksmith to cigarmaker to puddler. The reform school remained an institution for the working class.[17]

There were, however, two significant changes in the boys at Westborough. Obviously, raising the age limit to seventeen meant that there was an older population than earlier. Of 256 boys sent between

1877 and 1878, only forty-five were under fourteen years of age, and 122 were sixteen and older. The offenses boys committed were essentially the same, but the proportion of the boys with previous arrests and incarcerations increased. Sixty percent of the boys committed in 1864 had prior arrest records, while in 1879, 78 percent had arrest records and over a quarter had been previously incarcerated. Younger and less delinquent children were avoiding the reformatory, just as Howe and Sanborn had wished.[18]

Westborough's Decline

The transition from domestic reform to vocational training had a different impact on each of the public institutions. Domestic reform in the girls' reformatory could be trimmed without appearing to lose much; domesticity easily became domestic work without leading to a harsher environment because a maternal order more easily survived the change. With boys, stripping away the substance of domestic reform—affectionate discipline, personal attention, education, emphasis on self-regulation—left only the architectural shell—the cottages. Manual training was an improvement over the convict leasing system of the congregate reformatory; it did not involve the conflict between manufacturers and sweated labor inherent in convict leasing plans. Still, it was a narrow conception of education that emphasized order and discipline and not much was required for the reform school to descend into disorder.[19]

Westborough went through a wrenching period of transition. Westborough trustees wrote that they had to increase the number of officers, institute more serious disciplinary measures, add safeguards to prevent escape, and rearrange the number of hours devoted to study and labor. Visitors reported that the atmosphere at the school was tense, with one trustee writing the governor, "I did not tell you how much Mrs. Richardson and I have been pained by finding the surly, sullen spirit that exists among the boys. . . . Seeing them as you do in Chapel you could not feel the *absence of content* that we find so noticeable." The reform school no longer resembled the bourgeois family, but was a microcosm of industrial society.[20]

The violence that permeated American society in the 1870s also

affected the reform school.[21] On January 12, 1877, a group of boys in
the reform school started hurling bowls, utensils, and food at the
guards in the dining hall. Only about twenty youngsters joined in the
melee, and guards quickly restored order and marched the boys off to
their evening lessons. Soon trouble began again. Boys in the third floor
classroom shut off the gas lamps and some ran to barricade the doors,
while others advanced on the teacher, who escaped in the confusion.
A group of the rebels charged down the stairs, but were met with
guards' gunfire on the first floor and retreated. On the second floor,
the teacher locked his doors and managed to keep his boys quiet.
Other guards, alerted by inmates that a riot was in progress, trained
fire hoses on the roof of the building, encasing it in ice and making
escape impossible. The sheriff of Westborough and a posse of concerned citizens reinforced the guards, and, armed with axes, clubs,
revolvers, and rifles with fixed bayonets, charged the inmate barri-
cades. After bursting through, they trained fire hoses on the inmates
and forced their surrender.[22]

A legislative investigation followed the riot and evidence presented
at the hearing suggests the nature of the inmate subculture and the
ways in which inmates adapted to and resisted the reformatory's authority. The most obvious conclusion to be drawn from the testimony
offered at the legislative hearing is that the reform school relied on
brutality to keep order. Punishments included confinement in the
"lodge" (solitary), use of a straitjacket and gag, corporal punishment,
and confinement for several hours in a "sweatbox."

Solitary confinement at the reform school resembled that at other
penal institutions. Boys were put in cells apart from the other inmates
and fed a diet of bread and water and given the opportunity to reflect
on their misdeeds. However, confinement was never as solitary as
officials wished. Boys plotted together and continued the same type of
disruptive behavior they had in the old congregate institution. For
example, in April 1876 a group of boys in the lodge cheered, rattled
their doors, and made noise during a sermon by the local Protestant
minister. Afterwards, guards hooked up a firehose and wet them down
for their sacrilegious outburst. On other occasions troublesome boys
were restrained physically. A witness told the investigating committee
that boys were put in straitjackets, sometimes for several days, with

straps tied inside their mouths across their teeth.[23]

Flogging, administered with a heavy leather strap, was the most common punishment. Any official had the power to punish an inmate, and guards sometimes crossed the line between punishment and sadism. Cornelius Callahan described a beating by a guard in which

he kept on whipping me until the blood ran down my legs. When he got me down, he whipped me on the neck; and I have marks on my neck now. He gave me a pretty good strapping and after a while I begged. I got half across the floor, and he called me back and told me to take off my jacket and to take my pants down. I did, and he punished me again.

Cruel punishments, admitted guard John Ayres, were a constant problem at the reformatory and occasionally an employee had to be dismissed for the severity of his or her treatment of an inmate.[24]

Perhaps the most troubling means of punishing inmates was the sweatbox. This was a wooden box twenty-one inches by sixteen and a half inches, with a grate in the door and an opening in the top, in which a boy would be confined for several hours. The dimensions of the box made it impossible to lift up one's arms or to change position, and one inmate reported that after several hours of confinement his hands had swollen to twice their normal size. Inmate Frank Cunningham, one of the reformatory's trust boys, told investigators that he had been justly punished and that it had done him good. Nonetheless, he admitted that, after six and a half hours in the sweatbox, he had trouble walking for two or three days. Asked if he had seen the results of a prolonged stay, he replied that he had seen boys whose "legs were all swollen up, and they were black and blue, and the cords stood out on them so you could see them—black and blue all over."[25]

To be sure, the inmates could be equally cruel. The institution's physician, Dr. Edwin Harvey, described an attack on a matron by two inmates. The boys, who helped clean up the dining hall after meals, waited until they were alone with their supervisor, Mrs. Moore. Then the two threw her on the floor, stuffed a towel in her mouth to muffle her screams, knocked out her teeth, and beat and kicked her before the superintendent came to the rescue.[26]

As a result of both official and inmate actions, an aura of violence enveloped the reformatory. Incidents such as the attack on Mrs. Moore were used to justify harsh disciplinary measures. Following the attack on the matron, the superintendent took the inmate primarily responsible for the assault into his office and flogged him. Another witness told the committee that he counted forty-two blows. "As I said the boy screamed at first; but his voice gradually died out until . . . [the screams] stopped, and the superintendent came out." Dr. Harvey, who maintained that he was opposed to corporal punishment in principle, argued that floggings were necessary to control the inmates. Order was precarious, with inmates and officials in a constant struggle for power, and, with order itself the only goal for the institution, almost anything could be justified to maintain it.[27]

The inmate subculture was itself based on violence and the exploitation of weaker inmates. The testimony at the 1877 hearing shows that boys placed in positions of trust by the administration were as likely to be assaulted as were officials themselves. Even in ordinary times these inmates were sneered at and "called spies for assisting the officers." Colonel Shepherd, the superintendent, reported that he had "to get between those boys and protect them." After the riot, special precautions had to be taken. Elmer Lutz testified at the hearing that he had been punished for saying that one of the trust boys ought to be "thumped" for helping to put down the riot. Sexual exploitation of younger inmates was obliquely described by the administration. Norman Wood, assistant superintendent, told the committee that the older boys took "the smaller and more innocent boys, and [those] most free from vice," and "chummed" with them. The younger boys were "very affectionate" and the older ones took advantage of it.[28]

The administration could not control the inmate subculture, but attempted to infiltrate it. Colonel Shepherd had formed several special groups among the inmates, including the "tried and true," the "band of hope," and a Bible and singing class. These trust boys informed officers about inmate plans, and, as noted above, helped man the firehoses trained on the schoolhouse roof during the 1877 riot. While the trust boy was ostracized and sometimes assaulted, his presence meant the inmate subculture was never secure.[29]

The trust boys identified with the institution and the values of the larger culture it represented. They saw the punishments they received as justified and formed a loyal cadre of administration supporters. Conflict with other inmates undoubtedly reinforced their group identity, just as it probably helped secure other inmates in their deviant status. Trust boys signed a pledge not to steal, swear, lie, drink, smoke, or violate any of the institutional rules, and they agreed to influence other inmates to follow their example. A single misstep resulted in expulsion from this self-selected group, whose members obtained special privileges from the officers and earned an early parole. Trust boys experienced a cultural conversion and left the institution imbued with the fervor of their newly found faith. As Louis Otis told the investigating committee when asked what he would do when released in a few days, "I should take, sir, in anything I can get to do, no matter what the work is, until I can study for something else." Here was a boy who had adopted an ethic of industry, future orientation, and self-discipline, who accepted personal responsibility for what happened to him, and who exemplified to himself, to other inmates, and to the public the meaning of reform.[30]

Despite evidence of brutality, the state investigatory committee lauded the condition of the reform school. They noted the difficulty of keeping good discipline "by ordinary means," especially with older boys present. They recommended that the use of the sweatbox be abolished, that fire hoses be used on inmates only to quell riots, and that the right to use corporal punishment be restricted and all punishments recorded. While they agreed that Joseph Rawson had been justifiably fired for holding a gun to an inmate's head and then beating him severely, they found no fault with the other officers. Unlike in 1859, when similar evidence of misconduct at Westborough led to the firing of the superintendent and the forced resignations of the board of trustees, the 1877 investigation had no serious repercussions.[31]

The decline of the institution was explained in terms of its inmates, not their keepers. The immediate-placement policy left the institution incarcerating the worst of the juvenile population. Little hope was held out that these boys could be reformed, and the experience of the reformatory fueled the adoption of hereditarian and social Darwinian ideas. These were born criminals, not made ones, and harsh measures were needed to control them.

The change in reform thought is most easily illustrated through the experience of Joseph Allen, who was recalled to the superintendency in 1881. Allen was not able to duplicate his earlier success. Allen still kept the younger boys in "families" of about thirty inmates, each supervised by a couple and a female teacher and living a separate existence from the other families and the older boys in the main building. But the older boys resisted his paternalism, constantly sought to escape, and committed "crimes against nature," which Allen contended had not occurred during his earlier superintendency.[32] Allen blamed his failure on the boys' heredity. Some boys "come from superior parentage, inheriting the ability to appreciate motives addressed to the reason and conscience," while others came from poor homes in large cities, "inheriting for many generations scarcely more than the animal instincts." Methods appropriate for the first group were "lost upon the latter, who can rarely be reached except through the immediate fear of pain, or hope of pleasure."[33] Domestic reform remained a viable option for the boys of "superior parentage"; they enjoyed the ultimate in domestic reform, namely, placement in families. Only harsh discipline and crude conditioning kept the others from committing further crimes, while manual training fitted them to tend machines in factories.

The failure of reform ambitions led even Joseph Allen to mouth the hereditary determinism increasingly popular in the late nineteenth century. Allen came to see delinquents as representatives of an inferior species who could not be reformed, only controlled. Never had the gap between the worthy and the unworthy poor appeared as wide and as unbridgeable.[34]

Massachusetts reorganized its reformatory system again in 1884. The state sold the reformatory site and purchased a ninety-nine-acre farm, also in Westborough. The new reform school adopted a cottage plan and lowered the age limit to fifteen. Despite the architecture and the farm setting, the reformatory made no pretense of being a domestic reform school. The boys continued with their manual training, physical culture, and military drill, which were designed to produce "obedience, promptness and self-control." Boys who ran away were punished with a whipping and a loss of credits, a certain number of which had to be earned in order to be released. The state also opened the Concord Reformatory, for young men between the ages of fifteen and thirty, in 1884, thus "solving" the problem of older delinquents by treating them as adults. Westborough, like the Lancaster school, had become a waystation between placement and the prison, part of a system of institutions that sorted, classified, and labeled inmates and passed troublesome cases along to progressively harsher environments where they would be confined further.[35]

Between 1861 and 1884, the reform school at Westborough had undergone dramatic change. Instead of being the centerpiece of state juvenile corrections policy, the reform school became merely a place to jail adolescents who could not be placed in families or who were returned from placement. The rhetoric and substance of domestic reform were abandoned for the drab task of teaching work habits and industrial discipline. Moral regeneration and the creation of character were exchanged for orderly deportment and docility. For a brief moment the institution seemed to work, but the successful experiment was abandoned before the claims of less eligibility, the need for an industrial workforce, and a narrower vision of what was an appropriate education for working–class children. Thereafter innovation resided with the private agencies, while the public reformatory punished and labeled the failures. By the 1880s, the lines of deviance were firmly drawn.

PART III

The Organization of Welfare

THE Arlington Street Armory still stands as an eloquent reminder of bourgeois Boston's fear of the working class. Begun after the great railroad strike of 1877 and completed in the early 1890s, the Armory sits astride one of the few streets that crossed between the working-class South End and the Brahmin Back Bay. Jutting turrets enabled would-be defenders to catch invaders in a crossfire, while iron shutters for the windows, a moat, a drawbridge, and triply reinforced doors secured the building against assault. A cistern under the roof saved a month's supply of rainwater in case of siege and a system of semaphore flags provided communication links with the State House on Beacon Hill. Wealthy subscribers paid for building the fortress, which a private militia used for military drill. Although the Brahmin fort was never needed, it suggests the chasm that divided the classes in late nineteenth-century America.[1]

Just as notable (although leaving no architectural monuments) were the efforts to cross that chasm. The economic crises of the 1870s and 1880s spawned renewed efforts to organize private social welfare in order to tie relief to cultural reform. Protestant and Catholic agencies, at loggerheads since the 1850s, agreed to a peaceful coexistence and recognized their similar aims. This did not mean that religious tensions disappeared or that periods of rivalry were over. But the truce arranged in the 1870s lasted and Catholic charities were integrated into the larger organized charity movement.

Organized charity itself paid renewed attention to the children of working-class families, although its approach changed. Instead of trying to remove children from families, reformers blanketed urban neighborhoods with home libraries, industrial schools, boys' and girls' clubs, and settlement house programs designed to attract children into their sphere. These efforts to uplift the worthy poor were very different from what had been attempted by antebellum moral reformers, even such figures as Charles Francis Barnard. Uplift was secular and it was more limited, some might say more realistic, than before. While their goal remained cultural conversion, it was a narrower version of bourgeois culture and the methods differed greatly. These agencies still promoted thrift, hard work, and future orientation, but did so through military drill, manual training, and vocational education—essentially the same program found in reform schools. Instead of self-regulation and character, they promoted deportment and obedience to external commands. It was bourgeois culture tailored for the working class, and it carried the tacit admission of the permanence of economic inequality and class difference that was acknowledged explicitly in the construction of the armory.

CHAPTER 6

Catholic Welfare: Between Separatism and Accommodation

"Brands from the Burning," published by the Children's Mission to the Children of the Destitute in 1856, captures the hopes of Protestants and the fears of Catholics in nineteenth-century Boston. The story is about Pat, a Catholic boy, and the Protestant city missionary who met him when breaking up a fight among some boys. The missionary took the boys home with him to be cleaned up and fed, and offered to enroll them in Sunday school. Pat Connors, who lived with his widowed mother and six siblings, returned for the Sunday school lessons, which soon paid off. Not only did he stop taking the Lord's name in vain, but he persuaded his mother to stop as well. After a stay in a Protestant country home, Pat returned to the city and found a job as a brakeman on a railroad. During a train wreck, he heroically remained at his post and was crushed between two cars. The climax of the story occurs when his mother arrives at the hospital and curses the railroad that has taken her son's life. But Pat admonishes his mother, " 'Whisht again, mother, unless ye'd put a shadow on the last talk yer son would have wid ye. I have but an hour or two to live.' " Pat's mother then wants to send for the priest; again her son corrects her: " 'I can die in peace widout the praste. The blessed tacher used to say that we were to confess our sins to God; and sure I have just now done that same, and I am sure that God will forgive me." Pat's dying words are, " 'Ah, that blessed tacher!' "[1]

Protestants, particularly evangelicals, saw Catholicism as menacing American liberty and viewed the concentration of Irish Catholic poor in cities as a threat to social order. Responses in Boston were twofold. Working-class Protestants clashed directly and violently with Irish Catholics in the 1830s, while state and private social welfare agencies began to use institutions and family placement to transform poor Catholic children culturally and religiously. Since established Boston united in condemning working-class violence, the official Catholic response was muted. However, "soul-stealing" was taken as a more serious threat. Protestant evangelical societies expanded their activities in the 1850s and provoked the Catholic hierarchy into creating a separate system of schools, reformatories, and social welfare agencies to preserve the faith of their parishioners, particularly children.

Boston's Catholic leadership undertook this separatism reluctantly, preferring to continue the accommodation that had characterized Protestant and Catholic relations. The Catholic leadership shared basic values with bourgeois Boston, but this agreement was masked by the intense religious rivalry at midcentury. Only in the late nineteenth century, when Catholicism stopped being de facto evidence of deviance, were Protestant and Catholic social welfare agencies able to discover their similarities and cooperate in providing lessons in bourgeois culture. Ministers and priests agreed that Pat should be a loyal brakeman.

Cooperation and Conflict in Antebellum Boston

The intensity of religious rivalry around midcentury obscured the degree of acceptance Catholics had found before that time. The Massachusetts Constitution of 1780 eliminated legal restrictions against Catholics, the constitutional reforms of 1820 allowed Catholic office holding, and leading Catholics, such as Bishop Jean Louis Cheverus (1808–25), were welcomed into the homes of the Boston elite. Cheverus's cathedral, the Church of the Holy Cross, had been built with significant Protestant contributions from such well-known figures as John Adams, John Quincy Adams, Harrison Gray Otis, Theodore Lyman, John Lowell, and Thomas Handasyd Perkins. The Ursuline Convent School in Charlestown educated the daughters of Boston's leading families, and a slow but steady number of Brahmin converts trickled into the Catholic Church.[2]

The nineteenth-century bishops, Benedict Fenwick (1825–46), John Fitzpatrick (1846–66), and John Williams (1866–1907), reflected the tradition of friendly ties with Boston's Brahmins. John Fitzpatrick, the only one of the three who was the son of an Irish immigrant, in 1826 entered the Boston Latin School, where his contemporaries included the future political, social, and economic leaders of the city. Fitzpatrick's accommodationist policies as bishop reflected his admiration for Yankee culture and the conservatism gained through traveling in Boston's most elite circles. Throughout much of the century, prelates of non-Irish background held leadership positions in the Boston Church. The leading advisors to Bishop Williams, Fitzpatrick's successor, were three Yankee converts, George Haskins, Theodore Metcalf, and Joshua Bodfish. Ties between Catholic and Protestant leaders were cemented by friendship, culture, and sometimes class and ethnicity.[3]

This well-established, somewhat insular Catholic leadership experienced the arrival of Irish peasants as a shock. Boston's Catholic leaders were urbane and well educated and had accepted Boston's Anglophile culture. The Irish immigrants they encountered had been unchurched in Ireland and arrived in Boston as nominal Catholics, whose religion was heavily tinged with folk beliefs. Irish-born priests shared the peasant culture of their flock as well as their hostility to English and Protestant authority. The arrival of the Irish divided the Church as much as it did Boston and threatened decades of hard-won assimilation.[4]

Because of their accepted position, the Catholic leadership did not perceive early child-saving activities by the state and by private agencies as a threat. The St. Vincent's Female Orphan Asylum opened in 1833, and for over fifteen years it remained the only Catholic child-saving institution. The Catholic leadership was secure enough not to begin rival institutions, even though, starting in 1847, Catholic clergymen had difficulty getting permission to enter public institutions. In 1849, shortly before founding his own institution for boys, the Reverend George Haskins wrote a series of articles for the Boston *Pilot* giving the Boston House of Reformation and the State Reform School for Boys a favorable review.[5]

In his articles, Haskins assured his readers that children in the reform schools learned discipline, not Protestantism. Haskins contrasted the children of the "uneducated and vicious classes," who were "loathsome rowdies" standing intoxicated on streetcorners and insulting passersby, with the quiet, mannerly boys who stood at attention in their blue uniforms at Westborough. Haskins wrote that the school provided religious instruction only in a general way and that boys remained staunch Catholics.[6] To be sure, Haskins was predisposed to be sympathetic to public reform efforts. Before his conversion to Catholicism, he had been chaplain and superintendent of the House of Reformation, the House of Industry, and the Boylston School (for pauper children). Still, as an influential priest writing in the city's Catholic newspaper, Haskins provided a semiofficial imprimatur on the state's work. Elite Catholics such as Haskins believed that the necessity for lessons in order and discipline outweighed the potential ill effects of the generic Protestantism taught at the reform school.

The assurances of Catholic leaders rang hollow in the face of increasing proselytism. Attention has usually been paid to political nativism, but religious groups acted with equal fervor.[7] National evangelical societies, such as the American Bible Society, the American Home Missionary Society, and the American Tract Society, which had been founded to bring religion to the unchurched, became increasingly nativist in orientation.[8] In Boston, the Society for the Moral and Religious Instruction of the Poor, moribund since the mid-1830s, revived in the 1840s with a campaign to convert Catholics, while the Benevolent Fraternity of Churches, which had taken over Joseph Tuckerman's ministry to the poor, opened Sunday schools in Catholic neighborhoods. The Children's Mission to the Children of the Destitute also opened a Sunday school in the largely Catholic South End in 1849. In its first weeks the Mission attracted 125 children, but soon that number dropped to thirty-four, all Protestants. Two couples stationed near the entrance sent children home if they identified themselves as Catholic. Young toughs pelted the Sunday school with mud and stones and the missionary requested a police guard even when teaching Protestant children.[9] The Boston *Pilot* quoted a member of the city government as saying, "the only way to elevate the foreign population was to make protestants [sic] of their *children*." As religious tension heightened, the leadership of the Boston church was forced into a pattern of institutional separatism.[10]

The first official Catholic response to evangelicals came in a series of religious revivals. Catholic revivals, aimed at the many unchurched immigrants, illustrate the dual strategy of the Catholic leadership. While seeking to bind the immigrants to the Church, the prelates also wished to foster adaptation to the dominant culture that had served them so well. Missions did exactly this.

By strengthening the immigrants' ties to the Church, revivals confronted Protestant proselytism directly, and in that sense revivals fit a defensive pattern of separatism. Missions brought in teams of priests to hear confessions, preach rousing sermons, administer sacraments, and stir the faith of the nominally Catholic. In Boston, Catholic churches sponsored such missions in 1842 and again in 1851, 1859, and 1861.[11] But missions also introduced a new form of faith, one that fit well with bourgeois culture. In Ireland religious practices had been communal affairs, associated with agricultural festivals and family events such as births, marriages, and deaths. In American cities, the Church emphasized the individual's participation in sacramental duties, such as attending weekly mass, receiving the Eucharist, participating in novenas, reforming behavior through temperance, and carrying religious dictums into practice in daily life. The missions in particular emphasized personal religion, secured by faith and by adherence to a strict moral code involving self-improvement. Priests, like ministers, railed against drink, gambling, dancing, and sexual indulgence, while encouraging thrift, hard work, and individualism.[12] Peasant folkways and folk religion were under assault in the mission, and to the degree that the immigrant Irish listened, they were introduced to the values of a modern, bourgeois culture.

The tension between accommodation and separatism can best be followed in the institutions and educational and social welfare programs sponsored by the Church. Children on the streets and delinquent youth were particular targets of intervention by either private agencies or the state, and Catholics formed institutions to shelter them. On the other hand, the Catholic hierarchy was reluctant to build institutions, such as an alternative school system, that might prevent the acculturation of the majority of immigrant children who were otherwise in no danger of being converted. The leadership undertook separatism reluctantly, as a temporary strategy that was forced on them by Protestant proselytizers. After the Civil War, Catholicism lost its association with deviance and Catholic and Protestant social welfare agencies began a common effort to extend bourgeois culture to the poor.[13]

Institutional Separatism

The House of the Angel Guardian (HAG) served the dual function of protecting and isolating Catholic children while equipping them with bourgeois values. George Haskins opened the Angel Guardian in the North End of Boston in 1851, just two years after writing his positive review of the public reformatories. Haskins objected neither to the ends of the public reformatories nor to their congregate style. He acted because of the aggressive efforts of the Protestant sects to enroll Catholic children in their Sunday schools or to place them in rural Protestant families.

Haskins first tried to recruit the beggars and street traders most likely to be targeted by Protestant missionaries. He soon discovered that these boys "much preferred their own erratic life" and that if they came at all, it was on the condition that "they should have the liberty of at least the whole of this world, to say nothing of the next." Finding this group more independent than vulnerable, he next tried to have Catholic boys in the municipal almshouse transferred to the school, but the directors refused. Haskins asked bitterly, "had some broken down tradesman, turned missionary, some 'Father' This or 'Father' That—self-dubbed—applied for these boys, would he have been refused?" Haskins was doubly insulted; not only was this a clear example of anti-Catholic prejudice, but he had been employed prior to his conversion as chaplain and superintendent of the same institutions. Despite these initial problems, Haskins soon filled the Angel Guardian as parents of unruly boys swamped him with requests for admission. The institution did not become a working boys' home or a shelter for vagrants, but a combination temporary home and reformatory used by parents in times of family crisis.[14]

The Angel Guardian was a male preserve that paid strict attention to order and discipline. Upon entry boys received numbers by which they were known in the institution. They were supposed to work and eat in silence, under the surveillance of an officer. The boys arose at five-thirty and, after dressing and praying, marched to the washroom. Then they proceeded single file with downcast eyes to the chapel for mass and prayers. A recreation period followed until breakfast time. At a signal, the boys stopped whatever they were doing, ceased all conversation, and held whatever posture they were in until they heard the next signal. Then they formed a line and marched into the dining hall, where they ate while being read to. The rest of the day was similarly regimented, with periods for school, chores, and recreation. In the evening, the prefect called the roll and each boy reported his conduct, and received either merits or demerits. A balance of merits entitled a boy to some special privileges while demerits led eventually to the "Class of Penance," whose members sat by themselves in silence during recreation periods. After roll call, the boys said prayers and returned to the dormitories, where they undressed, folded their clothes, and went to bed.[15] Haskins was probably incorrect in claiming that few inmates knew each other's names, told their histories, or made lasting friendships, but the claims projected an image of boys as anonymous cogs in a large, smooth-running, silent machine.[16]

This description of the Angel Guardian indicates the values the institution sought to promote. Discipline and punctuality were supplemented by lessons in political economy, thrift, and future orientation as boys carefully toted up their merits, subtracted their demerits, and figured out the purchase price of good behavior. (The latter was literally true, since a balance of merits entitled a boy to some house currency that could be spent in the house store on various treats.) Haskins, from his experience at the House of Reformation, opposed vocational programs as expensive and unlikely to train boys for real jobs. Instead he instituted a unique work release program for the boys who had earned the most merit points. These boys held jobs by day in Boston and at night returned to the Angel Guardian, which deducted board costs and returned the balance to them on release.[17]

The House of the Angel Guardian exhibited none of the characteristics of domestic reform. There was no concern for the naturalizing effect of working the soil or for the feminine influence so many domestic reformers thought vital to remaking children. Even though he founded the Angel Guardian at a time when the family-style reformatory was in its ascendancy, Haskins did not discuss his institution in terms of family or domesticity. The Angel Guardian was similar in some ways to the House of Reformation under E. M. P. Wells, but it also reflected the emphasis on fitting inmates into an industrial economy that became commonplace after the Civil War. This tendency became more pronounced after the Christian Brothers assumed control in 1874 and introduced manual training.

There are several reasons for the Angel Guardian's character. The most logical explanation is Haskins's experience at the House of Reformation. Given Haskins's approval of that institution, it is not surprising that he modeled the Angel Guardian on it. Another explanation lies in Catholic tradition. The school, which was eventually taken over by a religious order, resembled a monastery; it was a congregate, silent, single-sex community. More pragmatically, Irish immigrants were urban settlers, despite their rural backgrounds and some efforts by Catholic clergy to promote migration to the country. A reform school that served as a transitional, rural "family" until a child could be placed in the country had no relevance for Irish Catholics, who formed the majority of the inmates. Finally, one should recall Haskins's opinions of the "rowdies" transformed by the reform school. Since the Angel Guardian served primarily as a temporary shelter for the children of the Irish working class, Haskins may have believed that promoting obedience and discipline was the best that could be hoped for.[18]

The Angel Guardian helped parents weather family crises. A random sample of 250 inmates incarcerated between 1872 and 1897 reveals that 54 percent of the boys left by the end of six months, while 80 percent left after a year. Since Haskins thought the ideal length of stay was between six months and two years, it is apparent that a majority of parents disregarded the institution's reform program and used the Angel Guardian as it fit into their plans. Parents or relatives had to pay at least a portion of a boy's upkeep, and this may have encouraged their independence. The Angel Guardian saved boys from the state reform school and the Protestant child-saving agencies and provided them with some discipline and schooling. For a parent able to recover a son after a short stay, it was not a bad bargain.[19]

As long as the larger society equated Catholicism with deviance, Catholics were forced into separatism. Haskins established the House of the Angel Guardian not because he disagreed with the goals of public institutions, but because he became convinced that they (together with the child-saving agencies) were threatening Catholic boys' faith. At the same time, Catholic working-class families turned to the Angel Guardian as the best alternative to state and private Protestant institutions. But even in the separate Catholic institutions, Catholic children were exposed to the values of the dominant culture.

The Creation of a Catholic School System

The public schools provided the main avenue for acculturation of immigrants. However, the overt Protestantism of the public schools led Catholics into frequent disputes with public authorities over curriculum, Bible reading, prayer, and textbooks.[20] In New York and Philadelphia such disputes led to violence, as nativists attacked Catholics and their institutions.[21] Ultimately Catholics developed their own school systems, but in Boston this process was delayed even after the national plenary council of bishops decreed in 1884 that each parish had to build its own school by 1886. Bishops Fitzpatrick and Williams graduated from the Boston public schools, respected the common school tradition, and rejected the demands of some priests that they assist in the development of a parochial school system. Separatism took a back seat to accommodation and acculturation.

The issue of Bible reading and Protestant sectarianism in the schools came to a head for many Boston Catholics in 1859. Although Bible reading, hymn singing, prayers, and recitation had been an integral part of public education, school authorities allowed Catholic children to read the Catholic Douay Bible and recite from their own texts, or to remain silent during school worship. However, Know Nothing political victories in the mid-1850s emboldened the School Committee to demand that all children participate in Protestant religious exercises. It is notable that a response came, not from the archdiocese, but from a parish priest. Father Wiget of St. Mary's Church in the North End instructed the children in his parish to recite only Catholic versions of prayers and commandments. The boys in the Eliot School agreed not to recite when called upon, and school authorities took Thomas Wall to be their ringleader, perhaps because of his reputed statement, " 'Faith and I wan't agoin to repate thim damned Yankee prayers.' " A schoolmaster used a rattan on Wall's hands until they were cut and bleeding and the boy agreed to read the Protestant version of the commandments. However, three hundred Catholic students who had followed Wiget's instructions were dismissed from school. Wiget formed his own school at St. Mary's for the children of the Irish North End neighborhood, and in 1861, Superintendent John Philbrick noted a decline in Irish enrollment in the public schools, "due in part, probably, to the establishment of Catholic schools" after the Wall incident.[22]

Nonetheless, very few parishes established schools. Only ten out of twenty-seven parishes in Boston had schools by 1880, and the Boston archdiocese did not encourage the creation of more. After the initial furor over the Wall incident faded, Bishop Fitzpatrick urged Catholic parents to return their children to the public schools. He told them that their children would have to obey the law until it was changed, and he suggested that the law's injustice might strengthen Catholic children's faith. Moreover, the School Committee eventually backed down, requiring that only teachers read from the Bible and say the Lord's Prayer, after Catholic voters elected George Haskins to the School Committee.[23]

Compromise was best for everyone. No Catholic school system could possibly educated all Catholic children. Even in Chicago, which had the largest parochial system in the country, only about half the eligible children attended. In addition, no school committee could allow such a large group of parents to become disaffected. The withdrawal of a large group of children into a rival system undermined the entire basis of public education while removing the very children who, according to the dominant view, needed acculturation and proselytizing the most. In addition, both John Fitzpatrick and John Williams had attended the Boston public schools, had significant ties to Brahmin Boston, and, as "Americanists" within the Church, believed that the

Irish would be best served by accepting the values of their new country, which would be learned in the public schools.[24]

Of course accommodation had its critics. Some Catholic laymen
noted that Fitzpatrick had not established any Catholic schools during
his tenure as bishop, and at least one priest charged that Fitzpatrick
had discouraged others' efforts at starting schools. These charges led
to a Vatican investigation, but apparently nothing substantive was
discovered. Fitzpatrick's successor, John Williams, faced similar accu-
sations. In 1876, Father Thomas Scully, representative of a younger
generation of parish priests more estranged from Yankee Boston, complained that Williams had neglected building schools so that Catholics
would not "disturb the *peace*, and lose the *good will* of our Yankee
friends." Williams had surrounded himself with Yankee Catholic advisors, men who shared his faith in American culture and who also
sought accommodation with Protestant Boston. Several pastors of Irish
parishes snipped at Fitzpatrick, Williams, and their Yankee Catholic
coterie, and occasionally won concessions, but accommodation remained the policy of the nineteenth-century Boston Church.[25]

The parochial school issue suggests the ambiguous position of the
Church leadership. Priests and laymen trained in the common school
tradition and accustomed to friendly relations with Brahmin Boston
responded reluctantly to the changing environment. They felt pres-
sured by nativism, by the hostility of Irish Catholics for Brahmin
Boston, by priests unsympathetic to their desire for accommodation,
and by the Vatican, which sought to orient American Catholicism
toward Rome. This leadership ventured into separatism reluctantly
and continued to work for an American Catholicism integrated into a
larger bourgeois culture.

The Basis for Cooperation

By the 1870s and 1880s there existed both a material and a religious
base for Irish Catholic acculturation. The "lace curtain" Irish enjoyed
some prosperity and shared with their American neighbors a belief in
domesticity, temperance, sexual purity, and industry. In addition,
post-1870 Irish immigrants differed significantly from the famine gen-

eration and brought with them values more in tune with Victorian America. While the culture of bourgeois Irish Americans remained distinctive, what they shared with the dominant bourgeois culture is more important than what distinguished them. These similarities became more apparent after the Civil War reduced Catholic-Protestant hostility.

The service of Irish Catholics during the Civil War promoted acceptance. Despite participation in the Draft Riots in 1863, the Irish proved loyal to their adopted country and served in large numbers in the Union armies. The former Columbian Artillery, banned by the Know Nothings in the 1850s, formed the core of the Ninth Massachusetts Regiment, and other predominantly Irish units were recruited as well. Over five hundred thousand immigrants fought for the Union and charges of un-Americanism were, at least for a time, laid to rest.[26]

Loyalty to the Union certainly helped Irish Catholics reach an accommodation with Protestant Boston, but the changing face of the Irish Catholic community was at least as important. Petty entrepreneurs, white collar workers, and conservative labor leaders defined themselves culturally in ways that were similar to bourgeois Protestants. By the 1870s and 1880s, first- and second-generation Irish families settled into modest homes in Roxbury, one of Boston's inner suburbs. Suburbanization was a reflection of growing prosperity and of the adoption of a domestic ideal. By 1890, about 10 percent of the city's Irish immigrants had white collar occupations, while nearly 40 percent of their children had white collar jobs, although the vast majority were of a fairly low status. Still, these jobs provided more job security than did unskilled labor, as well as the financial wherewithal for purchasing a suburban home. Gradually the material basis for adopting a bourgeois culture emerged.[27]

The Irish were also the middlemen for other immigrant groups. Because of their early arrival, their large numbers, their knowledge of English, and their ability to organize politically, the Irish captured increasingly higher rungs of municipal services and the Church bureaucracy. They acted as cultural and political brokers for other immigrants, formed alliances with established groups, and became entrenched as a socially and politically conservative force. They not only became acculturated but even assumed the position of acculturating others.[28]

Irish Catholic prosperity provided the opportunity for the emergence of a Catholic version of bourgeois domestic culture. Like Protestants, these Catholics valued a well-ordered suburban home to which a father retreated after his work. While Catholic women had a more restricted role than Protestant women in the organization of home religious devotions because of the sacramental and church-centered nature of Catholicism, they still set a moral tone for the household and taught domestic and religious values to children. Catholic domestic literature stressed parish, family, and home, rather than the tavern and male companionship that had been the focus of male life in Ireland and that continued to be the center of working-class male culture.[29]

Catholicism in Ireland also changed and promoted values that helped the post-1870 immigrants fit well in the United States. In Ireland, Paul Cardinal Cullen appointed young bishops loyal to him, constructed new churches, schools, and seminaries, began to reform the clergy, and introduced new religious observances in order to centralize authority, promote literacy, and redefine the loosely organized folk Catholicism of Ireland. Whereas only 40 percent of the Irish were churched in 1840, by 1890 that had increased to about 90 percent. The new devotionalism has been explained as both a cultural response to increasing Anglicization and as a substitute for the folk religious practices that had failed to ward off the tragedy of the famine. Whatever its source, the new devotionalism fostered a Catholicism that emphasized temperance, chastity, and obedience. Since these decades also witnessed a rising standard of living in Ireland, post-1870 Irish immigrants to the United States were quite different from the famine generation. They were more literate, wealthier, and more religious, and brought a culture that separated them more from the Irish American poor than from bourgeois Victorians.[30]

By the 1880s, the effects of increased wealth and intensified religious devotionalism were apparent. An Irish Catholic bourgeoisie had emerged that shared values with their Protestant American counterparts. They engaged in activities that spread their culture and, as a byproduct, fostered their acceptance by their Protestant peers. Visiting the homes of the poor and organizing charity were among the most important of these activities.

Charity Organization

Bourgeois Catholics defined themselves in part through visiting the poor, which they organized through the St. Vincent de Paul Society. Frederic Ozanam founded the Society in France in 1833 in answer to the charge that organized Catholicism cared little for the temporal needs of the poor. Brought to Boston in 1861, the Society was an organization of laymen who volunteered to visit poor families weekly for spiritual and moral counseling and to provide food, clothing, and, occasionally, money. The St. Vincent de Paul Society discovered through its activities that it shared a common ground with Protestant charitable agencies. This in turn prompted an agreement on child-saving that allowed Protestant and Catholic agencies to pay full attention to uplifting the poor.[31]

Visiting the poor and teaching them lessons in respectability assured the visitor of his own status. When recruiting visitors, the Vincentians stressed that they were to be "young gentlemen of social position, education, means, and leisure." The Society admitted that too often potential visitors were professionals just developing their practices, or shopkeepers who had to devote both night and day to earning a living, or young white collar workers who wished to spend free time on recreation or physical development. These individuals had little time to devote to charity, but they had to learn the obligations of bourgeois status, the "solid happiness" of serving God through "ministering to the wants of the afflicted, the neglected, the unfortunate." Service was proof of bourgeois respectability and of the seriousness of Catholic intent to share the burden of transforming the poor.[32]

The St. Vincent de Paul Society shared the methods and the goals of the Protestant ("nonsectarian") charity organization societies. It wanted to reconnect the wealthy and the poor, it restricted aid, which it saw as a means of leverage over the family, and it emphasized reconstructing working-class families, rather than removing children from them. Vincentians claimed that the presence of the visitor suggested to the poor that they were not a caste, cut off and despised by the rest of society. The visitor provided aid efficiently because he had personal knowledge of a family's circumstances. He assisted the worthy poor, found jobs for the unemployed, and resisted "the impositions of professional beggars and idlers."[33] The Vincentians discussed aid as a way of gaining entry into a family, winning "a welcome where otherwise our visit would be looked upon as impertinent meddling." Once a friendly relationship was established, the "real work" of preaching the gospel began. However, the visitors taught as much of a cultural gospel as a religious one. They preached temperance, thrift, piety, hard work, and self-reliance and made adherence to these values the price of assistance. Moreover, they saw charity in the same utilitarian way that Protestants frequently did. Almsgiving and visiting saved society from "the dry rot of communism or a war of classes."[34]

The Vincentians also wanted to cooperate with Protestant agencies. Theirs was not a sectarian battle, but a common effort to uplift the poor and prevent pauperism. Thomas Mulry, a Catholic prominent in social welfare, argued that without cooperation among agencies a form of "piracy" existed in which different agencies poached in the other's territories, and paupers and idlers were the only winners. "A catholic [sic] today, a protestant [sic] to-morrow, and a Hebrew the day after, [the pauper] could carry on his trade with impunity." The crusade against pauperism waged by the Vincentians struck a chord with Protestants. In its 1870 report, the St. Vincent de Paul Society thanked Protestants for contributing to its efforts and cited the Boston Provident Association for relieving the many families who could not be assisted by the Vincentians. Although the St. Vincent de Paul Society declined the invitation to join Boston's Associated Charites in 1879, the Society's president, Thomas Ring, became a member of the Associated Charities' executive committee and urged Vincentians to participate in its local chapters.[35]

An agreement on child-saving was key to cooperation. More than any other issue, the loss of Catholic children to Protestant agencies and families had led to the formation of separate Catholic institutions. In 1887, non-Catholic social welfare agencies in Boston agreed to report all cases of abandoned or destitute Catholic children to the local parish priest or to the president of the parish's Vincentians. Vincentians, in turn, agreed to refer cases to more appropriate private or public agencies, including the Society for the Prevention of Cruelty to Children and to public welfare authorities. This spirit of cooperation affected the separatist institutions as well. The House of the Angel Guardian raised a portion of its annual budget from Protestant contributors, while the admission statistics for the Home for Destitute Catholic Children (1864) offer another measure of the results of cooperation. Public or private "nonsectarian" agencies referred one-third of the children admitted between its founding and 1930. The city also began to work with the Catholics in 1888 by allowing a St. Vincent de Paul Society agent to attend children's trials, visit the lock-up, and take charge of Catholic delinquents. A Society member in the delinquent's parish acted as a probation officer, visiting weekly and making sure the child was in school or employed. When in 1889 the Overseers of the Poor provided the Vincentians' agent with an office in the Charity Building, along with the city's older Protestant groups, it symbolized the new status of Boston's Catholics.[36]

Poverty rather than Catholicism reemerged as the distinguishing badge of deviance. The rise of bourgeois Irish Catholics, solidly Victorian and themselves concerned about property and fearful of the poor, severed the connection between poverty and Catholicism and, to a lesser degree, between bourgeois culture and Protestantism. Bourgeois Catholics and bourgeois Protestants were not the same, but they shared enough of an identity and a class interest defined in relationship to the poor, that cooperation became possible.

Separate institutions had served their purpose; they had promoted acculturation while defending Catholics' religious interests. Once religion became divorced from class identity, these institutions, although they continued to provide a Catholic version of bourgeois culture, were incorporated into an emerging social welfare system.

To be sure, ethnic and religious rivalry emerged again, but never with the virulence of midcentury. In the 1890s the American Protective Association campaigned against the Catholics, and tensions rose again in Boston, culminating in a riot in 1895. But the APA did not achieve a wide following and its activities were more the dying embers of an earlier nativism than the harbinger of a new campaign.[37] And at the turn of the century, Irish Democrats shrugged off their alliance with Yankee Democrats, resorted to religious and ethnic appeals, and took control of city hall. But the basic accommodations on child-saving still held and Boston entered the Progressive era with a unified network of social welfare agencies.

CHAPTER 7

The Charity Network

A group of Methodist missionaries, touring the North End's "by-ways to hell" in 1867, discovered flourishing brothels, dance halls, and gambling dens. From spots all along North Street, boisterous laughter, squealing fiddles, and the sounds of dancing invited passersby to enter. The missionaries discovered a world where a mission had become a dance hall, where known criminals and notorious women assembled, and where men took their sexual pleasure. Everywhere blacks and whites mingled on an equal footing, and the missionaries commented on the number of mulattoes they found—further proof, apparently, of the totally dissipated natures of the vicious poor. They saw fifteen- or sixteen-year-old girls with toothless smiles and sunken eyes, the signs of moral "leprosy." The cost of dissipation was most obvious in a nine-year-old white boy with only one arm and a "face that bore the unmistakable signs of the idiocy of vice." He shuffled over to an elderly black woman, signaling that he wanted something. Taking the dime offered him "with a contortion of his features that was meant for a smile, but more resembled the grimace of a monkey," the boy headed for the bar, where he downed his drink "as if it had been mother's milk." Here was the antithesis of the progressive bourgeois world, one where fifty years of reform had been defied and where the inherited legacy of viciousness and vice left a physical imprint on the degenerating poor.[1]

Missionaries responded traditionally to this scene from Sodom: they created the North End Mission and distributed religious tracts, preached, and opened a refuge for prostitutes. The missionaries conceived of the North End's problems as moral and the solution as individual regeneration through religious conversion. Although they apparently held a Lamarckian view of heredity, in other ways they viewed the city no differently than the Society for the Religious and Moral Institution of the Poor had in 1817, and with less sophistication than Joseph Tuckerman in the 1830s. Poverty stemmed from vice, which was an individual moral problem.

Within a decade of their visit, however, the missionaries had changed their approach entirely. Shuttling rescued prostitutes off to the country to be trained as domestics, they concentrated on providing social services to the neighborhood's other inhabitants—the large Irish community and fledgling groups of Italians and Portuguese. By the mid-1870s, the Mission had become a secular neighborhood center.[2]

The history of the North End Mission exemplifies the shift from traditional charity to neighborhood social service in postbellum social welfare. Reformers realized that the poor could not be transformed by taking a few of their children and placing them in the countryside. Instead they attempted to change the environment that produced delinquent children by establishing a more pervasive presence in working-class neighborhoods. Their network of boys' and girls' clubs, industrial schools, home libraries, and recreational facilities invited children and their families into a bourgeois cultural sphere. Social welfare agencies also succeeded in organizing charity. Sectarian and organizational rivalries diminished in the face of the overwhelming social and economic crises of the period between the depression of 1873 and the end of the century. As seen in the previous chapter, Catholic and Protestant societies began to cooperate, and the Associated Charities, established in 1879, coordinated relief-giving by the agencies. Finally, reformers recognized that they were dealing with a new social structure. They still aimed to transform the poor, but they provided them with a distinctive working-class version of the dominant culture.

The Missionaries

The North End Mission's women visitors expanded the Mission's program to include secular goals as well as religious ones. Visitors from families of "comfort and culture and refinement" supplied moral advice and aid to the worthy poor much as the antebellum ministers to the poor had done. But the visitors found it difficult to explain poverty just in terms of moral failings, especially in the light of a national depression and widespread unemployment. As a result, they proposed measures alien to the spirit of laissez faire, and they moved beyond the positions taken by Joseph Tuckerman and the antebellum poverty workers.[3]

Temporary measures to provide work for poor women turned into permanent social service for women and children. The Mission formed an "industrial school" after the fire of 1872 destroyed much of Boston's downtown, including its garment district. Many of the North End's working-class women worked in the garment factories while their husbands, who were part of the North End's fishing fleet, were at sea. The garment factories were their sole source of support during many months of the year, and the Mission started the industrial school to offer them alternative employment. In a program that combined relief and entrepreneurship, the Mission provided the cloth and the women marketed the garments they stitched. Since the depression of 1873 followed on the heels of the fire, the industrial school became permanent and expanded. The Mission added a sewing class for the girls in the neighborhood in the hope of steering them away from jobs as singers and dancers in the concert halls, which employed girls as young as twelve. Here the choices facing working-class girls were starkly posed: training for the garment factory or the lure of the concert hall with the possibility of casual prostitution. The Mission also opened an inexpensive restaurant, with service provided by the neighborhood women, and in 1876, a summer camp for children, and the following year, a nursery school for working mothers. The generally sympathetic attitude of the women volunteers is indicated by one who asked what good tracts and prayers did " 'to a lot of poor bodies who haven't anything to eat, nor decent clothes to cover them.' "[4]

Where Joseph Tuckerman had feared to intervene in the workings of the marketplace, these women offered employment and the social services needed to allow poor women to accept it. It is not clear whether the missionaries provided child care and other services because they were able to identify with the needs of working mothers, or whether poor women forced the missionaries to respond to their circumstances. Most likely it was a combination of the two—the Mission, as a private agency, could only invite the poor into its doors and therefore it had to respond to their needs in order to attract them, while the women missionaries were themselves familiar with the burdens of caring for children and a home. As a result, the Mission challenged the tradition of providing the poor with only temporary aid and free advice. The social services provided were innovative and allowed poor women the opportunity to choose employment over pauperism or vice. But the missionaries left unquestioned the larger economic context that presented the poor with such a narrow range of choices.

The missionaries also did not question the tradition of cultural uplift. They approached the inhabitants of the North End with "throbbing hearts" and reached into the "foulest depths" to grasp any hand seeking help. Lessons in "industry, cleanliness, morality, and religion" were part of vocational training. The very fact that garment workers were "taught" sewing in a "school" is suggestive of the volunteers' unreflecting condescension. And while the women volunteers may not have handed out religious tracts, they had not become entirely secularized. They preached and read from the Bible to the many Portuguese women who sewed at the Mission, and commended them for being free of bigotry despite their Catholicism. (They noted without irony that readings were in English, which few of the women understood.) Child placement, while not an important part of the Mission's activities, offers another example of the volunteers' sense of cultural mission. The Mission's reports offered as examples of its success the cases of two Irish boys who adopted the Yankee surnames of their foster families. Through the placement, "what was a burden to society has been changed to a support." The Mission volunteers provided vital social services, which they traded for the opportunity to shape the culture of the poor.[5]

The Mission's shift from simple proselytizing to a complex array of services was common to religious organizations in this period. Urban parishes with dwindling congregations turned to social programs to revitalize their churches. The "institutional church" movement asked wealthy church members to sponsor trade schools and boys' and girls' clubs in order to provide vocational and cultural lessons to the poor. Perhaps immigrants could not be transformed into Protestant Yankees, but they could be provided with services and taught useful skills and work habits. This trend was most apparent in programs for children.[6]

The Child-Savers

One way of preventing delinquency was by providing alternatives to the streets where working-class children spent their time.[7] Home libraries, children's clubs, industrial schools, and gymnasiums, all introduced in the 1880s, provided recreation, manual training, and cultural uplift under the aegis of bourgeois reformers. The agencies cooperated with one another and their programs introduced children to the dominant culture, but in a version tailored to fit a working-class audience.

The most concerted effort to control children's time occurred with delinquents on probation. The Boston Children's Aid Society was the first organization to take large numbers of children on probation. The Society began interceding in court proceedings in 1865, but until the mid-1880s probation ("outdoor work") took a back seat to reforming children in the Society's institutions at Pine Farm and Rock Lawn. Charles Birtwell, hired as an outdoor worker in 1885, reoriented CAS activities. Probation enabled the agency to reach more children than it could through its institutional programs, while the increased number of neighborhood social service agencies meant that children on probation could be supervised more carefully than before. When Birtwell took children from court, he tried to become acquainted with their families and personal circumstances. Depending on his assessment, Birtwell placed children in the industrial classes, sewing groups, and evening programs run by different social welfare organizations. Children guilty of more serious offenses reported weekly to Society headquarters, while less serious offenders appeared every two weeks. They brought reports from their parents and teachers and were assisted in finding jobs, with their first obligation being the repayment of court costs and fines. In 1893 the Society had oversight of thirteen hundred children, nine hundred of whom were supervised at home, three hundred in other families, and only one hundred at the Society's institutions. The advent of social work provided the courts with an alternative to institutionalizing children, placing them in foster homes, or simply releasing them.[8]

The home library program, begun by the Children's Aid Society in 1887, attempted to shape children's leisure time. The Society deposited a case of twenty books in the home of the child who acted as librarian and circulated them among the group. The librarian hosted weekly book discussions led by a home visitor, and in 1893 seventy groups with over 630 children participated in the program. The Society viewed the home libraries as counteracting the harmful influences of popular culture, particularly dime novels. The Society also initiated the children into the world of thrift through the Boston Stamp-Savings Society. The children bought penny stamps from the visitors, pasted them on cards that eventually were redeemed for cash, and then opened savings accounts.[9]

Despite the emphasis on thrift and self-reliance, the cultural curriculum offered by the social welfare agencies differed in important respects from that taught earlier under domestic reform. Domestic reform demanded the development of character and the internalization of bourgeois values by encouraging children to use foster parents or the superintendents of a family-style institution as role models. In the 1880s, social welfare agencies emphasized manual training, vocational education, and military drill—the same program adopted by the reformatories. Educational and recreational reformers argued that repetitive physical activity developed a child's mental ability and moral sensibility, which was particularly appropriate for poor children and for older boys who otherwise became habituated to idleness and immorality. Exacting woodworking exercises and military drills in precise formations taught obedience and attention to detail that reformers hoped would become instinctive and ingrain moral rectitude for a lifetime. The skills learned in manual training classes had little or nothing to do with fitting youths for jobs in an industrial economy; rather, they developed work habits necessary for members of an industrial working class.[10]

Home Library Group, 19 Shaving Street, 1889. Boston Children's Services.

Home libraries were part of the effort to assert control over the leisure time of working-class children. This photograph captures the group's spirit: a mixture of defiance and pride with a willingness to see what reformers might be up to. Note the absence of older boys and the stance of the outsiders on the fence.

The North Bennet Street Industrial School offers a good example of the narrower approach to reform. The school began as the North End Industrial Home in 1880 and taught women how to operate sewing machines, cook, and do laundry. The Industrial Home emphasized self-help, selling sewing machines at cost to seamstresses, and charging ten cents for every dollar earned by the laundresses in order to encourage them to save and buy their own equipment. Recognizing the child care needs of working mothers, the Industrial Home established a nursery and kindergarten, while a restaurant, staffed by women from the cooking classes, offered inexpensive lunches.[11] Clay modeling classes, a shoe shop, and military drill were added to the curriculum in order to attract boys and, beginning in 1885, three hundred students from local public schools came weekly for the manual education program. The institution, signifying the change in focus, adopted a new name, the North Bennet Street Industrial School.[12]

The North Bennet Street Industrial School made clear its commitment to deportment and re-formed cultural values. Street boys "rough in manner and careless in appearance" learned, the School claimed, to become "quiet self-respecting youths, quick to obey and eager to learn." The institution viewed ethnic cultures dimly, as rivals to the dominant culture. As one volunteer remembered, "we play Crokinole and Parlor Pool and try to keep them happy and quiet. They mustn't get excited, chew gum, spit, swear, cheat or talk Italian." Like the North End Mission, the Industrial School saw itself in direct competition with street culture, dance halls, and the saloon. The directors noted with pleasure that the addition of a gymnasium and military drill attracted older boys of age fifteen away from street fighting and saloons. Similarly, evening recreation programs for girls who worked in the North End's chocolate factories or in the garment district kept them away from dance halls and the theater. With its vocational classes for school children and recreational programs for adolescents, the Industrial School declared it reclaimed hundreds of North End families. Children learned "habits of order, neatness, punctuality, honesty, gentler ways of speaking and acting," and their families benefited from their example.[13]

Work with children was not an end in itself. Reformers looked on it as a way of gaining entry into the working-class family. William

Tucker, founder of Boston's Andover House (later the South End House) wrote that the small boy was a "natural medium of communication" with local families, while Andover House workers reported that they felt like intruders in the neighborhood until boys' work enabled them to establish a natural relationship with families.[14] Children's Aid Society visitors used the book discussions as an opportunity to record the family's history and to examine its habits and living conditions. Visitors looked for evidence of destitution, truancy, waywardness, illegal liquor dealing, and moral exposure, which was then reported to the appropriate agency. The Society referred cases to the Associated Charities, the Society for the Prevention of Cruelty to Children, the Board of Health, and the Law and Order League, a private organization formed to root out illegal liquor selling, prostitution, and gambling. In 1900, workers from the South End House, a social settlement, began to serve as library visitors, and settlement workers noted that through the libraries they gained access to the "inner life of parts of the neighborhood which would otherwise have to be reached at arm's length."[15]

The effect of such intrusion into the neighborhood and the family should not be exaggerated. Certainly it added indignity to the difficulty of being poor, it reinforced the poor's wariness of contact with social welfare agencies, and it helped define the experience of class. But these were private agencies, without extensive resources, that had to attract the poor into their sphere. This forced reformers to negotiate with children and families over the use of recreational space and the distribution of goods and services.

The history of the Ellis Memorial Center demonstrates this process of negotiation. In 1885 Ida Eldridge, decided to open a boys' club in Boston's South End. Eldridge, a young religious woman looking for a calling, had been a successful Sunday school teacher for several years in her Back Bay parish. She reflected, however, that she knew only people who lived in the Back Bay or Beacon Hill and voted the Republican ticket. In order to enter into a wider world of social experience, she, with the help of her minister, overcame her father's objections and persuaded him to donate a vacant storefront and let her "have" a boys' club. Eldridge outfitted the storefront and brought refreshments for the club's first Wednesday evening meeting. The opening of the club attracted a flock of curious youngsters, and Eldridge, after introducing herself and her companions, asked the boys to line up and do the same. Each boy gave his name as either John L. Sullivan or James Corbett.

At a time when boxing was disreputable and the Marquis of Queensbury's rules were not universally accepted, the names of the Boston Strong Boy and Gentleman Jim conjured up a virile working-class world. Boxers were folk heroes who had achieved success and fame, not through industry, thrift, and temperance, but in spite of them. Prizefighting, promoted by saloonkeepers and gamblers, was part of the marginal world of organized crime and ward politics in which a working-class male could achieve success, and it was symbolic of the street culture reformers found so objectionable. Adolescent boys could have found few names more appropriate for twitting reformers' genteel sensibilities.[16]

To her credit, Miss Eldridge took it all in stride. She told the boys she realized that they might not yet be ready for a club but she invited them to enjoy the refreshments she had brought and to return the following week. Some did, and Miss Eldridge had her club, which eventually became the Ellis Memorial Center.[17]

Boy's programs had to be devised to attract and hold a demanding audience. Anything smacking of preaching and lessons in gentility was hooted down, and boys' workers found their greatest success with younger children. Older boys were interested primarily in athletics, and if a club could not supply athletic facilities, it had little chance of retaining adolescents. Clubs walked a fine line between making membership inclusive and maintaining control over their facilities. The Ellis Center started a branch club but eventually had to give it up. "After a while, there were elected in characters of a pretty tough reputation, and it was remarked at one gathering by a member, 'It is doubtful if a tougher crowd could be found together in any section of the city.' " Youths turned clubs into contested terrain.[18]

Children and their families negotiated with reformers on a more equal basis when the outcome was not vital to family survival. In conflicts over leisure time, the use of recreational space, or the type of training and services an agency provided, families had the option of refusing assistance, of pushing the agency into meeting their needs, or of trying their luck elsewhere. As in the past, the bitterest struggles were over charity and here reformers had the most power.

The Charity Organizers

The Associated Charities (1879) succeeded where Joseph Tuckerman had failed—in organizing Boston's relief-giving agencies. Charity workers, applying organizational skills developed in the Civil War, classified and counted the poor, formed a bureaucratic structure for relief distribution, and were relatively unsentimental about poverty.[19] At the same time, the Associated Charities relied on volunteer friendly visitors to uplift the poor. While the Associated Charities documented the extent of poverty and organized the network of agencies confronting it, it continued to assume that the surest escape from poverty was for the individual to adopt bourgeois values under the guidance of a well-to-do visitor. Only after the turn of the century did the Associated Charities surrender this traditional approach to reform.

Seen organizationally, the Associated Charities looks like a social welfare bureaucracy, with its hierarchical organization, rules for visitors, case methods, careful record keeping, and categories of assistance. The Associated Charities divided the city into districts, and a "conference," consisting of overseers of the poor from that area, the captain of police, and representatives from the various private agencies active there, presided over welfare in the district. At the weekly conference meetings, they reviewed applications for relief, determined the "worthiness" of each applicant, coordinated the activities of volunteer visitors, and passed information about applications on to a central register, which started a file on each case. A paid agent supervised the day-to-day operations of each district and advised the visitors how to proceed. Each conference sent three delegates to the Council of Associated Charities, which also included three Overseers of the Poor, a police commissioner, a trustee from the City Hospital, the Inspector of State Charities, the State Superintendents of Indoor and Outdoor Poor, and representatives from independent groups such as St. Vincent de Paul Society. The Associated Charities tied sectarian and public charity into a more effective network.[20]

The organizational perspective, usual for historians of social work, distorts as much as it reveals. By directing attention to the "modern" and bureaucratic functions of the charity organizers, it overlooks the distinctly traditional ideology of the Associated Charities. The Associated Charities used volunteer visitors when other agencies had begun switching to paid agents in the 1850s. The agency did not recognize the incongruity of combining investigation with friendly visiting, and while it stressed that its practices were businesslike and avoided sentiment, it argued that volunteer visitors could restore harmony between the classes.[21]

Home visiting was the key to both cultural reformation and charity organization. The Associated Charities argued that relief had to be tailored to the specific needs of an individual family, which could be discovered only by a home visit, and that aid had to be given personally, with appropriate moral lessons, in order to engender gratitude and devotion toward the benefactor. All other forms of relief ran into the danger of creating pauperism. Therefore it was especially important to cut outdoor public relief, even during a depression, since it could not be controlled and public authorities did not distinguish between worthy and unworthy applicants. Moreover, since public welfare was dispensed in the name of an anonymous public, it did not reinforce the ties between the wealthy and the poor, and the poor came to see it as a right. Only relief based on careful investigation, coordinated at all levels to prevent excessive help, and dispensed under the guidance of a visitor could exert a positive social influence. The Associated Charities promoted a slightly updated version of Malthusian welfare reform.[22]

The charity organizers viewed the poor as individual moral agents responsible for their fates and self-help remained the linchpin of reform.[23] Robert Treat Paine, president of the Associated Charities, offers insight into its philosophy. Paine, a Harvard-educated lawyer and scion of a once-wealthy Brahmin family, earned a fortune through shrewd investments and retired from business at age thirty-five. Thereafter he devoted his time to reform, serving on the boards of the Children's Aid Society, the Industrial Aid Society, and the Associated Charities. These three agencies sought to provide individuals with opportunities for self-help. The Children's Aid Society equipped children with work habits and a rudimentary education, the Industrial

Aid Society found jobs for the unemployed, and the Associated Charities ensured that the worthy received aid and advice. Paine's housing projects offer the best example of his principles. Paine urged that working men should have the opportunity to purchase decent, low-cost housing and capitalized a cooperative bank, the Workingmen's Loan Association, to provide them with mortgages. The houses Paine built sold for a small profit, and the cooperative provided mortgages at less than the market rate.[24]

Paine's housing reform, although admirable in itself and more than most of his contemporaries attempted, had more ideological than practical significance. The effort of a single individual could not even begin to address the need for low-cost housing in Boston. Like the women of the North End Mission, Paine intervened in the marketplace to provide an opportunity for a few worthy members of the working class to exercise bourgeois virtue. His social services assisted those individuals most capable of self-help and reinforced the ideological message of social welfare, namely, that the sources of poverty were individual and moral, as were its solutions.

As in the past, the principle of less eligibility shaped relief and underscored the message of self-help. Josephine Shaw Lowell, a founder of the New York Charity Organization Society, argued that the "honest laborer" should not see the children of the drunkard "enjoy advantages which his own may not hope for." Robert Treat Paine warned of the impact on workingmen and their children of seeing a professional beggar earning more money than they. Without realizing the irony of his comment on the inadequacy of workingmen's wages, Paine could only warn of the "poison" to children's minds of believing that "begging prospers while honest industry is cold and hungry." The Associated Charities reprinted an essay by Octavia Hill, the English charity reformer, which concluded that the poor remained in low-paying jobs in order to obtain charity, while Annie Fields, an American reformer, argued that men would struggle to support their families only if they found the "room cold and the table bare," and not if they thought their children would be cared for by charity. Charity had to be miserly because those who would not help themselves could only be driven to the marketplace by the pinch of poverty.[25]

Threatening families with the loss of their children was also a goad to reform. Robert Treat Paine wrote to Edward Frothingham of the Provident Society that taking children from their families was a last resort, but one that "should be held up squarely before the eyes of the father." Annie Fields, in her manual *How to Help the Poor*, suggested to potential visitors that they become well acquainted with the Society for the Prevention of Cruelty to Children. The friendly visitor could feel more effective knowing there was a "certain power behind their friendship." And one visitor advised calling on families when their children were present because children between six and ten were often unwittingly valuable sources of information about the family.[26]

The demand that relief be curtailed and charity organized subsumed the conflicting goal of uplifting the poor culturally. For the poor, a home visit meant being scrutinized for moral failings and having one's home life evaluated, with a month's rent or supply of coal hanging in the balance. Eventually the Associated Charities realized that when relief was tied to the expression of virtue, the poor fervently espoused it.[27] Social welfare professionals gradually replaced the volunteers and abandoned the rhetoric of friendly visiting, with its promise of cultural uplift through cross-class friendships. The Associated Charities, ostensibly the most modern of the social welfare agencies, was among the last groups to move from an uplift to a social service model. During the depression of 1893, Robert Treat Paine called for public works to deal with the crisis. Although his position was not endorsed by all members of the Associated Charities board, it represented a significant departure for the organization. In a world dominated by large-scale economic forces, traditional explanations of unemployment and poverty were found wanting, as were the usual exhortations to moral reform. Reformers settled for providing social services and preparing their clients to assume their places in an industrial working class.[28]

By the 1890s, social welfare agencies were omnipresent in Boston's working-class neighborhoods. Home libraries, boys' and girls' clubs, industrial schools, gymnasiums, settlement houses, and playgrounds attested to the effort to reshape the culture and leisure of working-class children and their families. Responses to reform were distributed across a continuum from passive acquiescence to active resistance. Since contact with these agencies was not mandatory, one obvious way to deal with them was to ignore their existence. When interaction became necessary, working people brought their own agendas. Boys enjoyed gymnasiums, carpentry, and playing soldier and remained blissfully unaware that they were supposed to be learning precision and to follow orders. Girls joined sewing clubs for sociability and to learn a skill that might provide income for the family economy or spending money, while they attended socials for the free refreshments and the presence of boys. Immigrants learned English and did not necessarily Americanize in the process. Poor people sought relief, listened to lectures, and then went about their business. Reformers, like the police, the truant officer, or city inspectors, were simply part of the urban landscape to be negotiated.[29]

Two contemporary discussions of Boston's social reform efforts provide opportunity for a final assessment of social welfare in the period 1870 to 1900. In 1894 Edward Everett Hale published *If Jesus Came to Boston* as a reply to William T. Stead's notorious *If Christ Came to Chicago*, which listed brothel locations and detailed municipal corruption. Rather than writing of Boston's corruption and its vice districts, Hale guided the reader through a North End transformed by the charities. Instead of finding "by-ways to hell," as did the missionaries in 1867, Hale discovered that the city was equipped with agencies for every emergency, the police were willing to crack down on the vice that existed, and children were being educated. The Boston of 1894 was a triumph of Victorian progress.[30]

Benjamin Flower's *Civilization's Inferno*, published a year earlier, reached a different conclusion. Flower described Boston's tenement districts as a "social cellar" out of which violent disorder could burst at any time. He gave accounts of poor families huddled together in a single room, of an invalid, with savings exhausted, driven to cut the throats of his children and himself, and of the poor turning to drink to ease their despair. Flower's Boston teetered on the edge of class war.[31]

Hale and Flower were both right. Hale, the grand old man of Boston moral reform, looked back to the days of Joseph Tuckerman and saw a successful campaign to organize charity and a remarkable decline in the open expression of prostitution and vice. North Street had been made respectable, and the slums blanketed by social welfare agencies that distributed relief according to scientific principles and offered an array of social services to the poor. Somehow he was able to ignore entirely that Boston was in the midst of a depression, with thousands of people unemployed. Flower, a muckracking journalist, was appalled by the chasm between rich and poor, and worried about the possibility of violence by the dispossessed. Flower saw the poor tossed about by the economic forces seemingly beyond anyone's control and found organized charity as irrelevant as moral reform to the problems of poverty and disorder.[32] Flower was a part of a rising generation of Progressives who thought that massive social and economic problems required more than voluntarism; they could be solved only by more positive intervention by the state. Delinquency was one such problem, and the juvenile court was part of a more activist public sector. Its creation organized the still-loose network of private and public, religious and nonsectarian, coercive and voluntary agencies into a juvenile justice system.

PART IV

Expertise and Scientific Reform

$\mathcal{F}$OR the Progressives, children and reform were practically synonymous. In the national effort to enact reform measures, tenement house reformers used photographs of children and their parents crowded into single-room apartments to show the need for improved housing. Lewis Hine indicted textile mill owners with photographs of barefoot boys and girls dwarfed by the machines they tended. "Newsies" hawking papers in saloons symbolized both individual entrepreneurship and the perils of street trading. Children playing next to decaying offal emphasized the need for playgrounds and sanitary reform. States expanded outdoor relief to prevent the breakup of families by funding mothers' pensions. The number of humane and other societies tending to child welfare expanded dramatically in the United States, with thirty-three founded in the 1880s, forty-nine in the 1890s, and seventy-seven in the first decade of the twentieth century. New institutions for wayward children were founded at a rate of twenty-two per year between 1886 and 1909. Existing institutions for children underwent an overhaul, with increased emphasis placed on keeping children in their own families or putting them in foster care rather than in institutions, and interest in child welfare culminated with a White House conference on the subject in 1909.[1]

There were three reasons for child-saving's particular appeal to Progressives. First, large numbers of potentially unassimilable immigrants and their offspring threatened to undermine bourgeois hegemony, and their children posed an obvious opportunity for reform. Second, while in the dominant culture the child was the devoted object of affection in a closely knit, smaller family, immigrant and working-class children flocked to the mills, sweatshops, and street trades in ever-greater numbers between 1870 and 1910. Ironically, the structure of the economy, technological innovation, and the creation of a vast unskilled adult labor pool through immigration undermined the basis for child labor in northern cities at precisely the time reformers discovered its evils. Nonetheless, the disparity between the bourgeois ideal of the sheltered child and the image of the precocious working-class one was an important spur to reform. A third factor was the creation of the concept of adolescence by social scientists. The theories of G. Stanley Hall, and the many popularizers who wrote about boys, emphasized adolescence as a period of primitive amorality among youngsters, making their deviance seem normal but highlighting the necessity of proper socialization. However, concern about exploited and/or morally exposed working-class children and changes in the reified world of social science would have made little difference to working-class children had it not been for social welfare agencies.[2]

Social welfare agencies were key players in putting child welfare on the political agenda. Progressive social welfare reformers sought to curb child labor, expand educational opportunities, provide support for women and children in their homes, and generally better working-class living conditions, while establishing themselves as experts/professionals who could intervene in working-class families. For them, child-saving was a happy union of benevolence and self-interest, and they lobbied to create a constituency for child welfare.[3]

The juvenile court and the mental health clinic emerged out of this context of expanded child welfare activity, a focus on the family, and the acknowledged failure of established institutions for juveniles. While the court and the clinic were in many ways the culmination of nineteenth-century child-saving, they also represented a new departure:

Stealing Coal from the Railroad Coal Yard, 1917. Lewis Hine Collection, Library of Congress.

The railroad yards served as sites for work and play. Hopping frieghts provided excitement while stealing coal served the family economy.

they applied scientific expertise to the problem of juvenile delinquency as part of a more active state. At the same time, the court, at least in Boston, was the product of careful political compromise that balanced the interests of different ethnic and religious groups and limited the court's potential for radical intervention into families.

CHAPTER 8

The Juvenile Court: Triumph of Progressivism

The strands of Progressive era child welfare reform were woven together in the juvenile court, which promised administrative expertise and efficiency. The court unified the system of social welfare agencies and juvenile justice institutions that had evolved in the nineteenth century, and it promised a "scientific" approach to the problem of delinquency, one that by definition was removed from conflicts of class, culture, and politics. The court was the perfect structural reform: it applied ostensibly neutral expertise to a difficult social problem.[1]

Of course, the court did not work as promised. The court itself was the product of partisan politics and as a result of political compromise it had a somewhat limited jurisdiction. More importantly, the court remained mired in the class and cultural conflicts it was supposed to rise above. The court was another weapon in the effort to reshape the culture, work habits, and leisure time of working-class youth and justices applied class and culturally specific norms as if they were universal. Some parents and delinquents realized this and refused to acknowledge the court's claim to scientific expertise about their problems. Although the court turned a loose network of agencies and institutions into a juvenile justice system, the promise of efficiency was thwarted by the sheer number of cases and the resistance of delinquents and their families.

Juvenile Justice before the Court

The creation of the juvenile court did not usher in a new era in juvenile justice in Massachusetts. It did not represent the adoption of innovative procedures, it did not signal the rise of an intrusive "therapeutic state," it did not break any major legal ground, and it did not establish the role of social welfare agencies within the juvenile justice system. At most, the court's establishment systematized existing practices and made cooperation among agencies dealing with delinquent children more routine.[2]

Massachusetts already had a system of separate trials, informal hearings, investigation, and probation. Since 1870 state agents had attended trials of juveniles, investigated their cases, and acted as advisors to both the court and defendants. Justices heard trials of juveniles in sessions separate from adults and frequently settled cases informally by placing them on file. That is, a case was continued without a finding for a period during which the state agent or a social welfare agency supervised the child. If no violations occurred, the court simply closed the case without a finding. Other children, formally found guilty of an offense, were placed on probation. John Augustus, a Boston shoemaker, began having minor offenders released in his custody in 1841, and after Augustus's death in 1859, the Children's Mission to the Children of the Destitute and then the Boston Children's Aid Society took over his probation work.[3]

Representatives of social welfare organizations were entrenched in this system. They investigated cases, supervised children's leisure-time activities, supplied children placed into families with necessities, and secured board payments from their families. The Children's Aid Society helped juveniles on probation find work and open savings accounts so they could pay court costs and fines. After the juvenile court was established, the justices continued these arrangements until regular probation officers were hired, and since the city had no juvenile detention facilities, the court used detention homes provided by the private agencies to hold delinquents awaiting trial.[4]

The powers of the juvenile court were buttressed by the traditional doctrine of *parens patriae*. *Parens patriae*, adopted from English Court of Chancery practice, had justified state intervention to protect a child's

welfare in the United States since *Ex parte Crouse* in 1838. In this case
the Pennsylvania Supreme Court upheld Mary Ann Crouse's commitment to the Philadelphia House of Refuge for the purpose of educating
her. The decision had the effect of allowing lax trial procedures for
children, securing the legal footing of the reformatory, and permitting
the incarceration of wayward and delinquent children in order to
provide them with training. The juvenile court built explicitly on this
tradition and removed delinquents, except for those facing charges
involving capital punishment or life imprisonment, from the criminal
process.[5]

The passage of juvenile court bills by the Massachusetts legislature
aroused little controversy in the press or around the state since they
essentially confirmed established practice. The Boston Children's Aid
Society, among other groups, lobbied for the passage of the bills, one
for the state, the other specifically for Boston, which accomplished
three reforms: they decriminalized juvenile proceedings, they abolished the lock-up for children under fourteen, which meant that children could not be incarcerated with adults even temporarily, and they
established a single court in central Boston with jurisdiction and expertise over children's affairs.[6]

Careful political compromise shaped the court. The juvenile court
was a structural reform, akin to good government schemes to stream-
line municipal government, centralize power in the mayor's office,
eliminate ward representation on the city council, and restructure the
school board in order to make government more responsive to business
interests and those of "better" citizens. Aware that the campaign for
the creation of a juvenile court had gathered legislative momentum and
that the state's Republican governor would appoint a Yankee Republican to the bench, Irish Democrats fought to keep the juvenile sessions
in the district courts and their Irish Catholic Democratic judges untouched, while yielding to Progressive reform in central Boston. Reformers agreed to the trade, probably because it allowed them to set
up the juvenile court in Boston as a demonstration project that could
be expanded at a later date. The new court had jurisdiction only over
Boston's downtown and central wards; the outlying neighborhoods of
Charlestown, Dorchester, South Boston, East Boston, and Roxbury,
all Irish Democratic bastions, kept their district courts. Boston's juve-

nile court was itself constituted as a model of political tact, with central Boston's leading ethnic groups all represented. While the presiding justice was indeed a Yankee Republican, he was assisted by two part-time justices, one Jewish, the other Italian, and a black clerk of the court, as well as probation officers drawn from Catholic, Protestant, and Jewish voluntary societies. From the reformers' perspective it was a good deal. Despite the rather diverse staff, the Boston Juvenile Court was not a model of pluralism. Like juvenile courts elsewhere in the country, the Boston court reflected the image of its presiding judge, who molded it in the shape anticipated by reformers.[7]

The Juvenile Court as a Progressive Institution

Like other institutions created by the Progressives, the juvenile court incorporated an emphasis on specialization, system, and expertise. Judges and staff worked exclusively with juveniles, presided over a network of social welfare and juvenile justice agencies, and discussed deviance in therapeutic terms.

The creation of the juvenile court made juvenile delinquency an area of specialization, while the judges themselves developed a distinctive identity as reformers as well as jurists. Boston's first presiding judge, Harvey Baker (1906–15), and his successor, Frederick Pickering Cabot (1916–32), studied social work practices and psychological approaches to delinquency, while other judges, notably Denver's Ben Lindsey and Chicago's Julian Mack, toured the charity and reform circuit and popularized the concept of a juvenile court.

The assignment of regular probation officers to the juvenile court was another step in the process of specialization. In Boston, officers whose sole function was to investigate cases and oversee those on probation replaced the overburdened state agents and the general agents of the social welfare agencies. Judge Baker argued that the probation practiced by the new court provided stricter oversight and was therefore quite different from permitting a child "to go free so long as he does not misbehave," which he claimed had passed for probation under the juvenile sessions. Probation officers, at least in theory, also developed expertise as family counselors. Herbert Lou, who surveyed the nation's juvenile courts in the 1920s, found that probation officers tried to reconcile separated parents, forced deserters to return home, encouraged families to move to better neighborhoods, and offered advice about health, law, finances, and employment.[8]

Even though the court hired its own probation officers, it remained dependent on the private social welfare system and raised the level of cooperation between private social welfare agencies and public authorities. The court relied on the Confidential Exchange (the investigational repository of the Associated Charities) for information about children and their families, since many delinquents had family records with member agencies. The court also made attendence at these agencies conditions of probation, and probation officers used these sites to visit with their clients. Private social welfare agencies had always played a part in the public sector, but the establishment of the juvenile court erased some of the distinctions between voluntary and coercive and private and public institutions.[9]

Supporters described the court with medical/therapeutic metaphors in an attempt to create an ideology that removed the court from class and cultural conflict. Baker wrote that a probation officer brought a child in for a "diagnosis." The court then followed the "procedure of the physician" by considering all the relevant information gathered about the child's health, family, and neighborhood before prescribing treatment. If the offense were trivial, the judge would have the child copy the violated ordinance and then present the work when it was finished, "just as a physician might do in the case of a burn or a bruise." If the offense were serious, the judge saw the child more frequently, "just as with the patient and the physician in the case of tuberculosis or typhoid." These were more than simple metaphors to describe the court's operations. The use of medical terminology was an attempt to shape popular conceptions of the court by cloaking it with the authority of science. It implied that the court was a neutral, benign agency, that the judge was an expert acting in the child's interest, and that the laws enforced by the court were as immutable and as natural as those of science. Resisting the court's "treatment plan" was like rejecting the advice of a physician about curing an illness, something that no good parent could possibly consider.[10]

Moreover, the analogy of cure and treatment by the individual physician fit a pragmatic and nonradical approach to deviance. Public health itself had shifted from a broad-based environmentalism that encompassed social and moral reform to a narrow emphasis on individual health and personal hygiene. Baker followed the example of many Progressives by focusing on the maladjusted ("sick") individual and the ways of educating him or her to deal with his or her environment. According to this view, immigrants suffered from cultural disruption and community disorganization, workers from a lack of understanding of the work process and their place within it, the diseased from poor sanitary habits, and children from the clash of old- and new-world cultures and the social influences of bad neighborhoods. Education under the guidance of experts, rather than social change, solved these problems. Deviance, even when produced socially and environmentally, had to be cured individually.[11]

The juvenile court epitomized the individual approach to deviance. By treating the offender rather than the offense as the heart of the case, the court could put guilt and innocence aside and consider the environmental and/or familial conditions that brought the offender before it. The court used information gathered by social workers about the delinquent's neighborhood and residence, the parents' drinking habits, their employment, sexual patterns, or cleanliness to determine whether the proper "treatment" for a delinquent was probation, placement, or incarceration. Since the court's objective was treatment rather than punishment, the particular offense that brought a child to the court's attention was practically irrelevant. It existed only as a symptom of an underlying pathology.[12]

The court was a uniquely Progressive institution, but it remained within the cultural reform tradition. Delinquency was an individual "illness," "adjustment" meant acquiring the proper cultural values, and "treatment" was delivered at the social welfare agencies, through placement or in the reformatory. The state had a more active role than before and it reinforced cooperation among social welfare agencies and public institutions such as the reformatories, but from the perspective of delinquents and their families, little had changed.

The Operation of the Court

The juvenile court reflected the personalities of its presiding judges. Harvey Baker, born in Brookline in 1869, was the son of a merchant from Cape Cod and a gentleman farmer's daughter. Baker, like many reform-minded New Englanders, was a Unitarian and he attended Roxbury Latin School followed by Harvard College and Harvard Law School, from which he graduated in 1894. Baker had been a visitor for the Children's Aid Society while an undergraduate and after law school he became secretary of a conference of Boston-area child-care agencies. He was therefore well versed in the techniques of social work and the therapeutic approach to deviance. Baker served as a clerk and then as a special justice in the Brookline police court before becoming the first justice of the Boston Juvenile Court, where he presided from 1906 until 1915. Frederick Cabot, scion of two Brahmin families, the Cabots and the Higginsons, was born in Brookline in 1868 and, after attending Harvard College, graduated from Harvard Law School in 1893. Cabot served as an assistant U.S. attorney in Boston before becoming a member of the firm of Hulbert, Jones, and Cabot. He inherited family money and was president and director of the Fisher Manufacturing Company and the Winthrop Mills. Cabot became presiding justice of the juvenile court after Harvey Baker's death in 1915 and served until his death in 1932. It is difficult to imagine two men more unlike the largely Irish, Italian, and Jewish delinquents they faced.[13]

 A child entered the court through a complaint made by a policeman, neighbor, social welfare agent, or family member. In cases where no arrest had been made, a complaint against the child was sworn and a summons issued if the clerk of the court believed the charge had merit. In cases of arrest, police notified the probation officer to come to the station house and he decided the immediate disposition of the case. Boys were generally released to the custody of their parents, unless they were repeat or serious offenders or had violated probation. In those cases, they either remained overnight in the police station in cells separate from other offenders, or were sent to the Charles Street Jail, where again they were kept in separate cells. The Children's Aid Society operated detention homes for boys who could not be sent home, but who were too young to be kept in jail, while Catholic boys were occasionally sent to the House of the Angel Guardian. Girls never remained in the station house following an arrest because of the absence of suitable facilities. If they could not be released to their parents, a matron from the Children's Aid Society picked them up and placed them in a detention home or with a suburban family.[14]

The Boston Children's Aid Society supervised the detention homes for the court. The homes were small, usually capable of holding no more than two or three delinquents in a family setting. The number of detention homes available to the court ranged from seven to twelve; three, run by widows with adult sons living at home or nearby, were specifically for delinquent boys. Two elderly unmarried ladies took in delinquent girls. Delinquents remained in the homes until arraignment, and since the juvenile court met six days per week, they stayed slightly more than two days in the homes, with the average driven up somewhat by girls with venereal disease, who were held while undergoing treatment. Only 15 percent of the delinquents arrested in 1919–20 were detained overnight, and over 90 percent of these were placed in the Children's Aid Society homes. The goal was not only to separate children from adult offenders but also to make the process of arrest, detention, and trial as dissimilar as possible from that in the criminal justice system.[15]

Baker's juvenile court emphasized informality. Although located in Suffolk County Court House, the juvenile court was in a different part of the building than the criminal courts. The court consisted of two parts, a large waiting room for children, their parents, and witnesses, and the judge's chambers in which the proceedings occurred. The court had no dock or detention area and only a railing separated the waiting area from the clerk of the court's desk. There were no uniformed officers of the court present. When a case was called for trial, the probation officer brought the child into the judge's chambers. There the three of them chatted without a clerk or stenographer to record the proceedings. The judge's desk sat on top of a small platform, much like a teacher's desk in front of a classroom, and the child stood at the side while the judge questioned him or her.[16]

Baker encouraged defendants to tell him their stories (or, from a harsher perspective, to incriminate themselves). Since this was not a criminal proceeding, Baker could justify interviewing the defendant because, like the physician he fancied himself to be, he had to make a diagnosis about what brought the defendant to court. Baker called the delinquent to come to his side for a heart-to-heart talk, and he sometimes asked the probation officer to leave so that they could speak in absolute confidence. The judge did not read the charge or ask for a plea, since the "technicalities" of a case were not important, but simply asked to hear about a delinquent's life and why an arrest had occurred. If a defendant proved reticent, Baker tried to coax a confession, asking who was more believable, the child or the witnesses in the case. Baker spent so much time extracting confessions because it preserved the impression that the procedures were not adversarial, and it created a feeling of confidence between the judge and the defendant, making it more likely that parents and children would accept the court's mandate. If a child refused to confess, the police and the parents were brought in for a formal hearing. Baker noted that a defendant had the right to be represented by counsel, who was consulted in all steps, but he found that even lawyers who were the "most technical" in other courts cooperated with him in trying to make parents understand that he had only the child's best interest in mind. If Baker's comments are accurate, and there seems no reason to doubt them, even defense attorneys were swayed by the ethos of the juvenile court. Certainly the process seems effective, or at least it produced a high conviction rate. During the court's first ten years, which coincided with Baker's judgeship, over 80 percent of defendants pled guilty each year and, of those who did not, only an average of 22 percent were found innocent. Convicted delinquents had the right of appeal to Superior Court, but this required an attorney, which was probably beyond the means of most working-class families, and in 1919–20 only 1.7 percent of all verdicts were appealed.[17]

Contemporaries considered probation to be the centerpiece of the juvenile court system. Probation involved reshaping the work habits, the use of leisure time, the family setting—in sum, the culture of working-class delinquents and their families. In many ways, probation officers were like the old charity workers, pushing families into the cultural sphere of social welfare agencies, but without the pretense of friendly visits, and with the threat of returning to court to enforce their "advice." Yet the effectiveness of probation was undermined by two factors: the very centrality of the probation officer to the juvenile court system and the frequency with which judges placed delinquents on probation.

Probation was the most usual outcome of a case. The decision to place a child on probation depended on several investigations of the case, either by social service agencies or by the probation officer. The court sometimes ordered physical examinations, particularly in the case of female sex offenders, to detect venereal disease. In later years, the court referred difficult cases to the Judge Baker Foundation, established in 1917 with William Healy and Augusta Bronner as codirectors. Healy and Bronner, whose work is discussed in detail in the next chapter, pioneered the "scientific" study of delinquents, combining intelligence testing with physical and psychiatric examinations. A visit lasted several hours and was followed by a case conference with the probation officer and social workers and recommendations were made to the court. If a child seemed physically and mentally capable and the home reasonable, a first offender almost always had the case filed or received probation. Each year under Baker's tenure, approximately half of all cases were simply filed without a finding, usually after a continuance of several weeks during which time the delinquent was on his or her good behavior. If those who were placed on probation and those who had their cases filed are considered together, over 80 percent of the cases handled each year in Baker's ten-year tenure on the court resulted in a minimal form of supervision.[18]

The probation officer's home visits were important in determining the "fitness" of working-class families to raise their children. However, the process of determining fitness was at best imprecise. Officers noted information about father's occupation, number of family members, presence of boarders, and the housekeeping, alcohol use, and atmosphere of the home. While probation officers were generally too overworked to record all this information systematically, they occasionally made revealing comments. When a probation officer visited Nicoletta Rota's home, she reported that its general appearance was "dirty — foreign," while Konstanty Ochowicz's mother was referred to as a "low grade peasant." Mrs. Connolly was "very pugnacious and thoroughly disliked by many of her neighbors." Another probation officer thought that Albert Franco's mother was "feeble-minded with a tendency to syphilis."[19] These comments were based on simple observations of the home, or neighborhood gossip, and while the degree to which these judgments affected the court is unclear, they indicate that delinquents and their families were measured against standards of fitness that poverty and peasant culture made difficult to meet.

The court tried to alter the influence on delinquents by mandating attendance at an industrial school or a settlement house as part of probation. Raphael Acardi was told by his probation officer that he had better report to the North Bennet Street Industrial School on Monday nights if he wished to have his case closed.[20] Frank Acetola attended Denison House, a settlement in the South End, under the guidance of one of its workers, a Miss O'Rourke. After reporting faithfully for six months, the boy started misbehaving and Miss O'Rourke wrote the court that he "might have to be committed."[21] The experiences were by no means all coercive. As Angelina Sappeti wrote, with apparent sincerety, "me and [Rosa Cappelini] belongs to the Girl Scouts. We going to the E. Boston High School and have beautiful time. I am glad to belong to the girls scout, they teach us to be good girls. And believe me . . . I am going to be a good girl and so is Rosa."[22]

Work was also in integral part of probation, although usually as a supplement to school and supervised recreation. The court enforced the discipline of the workplace and tried to encourage industry, punctuality, and steadiness in working-class youngsters accustomed to the freedom of the streets. The court, like the reformatory, the industrial school, the gymnasium, and other institutions that enrolled working-class youngsters, simply tried to get youngsters into the workforce and any case that ended with a delinquent working steadily was considered a success. Josephine Saccorso had a brother in reform school and another awaiting trial for larceny and truancy. She was placed on probation after appearing in court in March 1917 for larceny, and at last report, in November 1919, she had regular employment in a North End chocolate factory.[23] Another girl's words were recorded approvingly. Angelina Sappeti wrote, "I works and give my mother every cent I get," while George Gilbert's case of stubbornness was dismissed after sixteen months because he had worked for a year in the boiler room at the Massachusetts Institute of Technology.[24]

Although the terms of probation varied depending upon the case, some general rules applied. The court, like the social welfare agencies, actively combated the influence of the new mass culture. Children were forbidden to visit dance halls, cafes, nickelodeons, and other night spots, to drink or use tobacco, to be out late at night, and to leave town without permission. Of course they were expected to keep their appointments with the probation officer, usually weekly or monthly, depending on the nature of the case. More serious offenders were expected to appear downtown at the probation office, while other children reported after school at the local settlement house or public library. Appointments averaged five to ten minutes in length, and were supplemented by occasional home visits. The court supplied teachers with envelopes and blank report forms and requested that teachers supply weekly school reports. Older children received assistance in looking for work, and the probation officers checked with employers about the status of the child. The judge determined the length of probation, and in 1919–20 two-thirds of all offenders remained on probation for six months or less.[25]

While probation allowed the court to keep large numbers of children under supervision, the actual conditions of probation made strict oversight unlikely. Even taking the case of weekly visits of ten minutes' duration over a sixth-month period, probation officers lacked the time (and the training) to usurp family functions. They offered advice, encouraged children to work steadily or attend school, and tried their best to make sure that children on probation stayed out of trouble. But ten minutes a week was not a lot of time. From the perspective of the delinquent, and sometimes the family, probation officers may have been troublesome, meddling bureaucrats, but they hardly constituted the vanguard of an invasive therapeutic state. There were simply too many delinquents and too few probation officers.[26]

Female Crime, Manly Justice

The juvenile court, like earlier juvenile reform efforts, relied on the charismatic appeal of the reformer to be effective. The first generation of juvenile court justices used their charm and insight to get children to confide in them and to promote the court. Ben Lindsey filled his speeches with anecdotes about boys promising their fealty to him, or confiding secrets to him that their parents did not know. Most justices would have agreed with Chicago's Richard Tuthill, who declared that he always tried to act "as I would were it my own son that was before me in my library at home." Baker too was fond of placing a hand on a boy's shoulder while appealing to him to confess. The juvenile court exemplified personal justice, with a laying on of hands and man-to-man talks.[27]

The emphasis on manliness posed obvious problems for delinquent girls. Since the juvenile court had few established procedures and an emphasis on the judge's personality and ability to touch (sometimes literally) the defendant, it should not be surprising that girls were treated gingerly at best and unfairly at worst. Denver's Ben Lindsey claimed that he met with delinquent girls alone in chambers, as he did with boys, and that he had a good rapport with girls, who confided their misdeeds to him. If so, that was the exception and not the rule.[28]

Both Baker and Cabot were uneasy with female delinquents, particularly those who were sexually active. Baker stated that he never met with female delinquents in chambers unless a female probation officer was present, while a newspaper article, appropriately titled "He Understands Boys," described Frederick Cabot's embarrassment with delinquent girls. Cabot requested assistance from female friends when considering girls' cases, and he told delinquent girls to wash off "artificial coloring" before they came before him because " 'I can't be fair to you while you look like that.' " The two judges were straightlaced bachelors who applied the cultural standards of the Victorian era in which they were raised. Their decisions and treatment of delinquent girls suggest their deep mistrust of the new morality, the new woman, and the sexual revolution of the turn of the century and after. In policy and in practice, the juvenile court was shaped by the lingering hold of nineteenth-century bourgeois culture.[29]

Delinquent girls were subject to more careful examination and oversight than were boys, and differential treatment began with overnight detention. In 1919–20, only 13 percent of the boys were held overnight, but 35 percent of the female delinquents were detained. Female delinquents remained in custody longer because the court required physical examinations for delinquents charged with sexual miscon- duct, and treatment for those who were found to be venereally dis- eased. The court tended to send the more difficult cases for mental examinations, and in 1919–20, the Baker Foundation saw 38 percent of the boys who appeared in juvenile court. However, 70 percent of the girls were examined, which was probably an index of Judge Ca- bot's perplexity when handling girls' cases. The court committed only 4 percent (thirty-five out of 850) of the boys who appeared before it in 1919–20, but nearly 14 percent (fourteen out of 102) of the girls were institutionalized. In every instance, girls were scrutinized more care- fully than were boys.[30]

Girls were brought to court for offenses ranging from shoplifting to stubbornness to lewd and lascivious behavior, but their treatment depended on whether or not the offense was sexual in nature. In a sample of cases from 1907–37, girls who were truant or guilty of larceny were generally placed on probation or had their cases filed. Larceny, usually a shoplifting expedition to a downtown department store, was the most common offense (37 percent of all girls charged). Of the twenty-five girls arrested for larceny, only two were incarcer- ated and in one of these cases the court noted that she had engaged in sexual activity.[31] Lilian Anderson provides a typical example. Al- though her home was poor, her father unemployed and living on his children's earnings, her brother incarcerated for truancy, and she guilty of at least one earlier shoplifting incident, Lilian simply had her case continued. While this certainly posed a threat, as any future arrest would have reactivated the case, she was not even subject to the lax requirements of probation. Undoubtedly the court felt some sympathy for a girl who handed over her whole paycheck to her idle father and who then succumbed to temptation at Filene's Department Store.[32]

On the other hand, the court was far less understanding of girls accused of sexual offenses. Ten girls (14 percent of the total) were charged with lewdness or fornication and eight were committed, as were ten of the thirteen runaways. While lewdness is a sexual offense, running away is less obviously so. Yet runaways (19 percent of the total) frequently engaged in sexual activity while away from home. Marjorie Francolli ran away for a week and had "unusual relations" with several men. She was complained of as a runaway and committed to the House of the Good Shepherd and later transferred to the Lancaster School.[33]

Other courts were equally concerned with a girl's chastity, although justices were not always as discreet as Boston's bachelor judges. Testimony from the Milwaukee Juvenile Court shows that girls were interrogated quite explicitly about their sexual activities, given Victorian homilies about marriage and family, and then committed to the reform school. When Sophonisba Breckinridge and Edith Abbott surveyed Chicago's juvenile court records, they discovered that over a ten-year period nearly 43 percent of the girls brought to court were charged with incorrigibility and another 31 percent with immorality. In an effort to protect a girl's reputation, the court charged her with incorrigibility or disorderliness whenever possible—if her sexual activity was isolated or accidental. When Breckinridge and Abbott examined all of the charges against girls, they discovered that over 80 percent of the girls were brought to court on a morals charge. As in Boston, sexual delinquency was the most serious form of female deviance.[34]

The courts did not simply impose their ideals of female chastity upon delinquent girls and their families. Some ethnic groups, such as Italians, restricted the public roles played by women and probably saw the court as an ally in controlling the behavior of a streetwise daughter. It is rare to find a complainant listed in Boston's juvenile court records, but it is obvious that working-class parents, without other resources, turned to the court for help. Once in court, family members found they confronted not only their own family difficulties but also the concerns of the larger society about female chastity and "proper" family life.[35]

Mary Pasquale, whose mother had died when she was two, was the daughter of an Italian laborer who lived in the North End with his second wife and the couple's two children. Mary ran away from home and was complained of as a wayward child in 1925, when she was fifteen years old. The court put her on probation but she defaulted after a year, and at some point she was placed in a foster home. She ran away with a girlfriend and the two were discovered in a New York hotel with two men and returned to Boston. A physical examination showed that her hymen was intact and therefore she was allowed to return home to her parents. While at home she had intercourse with a boy who promised to marry her, but jilted her instead. At this time, her father complained to the court and Mary was brought in on the old default warrant. Her father's attitude certainly played a part in the court's decision. He told the court that he wanted his daughter put away until she was twenty-one, and when the girl fainted, he attempted to kick her. The court had tried family reconciliation and foster care, leaving few alternatives for the troubled girl. Strict Italian mores together with bourgeois concerns about adolescence and the judge's own difficulties in confronting sexually active girls led to Mary Pasquale's commitment.[36]

Girls' cases reveal the complex nature of the interaction between social welfare/juvenile justice institutions and the working class. Bourgeois society was concerned about family stability, curbing prostitution, protecting the vulnerable, and codifying its own cultural standards into law. Therefore reformers invented juvenile courts as part of a more active state and extended the services provided by social welfare agencies. Working-class families worried about the economic contributions of their members, their respectability, and the ample opportunity for a young girl to go wrong. The twentieth-century city provided less economic opportunity for youngsters while it opened up a tantalizing world of commercialized leisure and consumption that working-class girls in particular lacked the resources to enjoy. Expected to stay at home to care for their younger siblings or to turn their pay envelopes over to the family if they worked, working-class girls were at the same time seduced by the abundance of American society. Some girls went on shoplifting expeditions while others exchanged sex for ice cream, automobile rides, and entertainment, and they all became vulnerable to the intervention of social welfare agencies or the state. As in the nineteenth century, parents cooperated with private agencies and public authorities—while not necessarily sharing all of their goals—to keep girls off the streets and prevent them from trading on their sexuality.[37]

Ironically, the juvenile court stood as a bastion of Victorian culture at a time when that culture's basic assumptions were being challenged, not only from without but also from within. College-educated men and women, in particular, broke down the sexually segregated social spheres of their elders in the first decades of the twentieth century. The rise of dance halls, night clubs, amusement parks, and other entertainment establishments, not to mention coeducational institutions, sexually integrated the social lives of young bourgeois Americans in unchaperoned settings. Not surprisingly, more contact also meant more intimate contact. The state was enforcing traditional cultural values at a time when the bourgeois consensus supporting those values was eroding. The court sought to impose on working-class youth a morality and culture bourgeois parents were unable to fasten on their own offspring. As a result of these shifts in the dominant culture, the juvenile court became increasingly marginalized as a mechanism for reform.[38]

Boys and the Streets

Boys committed offenses against property and public order, which brought them into direct conflict with public authorities. Larceny (31 percent), breaking and entering (9 percent), auto theft (5 percent), and vandalism (4 percent) accounted for half of the boys' cases in my sample. Another fifth committed status offenses, such as "gaming" on Sunday (usually shooting craps or playing cards), selling newspapers without licenses, or sledding in the public streets, while 5 percent evaded fares on the trolleys. The only other "major" category was assault and battery (6 percent), which sounds more serious than it was, since nearly all of the cases involved fistfights, snowball fights, or rock-throwing incidents among boys. Boys contended directly with public authority because of their use of the streets for employment, recreation, and criminal activities, and they were hauled into court in much greater numbers than were girls.

While poor parents found it easy to overlook petty theft in the name of the family economy, the court did not. Charles Pulanski, arrested for loitering, sold papers and begged for change in the theater district. He and his brother also picked up coal and brought it home for heating fuel. The father, an illiterate laborer for the American Sugar Refinery, did not make much and the family was saving to buy the home in which they lived. Neither boys nor parents were too particular about the sources of the coal, and the probation officer found two tons of it

Boy Wood Pickers Loading, October 1909. Lewis Hine Collection, Library of Congress.

Children contributed to the family economy by scavenging wood for kindling, taking pipes and fittings from abandoned or uninhabited buildings, grabbing fruit and vegetables discarded in the market, and scouring the city dump. Scavenging easily slipped into petty larceny.

in the basement. Charles was placed on probation, but when rearrested for larceny he received a suspended sentence to the reformatory and a warning that further misconduct meant imprisonment.[39]

Other boys, arrested for rolling drunks, could not be made to understand that they had done anything wrong, and the court was confounded by their "moral density." At least one parent defended her son. Mrs. Weinstein told the probation officer that the family's only income came from a fifteen-year-old daughter who earned five dollars a week in a chocolate factory, and she "thinks it not so terrible if Sammy and other kids did take money when a man was throwing it about when drunk." In such a case, where juvenile delinquency was compounded by parental obdurance, the court had little choice but to commit. Families and the court each found the other's standards of morality incomprehensible.[40]

However, both parents and the court agreed that boys, especially older ones, had to work, and this shaped sentencing patterns. Members of the working class rarely found a full year's employment, and families had few resources to tide them over a father's unemployment that lasted several months.[41] Stealing coal, stripping copper pipes from unoccupied buildings, scavenging for junk, and extorting change from drunks bought children treats and provided excitement but also contributed to the family economy.[42] Therefore the families of boys opposed efforts to have their sons incarcerated. (This was unlike the families of female delinquents, who were willing to cooperate with the court and have daughters charged with stubbornness or running away to prevent sexual activity.) Because the court placed a high value on employment, most of the time it acceded to parents' wishes. Only 10 percent of the boys' cases, involving either more serious or repeat offenders, concluded with incarceration. By comparison, over a third of the girls in a sample of records were incarcerated. The court agreed that males had to be prepared for the marketplace, and it sought to ensure that they learned the discipline and work habits needed for industrial employment.[43]

Discipline was not learned on the streets, and the courts tried to limit their use. Working-class youth loitered, gambled, drank, smoked, stole, and had sexual relations on the streets and developed a worldliness that shocked reformers. Ben Lindsey, in an argument that is representative of child-savers' beliefs, found that street traders' lives were "impure and unclean" compared to what he thought child life should be "and what any decent parent would want it to be." For this he blamed not the youths but their parents, who encouraged youngsters to profane "the sacred period of adolescence." Working-class childhood and youth had not changed very much since the nineteenth century, which was precisely the point. It was at odds with the sacralization of childhood that had occurred in bourgeois culture. Progressive reform sought to curb the independence of working-class youth, to gather them under adult supervision in classrooms and playgrounds, and to control the conditions and timing of their work. Reformers were extending the experience of a more dependent and sheltered adolescence across class lines, and they encountered both resistance and bewilderment from delinquents and their parents.[44]

The juvenile court participated enthusiastically in the drive to make the streets off limits. In the first five years of the court, cases of truancy, license violations, or gaming on Sunday comprised over half of the caseload. While these were not treated as serious offenses, the court reinforced the message delivered in school and recreation centers that the streets were the property of adults and that working-class youth would be supervised whether they liked it or not.[45]

Gradually these kinds of cases declined. From 1911 to 1916, only 31 percent of the Boston Juvenile Court's cases fell into the ordinance, license, and truancy categories. The supply of such cases to the court fell dramatically during these years as other agencies took over the court's work and thus precipitated a wholesale decline in the number of cases heard by the court. The Newsboys' Trial Board, in which the newsboys policed themselves, was established by the School Department in 1908 and by 1912 was siphoning off over four hundred cases per year. In addition, the School Department established new regulations regarding the handling of truancy. Instead of going directly to court and having a child committed to the Parental School (the city's institution for truants), the department established disciplinary day schools to handle truants. Only if a child failed there did the department complain to the court. The average number of truant cases heard fell from over fifty to twelve per year during the same period. For these kinds of cases, the juvenile court became the arena of last resort, used only after other mediation had failed.[46]

Child gamesters and traders did not disappear from the streets, but reform and economic forces combined to limit their activity. The role of reformers in this process was secondary—their efforts to enforce child labor laws and city ordinances regulating the street trades were notoriously ineffective. Adult competition and technology led to the decline of child labor, and changing newspaper managerial practices resulted in the near extinction of child street traders. Only 11 percent of ten-to-fifteen–year-olds nationally reported wage-earning activity in 1920, down from 18 percent in 1900. In 1930 that fell to 4.7 percent as schools enrolled an ever-increasing segment of the school-age population and as the economy collapsed. Reformers did create alternative recreational sites, and schools sponsored safety badges, safety days, and student safety councils to have students police themselves about using the streets. Youthful loiterers and delinquents were never driven from the streets, but by the end of the Progressive era working-class youth were under greater adult supervision than before.[47]

The Ambiguous Legacy of the Juvenile Court

Ignos Ontewicz, who had lost an arm and a leg while hopping a freight train, contributed to the family economy by selling newspapers in Chinatown at night. Hawking papers to patrons leaving the nearby entertainment district was, in the police's opinion, a pretext for begging and Ignos was arrested and committed to the Industrial School for Crippled and Deformed Children. He caused so much trouble there that the school expelled him after a short stay and he returned home and resumed his newspaper sales. Several warnings by the police and his probation officer, fines, and the continuation of his probation for over two years had no effect. The family was poor, and Ignos was too successful at getting tips for him to stop. Finally the court gave up and filed the case, concluding, "we are not entirely satisfied with what he has done while on probation, but we believe it is almost impossible to get this boy to change his entire view of life."[48] The court faced similar problems in trying to get parents and children to move out of "bad" neighborhoods or to return to their countries of origin. The court suggested, cajoled, and threatened but ultimately its power was limited, particularly in the case of minor offenders.[49]

Boston's juvenile court had the reputation of being one of the more progressive courts in the country. It was attuned to the newest developments in social work and it searched actively for the social and psychological roots of crime through its investigations and referrals to the mental health clinic. The court commanded the cooperation of an extensive public and private social welfare network, which it linked to the public reformatories, and it moved individual delinquents around within this system. The court utilized community resources, such as settlement houses and boys' and girls' clubs, to supervise the activities of hundreds of youngsters each year and to assert control over the leisure time of adolescents. From this perspective, the court was a triumph of Progressivism.

When seen from the perspective of Ignos Ontewicz and other delinquents, the court was less awe inspiring. The court treated delinquents to Victorian-style homilies, subjected them to fairly cursory visits with probation officers, counseled them to attend school or spend free time at a settlement house, and threatened them with being "sent away" if they did not improve. But unless the Court enlisted parents' support for its reform program, its threats were hollow, as most delinquents probably learned.

The rhetoric surrounding the court was vastly inflated. Despite the veneer of science and expertise, the Court enforced values that were decidedly Victorian into the 1930s. No trace of a modern, consumer culture can be found in the practice of the Boston court, which was more an artifact of the nineteenth-century child-saving movement than a harbinger of the therapeutic state. The court was overcrowded, underfunded, dispensed with most cases quickly, and provided only limited oversight. Even with its disregard for procedure and defendants' rights, the court did not invade the province of the family. The court convicted many delinquents, but it reformed very few of them. It was the best instrument reformers and social workers could devise, and it served their purposes by linking a disjointed collection of private and public institutions under Brahmin leadership, but to delinquents it delivered neither justice nor therapy.

CHAPTER 9

Child Guidance and the Court

Reviewing their work in 1935, William Healy and Augusta Bronner concluded that they had failed. Efforts to diagnose delinquents clinically and to recommend treatment plans to the juvenile court had not succeeded in curing delinquents of their deviance. The presiding justice of the Boston Juvenile Court, John J. Perkins, agreed. "The value and power of psychiatry were exaggerated to the point of magic, and like the juvenile court, psychiatry was oversold to the public." Popularization of psychological theories of deviance encouraged the public to believe that if the court sent a maladjusted youngster to the clinic, the mental conflict causing the delinquency could be removed "like having a tooth pulled by a dentist." Therapy proved no more able than Protestantism, lessons in bourgeois culture, vocational education, supervised recreational activities, placement, or probation in solving the problem of the deviant poor and their delinquent children.[1]

Psychiatry and psychological approaches to human relations became part of American culture in the early decades of the twentieth century, and few institutions were shaped more profoundly by this innovation than those dealing with deviants. Psychiatry emphasized that people suffering from neuroses had not adapted to their environments. Since an individual's neurosis had social causes, treatment could have involved both social reform and readjustment of the individual. But psychiatry, in the period after World War I, and social work, which found its professional direction through psychiatry in the 1920s, focused on analyzing and resocialing the individual and/or the family. Psychiatry interested judges, social workers, and reformatory officials because it refuted the findings of the early mental testers that feeble-mindedness caused a large proportion of deviance and criminality and it offered new hope that delinquents could be reformed through science.[2]

The psychological replaced the medical idiom in discussions of delinquency in the 1920s, as "adjustment" became the new justification for the juvenile justice system. The juvenile court was central to the process of adjustment, for it directed juveniles to the proper venues: the clinic for diagnosis, the probation office or the settlement house for advice and supervision, the foster home to develop new social relationships, or the reform school for a "curative" environment. The therapeutic also demanded a new language, so reformatory officials urged that the terms "criminal," "delinquent," and "bad" boy or girl be replaced by "maladjusted." The reformatory sought to create sound personalities, defined as individuals who could fit in with society, which began with acquiescence to institutional regimen. When critics raised the issue of absence of due process in juvenile court proceedings or asked if reform schools were anything more than prisons, defenders argued for their therapeutic value. Since these institutions were designed to help individual delinquents overcome their mental conflicts and personality disorders, they were by definition in the delinquent's best interest.[3]

Progressive-minded child-savers created child guidance clinics in response to the demand for psychological evaluations of delinquents. The first clinics, such as those established in Chicago in 1909 and in Boston in 1917 by William Healy, were supported by coalitions of settlement and social workers and were affiliated with juvenile courts. Their original purpose was to advise the court on the disposition of difficult cases, but they also provided the opportunity to gather data on delinquents and to test different criminological theories. Most child guidance clinics eventually grew away from their early affiliation with the court, with delinquents forming only a small percentage of their clients, but at Boston's Judge Baker Foundation delinquents remained an important part of the clientele into the early 1930s.

The apparent success of the initial clinics led to their proliferation and support by private funders. In 1920, the Commonwealth Fund created an advisory committee, which included Healy and Bronner, to examine what could be done about juvenile delinquency. The committee developed a five-year plan for psychiatric study of predelinquent and delinquent children, among other recommendations, and between 1922 and 1927, the Commonwealth Fund established eight mental health clinics on an experimental basis around the country. By 1933 there were over forty clinics in existence as reformers followed Healy and Bronner's example.[4]

The Work of William Healy and Augusta Bronner

William Healy and Augusta Bronner were prophets of the new science. Healy, born in England in 1869 to poor tenant farmers, had come to the United States at age nine, left school at thirteen to help support his family, and worked his way through Harvard College and Rush Medical School in Chicago. He was an American success story who embodied the values of a Victorian bourgeois culture that had served him well. It is not surprising that he viewed the poor through the lens of his own accomplishments. A strain of Victorian moralism remained predominant in his thought and practice, and his views fit well with those of the Boston court justices.[5]

Augusta Bronner, Healy's student, collaborator, and, later, wife, was born in Louisville, Kentucky, in 1881 to parents of German Jewish ancestry. Bronner's family enjoyed modest wealth and social position and encouraged her to pursue a career as a teacher. After attending Columbia University's Teachers College, she taught English in Louisville for several years before returning to Columbia to study with Edward Thorndike, an educational psychologist. She also attended William Healy's lectures at Harvard summer school in 1913 and he offered her a position as a psychologist at the Chicago Juvenile Psychopathic Institute upon the completion of her Ph.D. in 1914. Bronner specialized in working with delinquent girls and she was well known in the mental testing movement, although Healy was the more prominent member of the Baker team.[6]

Like many practitioners in the United States, Healy and Bronner were eclectic, acknowledging a debt to Sigmund Freud but also using mental testing and applying concepts derived from Carl Jung, W. I. Thomas, and Alfred Adler. At first, Healy and Bronner consciously avoided too great a reliance on theory (as was true of "dynamic psychiatry" in general), and advanced the case method for analyzing the individual delinquent. Their team approach included a battery of intelligence and aptitude tests, physical examinations, investigations by social workers, and a long interview with the client, followed by a case conference. By the time they arrived at the newly established Judge Baker Foundation in 1917, they had become more psychoanalytical in approach and examined delinquents for mental conflicts, which they claimed were caused by unfortunate childhood sexual experiences and lay at the heart of a child's delinquency.[7]

Healy and Bronner were confident that science would solve the problem of delinquency. The first step was use of a scientific method, which they defined as collecting facts, analyzing them impartially, and then deriving generalizations and laws. As therapists, they believed that analysis of a case not only provided data for larger scientific purposes but was itself therapeutic in that it gave the delinquent insight into the causes of antisocial behavior. The interests of science, of society, and of the delinquent were one. The publication of numerous case studies testifies to Healy and Bronner's faith that a "science of treatment" would emerge from their work.[8]

Believing that the roots of misconduct lay in family dynamics, Healy and Bronner moved inevitably from treatment of the individual delinquent to work with entire families. A team of psychiatrists and social workers sought to remake the family's internal relations and to shape their responses to social welfare agencies. They discussed the parents' social problems, such as alcoholism or illicit sexual relationships, and explored parental feelings of guilt or inadequacy that might have contributed to a child's delinquency. Practical assistance accompanied psychological analysis and the clinic provided families with medical care and referrals to social welfare agencies for financial aid. Social workers also offered instruction in household budgeting, child care, and child psychology, and acquainted families with local clubs and recreational facilities. If these interventions failed, workers sought permission from the court for foster placement.[9]

The "treatment plans" that Healy and Bronner recommended to the court were described in different terms, but turned out to be identical to the solutions to delinquency promoted by earlier generations of child welfare workers. Home visitors had always referred families to the charities, to public dispensaries or hospitals, and to settlement houses, industrial schools, and other culturally uplifting organizations. Moreover, home visitors aided families with their budgets, offered housekeeping tips, consulted school authorities, and sought to develop relationships with the poor. And since the 1830s agencies had placed children of the urban poor with families in the country in order to provide them with different parental models and new cultural values. Eventually, more extensive therapeutic services became available at the child guidance clinics as child guidance shifted away from its behavioralist roots, but psychotherapy proved to be no panacea.[10]

The Practice of Therapy

Healy and Bronner's diagnoses and comments to the court indicate how rudimentary the practice of psychotherapy was in its early years and the extent to which traditional attitudes toward the poor influenced twentieth-century science. Patrick Brennan's case is illustrative. Brennan was arrested for begging in 1917 but had two earlier convictions for larceny, and the juvenile court sent him to the clinic for evaluation. The probation officer investigating the case reported that the Brennan family was chronically poor, "without food or money, although the father worked steadily and Beatrice [the eldest daughter] and Patrick also worked part of the time." Both the Associated Charities and the St. Vincent de Paul Society provided advice and support for the family, suggesting their belief that the Brennans belonged to the worthy poor.

In contrast, Healy's discussion of the causative factors in the boy's delinquency emphasized the family's shiftless character. The first cause was heredity—the father was an irregular worker who "relies much on charities," the mother was a "weak type, either defective mentally, or constitutionally inferior," and the maternal grandfather was a reputed alcoholic. A second cause was developmental—Patrick's mother had worked while she was pregnant, and consequently had produced a small, delicate child. The home condition—"shiftless and dirty"—

was the third cause, and lack of parental control the fourth. Patrick lacked normal home interests and consequently participated in an "excessive amount of street-life," and he smoked and drank tea. Healy admitted that poverty was always a big factor, "but secondary, of course, to the parents' own inferiority."[11]

For Healy parental inferiority was both genetic and cultural. Healy, who had been a member of the American Breeders' Association, an early eugenics organization, came by 1915 to the more moderate position that the hereditary causes of deviance could not be easily separated from the environmental.[12] In the Brennan case, the father's irregular work habits, an Irish family's history of alcohol use, the mother's lax housekeeping, her employment during pregnancy, and the boy's participation in street culture provided evidence of pathology and were causes of delinquency.

Healy and Bronner's psychological approach to delinquency offered so little advance over the cultural reform tradition because it was so deeply embedded in it. For them, poverty was the product of individual moral failure and it was as much a symptom of deviance as was delinquency. Healy and Bronner's evaluations of families contained the usual fear that welfare pauperized the poor, even when social welfare agencies found that a family deserved aid, and they believed that the economic failure of the male breadwinner eroded family discipline. Their comments showed no awareness that periodic unemployment plagued the working class or that economic contributions from all family members, including children, were vital to a working-class family's upkeep. They were not sympathetic to working mothers, who were presumed to neglect their children. Housekeeping, whether or not a woman worked and regardless of a family's resources, remained a key index of moral worth. And as in the Brennan case, ethnic stereotypes helped shape evaluations of delinquents' families.[13]

The case studies published by the Judge Baker Foundation provide evidence of how much the new science derived from the cultural reform tradition. This is not meant to suggest that Healy and Bronner were shoddy social scientists, only that the dominant culture shaped the questions they asked and their interpretation of the material they found. Despite the change in methods, the novelty of asking delinquents to explain themselves, and the extreme positivism exhibited by

Healy and Bronner in their obsessive search for facts, when it came time to interpret their data, they applied the class and cultural standards they had inherited. The case of Tom Rainer provides another example.[14]

Rainer was eight years old in November 1920, when he was first referred to the clinic. Tom had been picked up for begging at a railroad station about forty miles from Boston and returned to his parents, who brought him to the clinic at the suggestion of a child welfare agency. The father had worked as a night watchman for the same company for fifteen years, and his father, who had emigrated from Great Britain, had been a stationary engineer. The mother, whose parents were Nova Scotian farmers, was reportedly in poor health from her nine pregnancies, and had worked as a domestic before marriage. Of the seven living children, one was feebleminded and five, including Tom, were undernourished and less than average in weight and height. The three oldest children worked, one in a candy factory, one as a machinist, and one as a factory operative when her health permitted. The social worker who visited the family commented that the house they lived in was in need of painting and repair and that the kitchen was in disorder, that dirty clothing lay about the house, and that the household was ill kept. The mother's housekeeping was deemed inadequate and her discipline lax, with little parental attention given to the younger children. Tom began his delinquent career at age five, when he first started running away from home for several days at a time. He earned money by begging and singing on the streets.

Healy and Bronner's analysis of the case emphasized Tom's pleasant personality, his playfulness, and his mental alertness. Although he did not test well, his IQ was within the limits of normality and he showed good learning ability. They concluded that while he had heard about "bad sex affairs," he was fortunate enough to have "escaped contamination." They listed as the probable causes of Tom's delinquency his love of adventure, good singing voice, the pleasant way strangers responded to him, dislike of school, and poor parental oversight. Their prognosis was that his future was poor under the old conditions and that he should be placed on a farm.[15]

The insights of the psychiatric team were no deeper than those of nineteenth-century moral reformers. Healy and Bronner had collected an enormous amount of data on Tom Rainer, including the delinquent's "own story," but most of the information was irrelevant to the outcome of his case. His family background and social and developmental history offered few clues for treatment, other than the obvious one of foster care. Only the questions about childhood sexual experience indicate a search for possible mental conflicts in Rainer's past, but as Healy and Bronner recognized, this approach offered no particular help in understanding Rainer's case.

Girls sent to the Judge Baker Foundation encountered the usual concern about their sexuality. Healy and Bronner's Freudian fascination with childhood sexuality reinforced the tendency to subject delinquent girls to more careful scrutiny than boys and to incarcerate them for relatively minor offenses if they were sexually active. Here again, the new approach to delinquency incorporated many of the assumptions and cultural standards of the old. [16]

Tillie Mardon's referral to the clinic was a back door into the juvenile justice system. Even though girls generally were referred by social welfare agencies, rather than by police or the court as was the case with boys, they found themselves enmeshed in a court process, particularly if they were sexual offenders. In order to put some clinic recommendations into effect, parents had to enter a stubborn child complaint in juvenile court. In Tillie Mardon's case, several unexplained disappearances from home led a social worker to bring Tillie and her mother to the Baker Foundation. After an evaluation, the mother took Tillie to court, where she was committed to Lancaster, the usual fate for sexual delinquents. [17]

Tillie's family history illustrates the misfortune that troubled the families of Baker Foundation clients in the early years of its operation. Tillie's parents were both born in Canada, her father on Prince Edward Island in 1877, and the mother in Montreal in 1878, and the family moved to Boston in 1902. Mr. Mardon had trained as a cabinetmaker, but worked irregularly because of tuberculosis and heart disease, and the family had received assistance from various welfare agencies for twelve years. At the time of Tillie's interview, he had been hospitalized for about five months. James Mardon, the oldest living son, supported the family although he too was in ill health. Social workers reported that the family attended church regularly, that the six children were well brought up, and that Mrs. Mardon did not work outside the home and was a good housekeeper. These were the worthy poor and Tillie's delinquency could not be attributed to "poor stock."

Tillie's problems began after her father's hospitalization. She started skipping school, lying about her whereabouts to her mother, stealing from her employer, and staying out at night. Then she disappeared for ten days, living in a hotel room with a sailor, afraid she was pregnant and contemplating suicide, before writing a desperate note to her mother. She returned to her neighborhood, apparently waiting to be found, and her mother brought her into the clinic.

When Healy and Bronner analyzed Tillie's case, they noted her wish for pretty clothes, "a most natural desire among adolescent girls," and they lauded the fact that she was too proud to request new shoes from a social welfare agency. Her main problem was her "sex urge." The clinicians described Tillie as sensual, with a broad face, thick lips, and large breasts, and discovered that at age twelve she had overheard a neighbor accuse his wife of having affairs with other men and had heard "bad stories" from other girls in the neighborhood. This formed the basis of her later "sex consciousness and sex interest," which was defined as a combination of fantasy, curiosity, and a desire to be popular with men. When listing the reasons for her delinquency, Healy and Bronner counted adolescence, bad companions, unfortunate sex knowledge, lack of parental control, and premature development of sex characteristics, "making her attractive to men." The only remedy for the girl was a prolonged stay in a reform school.

Tillie Mardon had several problems, but the clinicians focused on her sexuality. Certainly Healy and Bronner did not approve of her larceny or adolescent rebelliousness, but these were comparatively minor issues in their analysis. Intervention in Tillie's case might have taken a number of forms: probation, with the family moving to a more desirable neighborhood, attendance at a settlement house recreational program, vocational training, continued therapy to bolster her self-image, or foster care, if the home situation were beyond remedy (which, according to the case workers, it was not). Instead, the clinicians recommended incarceration, even though they thought Tillie's sexual delinquency stemmed more from a desire to be popular than from any "primary physical sex feeling" and the evidence suggested that she had been intimate with only one individual.[18]

Healy and Bronner's analysis of female deviance proved no more understanding of adolescent needs and desires than those of earlier reformers. The new psychology did not replace an older Victorian framework, but evolved out of it. The acceptance of female sexuality in the new psychology did not equal acceptance of female sexual expression outside of heterosexual relationships leading to marriage. Girls on the streets may have been called maladjusted rather than criminal or bad, but they remained deviant and subject to incarceration.[19]

Psychiatrists and psychiatric social workers, who had billed themselves as experts on the emotional life of the family, found themselves as puzzled by delinquents as reformers generally had been. They perceived that parents felt vulnerable and uncertain about their children, and they seized the opportunity offered by misfortune to provide expert prescriptions for the cure of deviance.[20]

By the late 1920s, therapists at the Baker foundation, like child guidance clinicians elsewhere, began to probe beneath the symptoms of deviance. Psychiatrists encourage younger children to act out their version of family dynamics through play, sometimes with dolls representing different family members. Older delinquents worked through their conflicts in their relationships with the therapist. Samuel Hartwell, who worked with Healy and Bronner at the Baker Foundation before becoming director of the Worcester Child Guidance Clinic, developed a four-stage model of patient-therapist relations. Each step, from "friendly belief" to "dependent attachment," involved a closer bond with the psychiatrist, who sought to resolve the patient's conflicts at the simplest level before guiding the therapy to the next stage. The clinician's goal, beyond that of ending antisocial behavior, was to make the child aware of the family dynamics causing delinquency, and to make the child accept foster care or any environmental changes that might be needed. Like domestic reform, psychotherapy encouraged the delinquent to identify with the reformer/therapist and to adopt his or her values.[21]

Psychotherapy, like other versions of cultural reform, worked with some children. That is, science could not solve the problem of delin-

quency any better than religious conversion or the adoption of a
bourgeois culture, but it could provide clues for assisting an individual
delinquent. Hartwell's case studies show the increasing sophistication
and success of the Baker Foundation's work with delinquent boys.

Herbert Eilers, age ten, was referred to the clinic after a career as a
thief, a fence, and a truant and after having been on probation and in
a truant school. Herbert's parents had quarreled frequently—the father disputed the paternity of Herbert's younger sister—and his mother
died shortly after she separated from her husband. Herbert lived with
an enfeebled grandfather and spent most of his time on the streets,
where he became adept at petty crime. Hartwell discovered in his
interviews with the boy that he was frank and reliable and thought
that his main problem was that he had not been able to form close and
trusting relationships with adults. Hartwell decided to establish a deep
rapport with the boy to overcome his pattern of having only superficial
relationships. "What Herbert most needed was someone towards whom
he could develop a genuine loyalty and trust. That person could
transfer these loyalties to others and thereby lay the foundation for a
much more normal life." Hartwell encouraged Herbert to discuss what
caused his delinquent activity and how he felt about it. Herbert related
that he stole because it was the only way he had to get things he
wanted and he pretended he liked people because that way he could
use them for his own ends. The boy was convinced that he should try
to find his father and see if he could live with him because "his father
had lots of money and would buy him things."

Herbert came to realize that Hartwell liked him despite his misbe-
havior, even though he did not approve of the behavior itself, and this
was the beginning of Hartwell's therapeutic breakthrough. Hartwell
heard from the social worker that Herbert had started to stay home in
the evenings to read to his grandfather. When he asked the boy about
this, he replied that his grandfather was lonely and " 'I thought maybe
you would like me better if I did.' " Transferring Herbert's loyalties
to another person in his life was the next, more difficult step. Fortunately, the father proved to be a reasonable man who had remarried
and indicated an interest in the boy. Hartwell laid the groundwork for
their reunion by discussing with Herbert what fathers meant to boys
and the reasons why fathers sometimes neglected their children. Har-

twell arranged to have the father present at one of Herbert's sessions, and the boy eagerly embraced the father after learning his identity. After two followup sessions, Hartwell decided that therapy was successful and stopped the visits. While Herbert lived in a foster family rather than with his father, he developed a good relationship with both the father and the foster family and his delinquent behavior ceased.[22]

Hartwell obviously counted Herbert among his successes. He noted that without therapy the efforts to find a good foster home and to reestablish contact with the father would have been failures. Without the intervening stage of loyalty and deep rapport with Hartwell, Herbert would likely have continued his delinquencies in his foster home and simply viewed his father instrumentally. Hartwell was equally frank in discussing his failures, but overall he counted forty-four of the fifty-five cases as at least partial successes.[23]

It is notable that Hartwell's successes came with boys. Baker clinicians continued to find girls' cases difficult to handle sympathetically, perhaps because of the gender biases of Freudian-influenced therapy. Clinicians routinely overlooked or reinterpreted evidence of incest or other sexual abuse in delinquent girls, confusing the girls' experience with fantasies.[24] Therapy may have worked with boys because therapists could avoid the knot of patriarchal family relations that their training did not prepare them to untangle. But more extensive analyses of the clinic's work prove that claims of success with boys were exaggerated. Psychotherapy may have worked in some cases, such as Herbert Eiler's, but few delinquents received as extensive care and attention. The principle of less eligibility limited the provision of psychiatric services, and for most delinquents visits to the clinic involved far more modest achievements.[25]

Evaluations of the Therapeutic Approach

The emphasis on science and scientific method meant that for the first time the results of reform could be measured and analyzed. No one had conceived of counting how many poor children remained evangelical Christians five years after attending a Sunday school or seeing whether placement in a foster family resulted in a permanent reformation of character. In the 1920s and 1930s, however, social scientists

began to study the effects of intervention into delinquents' lives. Much
of William Healy and Augusta Bronner's research involved comparing
groups of treated and nontreated delinquents, and several independent
studies were done of the clinic's work. Never before was failure dem-
onstrated so precisely.

Early reports indicated mixed success for the therapeutic approach
to delinquency. When Healy and Bronner compared the careers of
male delinquents they treated in Chicago with those of male delinquents seen in Boston, they found that nearly twice as many Chicago
delinquents had adult court records (50 percent vs. 26 percent). Healy
and Bronner could not attribute the improved results to greater experience or their psychoanalytic methods, for their analysis of an un-
treated group of delinquents in Boston showed an even lower recidivism rate (21 percent). Rather, they cited an improved police/judicial/
social welfare environment that encouraged early intervention in a
delinquent's life. Boston delinquents did not have their trivial offenses
dismissed, as occurred in Chicago, but were placed on probation;
Boston social welfare agencies cooperated with each other and with
public authorities; the Boston Juvenile Court utilized probation, rather
than incarceration, even for more serious offenders, and more boys
thereby avoided the corrupting influence of the reformatory. Healy
and Bronner concluded that the more active social welfare/juvenile
justice network, if not therapy itself, disrupted potentially criminal
careers.[26]

An intensive study of children placed into foster homes after diagnosis and treatment at the Baker Foundation also revealed successful
outcomes. The research team found that 90 percent of the mentally
normal children were successful, which they defined as becoming
desirable members of the foster family and community and making
some progress toward mastering the antisocial behavior or personality
difficulty that had led to delinquency. Among those who were mentally defective, or exhibited mental abnormality or abnormal personalities, the success rate dropped to 49 percent. Still, Healy and his
coworkers concluded that delinquents could be placed with great success: neither sex, age, heredity, nor type of delinquency proved to be
an obstacle to reform. Only when delinquency was compounded by

mental abnormality or personality disorders, as occurred in 40 percent of the cases placed by the agencies, was the prognosis negative.[27]

Child guidance, however, did not live up to its initial promise. One warning came from Bella Boone Beard's study of five hundred delinquent boys and girls seen at the Baker Foundation between 1924 and 1929. Beard interviewed her five hundred delinquents five years after treatment at the Baker foundation, which was a significantly longer period than that used by Healy and Bronner, and she was critical of Healy and Bronner's standards of evaluation.

Beard's findings show that Healy and Bronner were too optimistic in analyzing their own work. While she concluded that over 40 percent of the boys and three-quarters of the girls were "permanent" successes (in that they committed no further delinquencies during the study period), she found that many of the recommendations of the clinic were not carried out and it was not clear that a diagnosis by the Baker foundation had any impact on delinquent behavior. Parental opposition was a significant factor in the failure to follow the clinic's recommendations. In one-quarter of the cases, the clinic proposed institutionalization or foster care, but the court acceded to parental wishes that the delinquent be allowed to remain home on probation. In nearly one out of every five cases, the clinic had the court order families to move out of their neighborhoods, and a quarter of the families refused. Healy and Bronner (reflecting their low expectations of working-class children) were also too eager to see employment as a sign of reform. Many cases were closed after a boy or girl obtained work, with no followup to determine whether or not the job was appropriate or whether the delinquent held the job for any length of time. Beard's study showed that unemployment was four times as high among the recidivists as among the successes, and she argued that more careful supervision might have prevented these failures. While the clinic made sweeping recommendations, parental indifference or opposition and low expectations by the clinic staff meant that therapeutic intervention touched many delinquents lightly. Beard's conclusions, however, were not the most devastating.[28]

Criminologists Sheldon and Eleanor Glueck conducted the most extensive analysis of intervention by the Boston Juvenile Court and the Baker Foundation. In their work, published in 1934 as part of Harvard Law School's Boston Crime Survey, the Gluecks examined the probation records of one thousand boys (unfortunately they decided that girls presented "special problems" and did not include them) sent to the Baker Foundation by the Boston Juvenile Court between 1917 and 1922 to see whether the delinquents committed any further delinquent acts in the five years following the end of their treatment period. Their conclusions were startling.

The boys sent to the clinic comprised a peculiar subset of Boston's population. As a group they were ill educated, with 83 percent of them stopping their schooling with, or before completing, the eighth grade, when 93 percent of Boston's school children entered the ninth grade. They were the products of poor families, three-quarters of whom were defined as marginal (living on daily earnings) or dependent on charity, and with two-thirds of the boys dropping out of school for economic reasons. Seventy percent of the boys had at least one foreign-born parent at a time when this was true of only 29 percent of Boston's male population. Not surprisingly, given their class and ethnic background and the cultural biases of intelligence tests, they scored poorly on the Stanford-Binet IQ test, which showed that 13 percent were feeble-minded (IQ of 70 or less) and 17 percent borderline (IQ of 71–80), when only 7 percent of a sample of Massachusetts school children fell into these two categories. Most notably, 87 percent had family members or siblings who had committed delinquent or criminal acts. The delinquents studied by the Baker Foundation were drawn from the most recent arrivals (40 percent of the fathers were born in Italy and 24 percent in Russia, Poland, or Lithuania), the poorest, and the most desperate.[29]

The Gluecks' most important discovery was the utter futility of the juvenile justice system's treatment of these cases. Over half of the delinquents committed further delinquent acts during the time of their supervision by the court, and in the five-year followup period, 88 percent engaged in delinquent activities, with seven-tenths of these activities being felonies rather than minor status offenses or misdemeanors. Delinquency may have been diagnosed but it certainly was not cured.[30]

The Gluecks did not blame the clinic itself, but focused on the lack of coordination among juvenile justice agencies. Despite Judge Cabot's role in bringing Healy and Bronner to Boston and in establishing the Baker Foundation, he often did not follow the clinic's recommendations about the delinquents he asked them to study. One problem was jurisdictional—for example, the court had to ignore proposals to send delinquents to institutions for the feebleminded because it lacked the power of commitment. A second issue arose over "creaming"—the practice of private social welfare agencies taking only the most favorable cases and leaving the difficult ones to public authorities. This limited the court's flexibility in arranging placements. Parental opposition to clinic plans, especially foster placement, was of primary importance. Working-class families were especially loath to lose an income-producing male adolescent, and the court succumbed to their insistence on having boys placed on probation even when the clinic recommended otherwise. In one-fifth of the cases, a recommendation to remove a delinquent from home was ignored completely, while in another fifth, the length of time (three months or less) spent in foster care was considered too short to have been effective. In other words, families were quite successful in evading recommendations and in short-circuiting the juvenile justice/social welfare/mental health connection. In total, over half of the clinic's recommendations went unheeded.[31]

That the court ignored the "treatment plans" of its own advisors is a telling commentary on the limits of state intervention into families. The juvenile court certainly had the power to remove children from their families, but wholesale disruption of working-class families was untenable in a democratic society. The court found it wiser to attempt to gain parental cooperation in reforming a delinquent youth than to ride roughshod over parental wishes, and this gave families the opportunity to negotiate with the court in settling a case. Even in the more active Progressive state, delinquents and their families asserted their interests successfully.[32]

A troubling conclusion for reformers was the Gluecks' finding that carrying out the clinic's recommendations did not make much of a difference anyway. The Gluecks discovered that delinquents who followed the clinic's proposals about residence had nearly the same recidivism rate as those who did not. When analyzing the impact of the other recommendations, the Gluecks discovered that only when they had been carried out fully did the recidivism rate drop—and even then three-quarters of the delinquents were rearrested.[33]

Three positions emerged in the debate over the Gluecks' report, one calling for an expansion of the therapeutic state, a second defending the status quo, and the third recommending that the court surrender the idea of therapy. The Gluecks put their faith in progress. They argued that the court was a step in the evolution of criminal justice toward more humanitarian and scientific treatment of delinquents, and that if the principles behind the clinic and court were applied more extensively, they could succeed. They recommended that the clinic become part of the court so that it could guide treatment as well as diagnosis of delinquency, that the juvenile court serve the greater Boston area, that more family clinics be made available to advise parents about childrearing, that recreational facilities and settlement houses/clubs be expanded, and that all elements of juvenile justice be united in a ministry of justice. Dr. Richard Cabot, in an influential review in *Survey*, called the court and clinic "an appallingly complete and costly failure" and, like earlier generations of frustrated reformers, he laid the blame on the social and hereditary characteristics of the delinquents. Despite his pessimism, he did not call for the abolition of the court, but, like the Gluecks, wanted to see treatment and diagnosis unified in one powerful therapeutic agency.[34]

Others saw nothing wrong with the operations of juvenile courts and mental health clinics. Commentators to *Survey* argued that Boston's failure could not be writ large. In absolute contrast to earlier claims, they stated that the Boston Juvenile Court was neither a model for other courts nor even representative of their work, which was much more advanced. Moreover, they claimed, juvenile justice had progressed since the period analyzed by the Gluecks and therapeutic models were being used more effectively.[35]

The third position was represented by Thomas Eliot, a prominent sociologist, who suggested that treatment be completely separated from adjudication. Like earlier legalist critics of the juvenile court, Eliot believed that justice was served best by having the court supervise the investigation of cases, decide conflicting claims, and enforce decisions. Social work and psychiatric services belonged in the domain of public welfare. However, this position meant surrendering social work's claim to power and it attracted few adherents.[36]

William Healy and Augusta Bronner responded to the Gluecks' report by admitting the failure of their efforts to cure delinquents. They concluded that the Boston Juvenile Court "has not achieved the end desired" and that "clinical diagnostic service is not in itself thera-peutic." Perhaps moved by the misery of the Great Depression, they suggested that if "the roots of crime lie far back in the foundations of our social order, it may be that only a radical change can bring any large measure of cure. Less unjust social and economic conditions may be the only way out, and until a better social order exists, crime will probably flourish and society continue to pay the price." Despite this conclusion, Healy and Bronner did not give up; like the Gluecks, they believed in scientific progress and argued that intensive case work had not been given a fair chance to succeed.[37]

The therapeutic model revitalized the cultural reform tradition, but did little more than that. Reformers continued to view the sources of deviance as individual or familial, but instead of stemming from intem-perance, idleness, promiscuity, or viciousness, deviance arose because of parental inability to supply emotional sustenance to children or parental failure to provide proper conditioning. The therapeutic model allowed professionals to assert claims of expertise while continuing to justify intervention in families in a society that was becoming more pluralistic. Therapists did not claim to be enforcing a superior cultural standard; rather, they instructed parents about emotional and familial adjustment. Their intervention, however, was not notably more effec-tive than that of earlier generations of moral/cultural reformers. The treatment plans submitted by the clinic were ignored as frequently as they were followed. Parents simply rejected proposals that they change residence, return to the old country, or surrender their children for placement, and the court enforced radical intervention for only more serious offenders. Proposals for a centralized ministry of justice were not taken seriously, as the democratic polity remained an important obstacle to the rise of an intrusive therapeutic state.

Despite its problems, the therapeutic model retained its lure for reformers, and not just because it sustained their professional status. Its appeal stemmed from the nature of the reform process itself. Reformers had generally seen problems with their plans as stemming from inadequate funding or other interference with the proper implementation of reform. They rarely doubted the validity of the cultural reform tradition. Only when reformers looked failure in the eye— such as Healy and Bronner did after the publication of the Glueck report—did they begin to question their paradigm and look to an alternative explanation for the sources of deviance and the reasons for failure. Such openings for a more radically political interpretation of deviance closed quickly. Healy and Bronner argued that the therapeutic model had not been given its due. Like earlier generations of cultural reformers, they ignored the constraints less eligibility put on reform and continued to treat the symptoms of deviance, even as they left its causes untouched.

Conclusion: The Failure of Cultural Reform

On the eve of the Great Depression, Boston's social welfare agencies formed a network of public and private, sectarian and secular, coercive and voluntary institutions that responded to the city's social problems. Cases were routinely referred from one agency to another, the courts used private agencies for public purposes (such as supervising individuals on probation), private agencies initiated court cases against working-class parents accused of neglecting or abusing their children, and delinquents shuttled back and forth among schools, the mental health clinic, social welfare agencies, settlement houses, and the reformatory. However impressive this triumph of bureaucracy and rationalization may seem, its system and order must not be overemphasized. Despite sophisticated techniques of intervention and the extensive reach of social welfare institutions, reformers failed to reshape the lives of the poor and delinquent.

There are two reasons for the failure of reform. One is that reformers underestimated the impact clients had on reform programs. The poor, forced by family disaster or economic necessity to turn to the state and/or to private social welfare organizations, were not in the best position to resist reformers' demands, but they defended their own interests as best they could. The contest between reformers and delinquents and their families, while unequal, determined the ways social welfare institutions functioned.

The second reason for failure lies in the cultural reform tradition itself. Reformers reworked the cultural reform tradition many times between the 1810s and the 1930s, but throughout they emphasized the individual, moral sources of deviance and consequently the individual, cultural sources of reform. Moral entrepreneurs used religious conversion as their model for regenerating society, domestic reformers emphasized putting children into either real or institutional model families, charity organizers linked social welfare agencies and created alternative cultural centers in working-class neighborhoods, and the Progressives tied the system together and offered flexible treatment plans and psychological adjustment as the cure for deviance. Only rarely did reformers question the larger structure of economic inequality and instability that forced working-class families to rely on charity or on child labor. Even after reformers began to champion a more activist state to confront social problems, traditional moral categories of deviance conditioned reformers' responses to the poor and the delinquent.

The cultural reform tradition frequently produced humane experiments for reeducating delinquent youth. The early House of Reformation, the farm schools of the Children's Aid Society, the placement programs of private and public authorities, home libraries and children's clubs, and individual psychotherapy with troubled youths produced modest successes with a limited number of individuals. But these were only individual successes. The principle of less eligibility prevented the expansion of these programs, and sometimes forced their reorganization, particularly in the public sector. Reform of delinquent youth was held hostage by the need to control the welfare system and to prevent any challenge to the hegemony of the marketplace.

The poorhouse and the reformatory dominated the welfare and the juvenile justice systems. These institutions stigmatized rather than reformed, and they established the boundaries between the worthy and the unworthy poor. (One need only recall from the introduction Mrs. Kern's horror of public institutions to realize how much the poor internalized the fear of contact with public agencies.) The humiliation of those in public institutions helped create the division between the respectable working class and the disreputable underclass that is a salient fact of contemporary society and that prevents the extension of decent housing, basic medical care, an adequate income, and an education as inherent rights of citizenship.

Today there is another crisis in juvenile justice and we continue to think about it in moral terms. Instead of confronting deindustrialization and the collapse of an urban job market, the deterioration of housing stock, the failure of urban schools to educate, the inability of welfare to relieve the poor, and the perfectly understandable lure of illegal drug trading, we launch campaigns to have poor adolescents say no to drugs. Despite evidence that the poor work eagerly when work is available—even if the jobs do not pay enough to sustain them—we cling to the myth that the poor somehow choose their fate.[1] We continue to locate the urban crisis in the absence of moral fiber among the poor, and that means we will fail to address the source of that crisis as certainly as the reformers studied here did. Surely we can do better.

Notes

Introduction: The Web of Class

1. Reformers are interpreted here as aggressive proselytizers who sought to infuse both public and private institutions with their values. Antonio Gramsci used the term *hegemony* to refer to the ability of a dominant social group or class to establish its values as universal and to win the consent of subordinate groups in society to its social and cultural leadership. Because of the emphasis on consent, hegemony is far more subtle than the simplistic notion of social control employed by many historians. It suggests an aggressive attempt to proselytize as well as the give and take of alliance building among different groups even if those groups possess unequal power. Hegemony also points to the role of private institutions ("civil society")—as apart from governmental institutions ("political society")—in reinforcing economic power and structuring the ways in which society and the possibility of social change are conceived. See *Selections from the Prison Notebooks of Antonio Gramsci*, ed. and trans. Quentin Hoare and Geoffrey Nowell Smith (New York, 1971), 12–13, 52–60, 180–82, 192–95, 207–8, 243–47, 258–65. The best recent introduction to Gramsci is T. J. Jackson Lears, "The Concept of Cultural Hegemony: Problems and Possibilities," *American Historical Review* 90 (June 1985): 567–93.

My interpretation is based on Gwyn A. Williams, "The Concept of 'Egemonia' in the Thought of Antonio Gramsci: Some Notes on Interpretation," *Journal of the History of Ideas* 21 (October–December 1960): 586–99; Raymond Williams, "Base and Superstructure in Marxist Cultural Theory," *New Left Review* 82 (November–December 1973): 3–16; idem, *Marxism and Literature* (New York, 1977), especially part 2; Walter L. Adamson, *Hegemony and Revolution: A Study of Antonio Gramsci's Political and Cultural Theory* (Berkeley, CA, 1980), especially 170–79. Ira Katznelson, *City Trenches: Urban Politics and the Patterning of Class in the United States* (New York, 1981), 208–9; and Christine

Buci-Glucksmann, "Hegemony and Consent: A Political Strategy," in *Approaches to Gramsci*, ed. Anne Showstock Sassoon (London, 1982), 116–26, especially her remarks on the function of the state.

Aileen S. Kraditor has offered a trenchant critique of her version of the Gramscian model in *The Radical Persuasion, 1890–1917: Aspects of the Intellectual History and the Historiography of Three American Radical Organizations* (Baton Rouge, LA, 1981), 63–96. For a rejoinder, see Lears, "Concept of Cultural Hegemony," 581–83.

2. Intellectual histories include Joseph M. Hawes, *Children in Urban Society: Juvenile Delinquency in Nineteenth–Century America* (New York, 1971); Robert M. Mennel, *Thorns and Thistles: Juvenile Delinquents in the United States, 1825–1940* (Hanover, NH, 1973); LeRoy Ashby, *Saving the Waifs: Reformers and Dependent Children, 1890–1917* (Philadelphia, 1984).

Studies of deviant populations include Blake McKelvey, *American Prisons: A Study in American Social History prior to 1915* (Chicago, 1936); Orlando F. Lewis, *The Development of American Prisons and Prison Customs, 1776–1845* (Montclair, NJ, 1967); David J. Rothman, *The Discovery of the Asylum: Social Order and Disorder in the New Republic* (Boston, 1971); idem, *Conscience and Convenience: The Asylum and Its Alternatives in Progressive America* (Boston, 1980).

Studies of reformatories as part of the education system include Michael B. Katz, *The Irony of Early School Reform: Educational Innovation in Mid–Nineteenth Century Massachusetts* (Boston, 1968); Stanley K. Schultz, *The Culture Factory: Boston Public Schools, 1789–1860* (New York, 1973).

Institutional biographies include Negley K. Teeters, "The Early Days of the Philadelphia House of Refuge," *Pennsylvania History* 27 (January 1960): 165–87; Robert S. Pickett, *House of Refuge: Origins of Juvenile Reform in New York State, 1815–1857* (Syracuse, NY, 1969); Jack M. Holl, *Juvenile Reform in the Progressive Era: William R. George and the Junior Republic Movement* (Ithaca, NY, 1971); Robert M. Mennel, " 'The Family System of Common Farmers': The Origins of Ohio's Reform Farm, 1840–1858," *Ohio History* 89 (Spring 1980): 125–56; idem, " 'The Family System of Common Farmers': The Early Years of Ohio's Reform Farm, 1858–1884," *Ohio History* 89 (Summer 1980): 279–322; Barbara M. Brenzel, *Daughters of the State: A Social Portrait of the First Reform School for Girls in North America, 1856–1905* (Cambridge, MA, 1983).

On the juvenile court, see Peter Gregg Slater, "Ben Lindsey and the Denver Juvenile Court: A Progressive Looks at Human Nature," *American Quarterly* 20 (Summer 1968): 211–23; Sanford J. Fox, "Juvenile Justice Reform: An Historical Perspective," *Stanford Law Review* 22 (June 1970): 1187–1239; J. Lawrence Schultz, "The Cycle of Juvenile Court History," *Crime and Delinquency* 19 (October 1973): 457–76; Ellen Ryerson, *The Best-Laid Plans: America's Juvenile Court Experiment* (New York, 1978). Anthony M. Platt, *The Child Savers: The Invention of Delinquency* (Chicago, 1968), has a slightly wider focus but basically belongs in this category as does David John Hogan, *Class and Reform: School and Society in Chicago, 1880–1930* (Philadelphia, 1985). On the mental health clinic, see Margo Horn, *Before It's Too Late: The Child Guidance Movement in the United States, 1922–1945* (Philadelphia, 1989) and Theresa R. Richardson, *The Century of the Child: The Mental Hygiene Movement and Social Policy in the United States and Canada* (Albany, NY, 1989).

Works that use client records perceptively include Steven L. Schlossman, *Love and the American Delinquent: The Theory and Practice of "Progressive" Juvenile Justice, 1825–1920* (Chicago, 1977); Steven L. Schlossman and Stephanie Wallach, "The Crime of Precocious Sexuality: Female Juvenile Delinquency in the Progressive Era," *Harvard Educational Review* 48 (February 1978): 65–94; Brenzel, *Daughters of the State*; Horn, *Before It's Too Late*; and Linda Gordon, *Heroes of Their Own Lives: The Politics and History of Family Violence, Boston, 1880–1960* (New York, 1988).

3. Roy Lubove, *The Professional Altruist: The Emergence of Social Work as a Career, 1880–1930* (New York, 1975), 26–31, 34, 43–45, 138–41; Nathan Irvin Huggins, *Protestants against Poverty: Boston's Charities, 1870–1900* (Westport, CT, 1971), 12–13, 62–63; Gordon, *Heroes*, 7.

4. All societies define deviants as a way of establishing boundaries and reinforcing norms. Sometimes deviance is constructed formally through established legal codes and sometimes informally through community rituals. In either case, the definition of deviance constitutes the formation or reinforcement of a cultural consensus. See Emile Durkheim, *The Division of Labor in Society* (New York, 1964), 102–5; Howard S. Becker, *Outsiders: Studies in the Sociology of Deviance* (New York, 1963), 1–18; Kai Erikson, *Wayward Puritans: A Study in the Sociology of Deviance* (New York, 1966), 6–7, 10–13.

5. The term "dominant culture" requires explanation. For much of the nineteenth century, it refers to a set of values favoring private property, temperance, enterprise, individualism, future orientation, industry, thrift, and chastity. See Daniel Walker Howe, "American Victorianism as a Culture," *American Quarterly* 27 (December 1975): 507–32; Walter E. Houghton, *The Victorian Frame of Mind, 1830–1870* (New Haven, 1957); Burton J. Bledstein, *The Culture of Professionalism: The Middle Class and the Development of Higher Education in America* (New York, 1976), 26–39.

However, the dominant culture was not the only culture. Populists, working-class radicals, and Socialists formed oppositional cultures and challenged many of the dominant culture's basic values. In addition, there existed a variety of alternative cultures that incorporated some of the same values but gave them different meaning. These included the republican culture of the antebellum artisanry and the variety of peasant cultures brought by different immigrant groups. The difference between an alternative and an oppositional culture is developed in Raymond Williams, "Base and Superstructure in Marxist Cultural Theory," 10–11. Roy Rosenzweig makes use of these distinctions to study the limits of hegemony in *Eight Hours for What We Will: Workers and Leisure in an Industrial City, 1870–1920* (Cambridge, England, 1983). On artisan radicalism and its relation to the rise of the working class, see Sean

Wilentz, *Chants Democratic: New York City and the Rise of the American Working Class, 1788–1850* (New York, 1984); on Populism, see Lawrence Goodwyn, *Democratic Promise: The Populist Moment in America* (New York, 1976); on working-class communities and ethnic cultures, see Herbert G. Gutman, *Work, Culture, and Society in Industrializing America* (New York, 1977), especially 3–78; on socialism and working-class radicalism and their relation to ethnicity, see Richard Jules Oestreicher, *Solidarity and Fragmentation: Working People and Class Consciousness in Detroit, 1875–1900* (Urbana, IL, 1986).

Obviously the values of the dominant culture did not remain static. On the shift toward a culture emphasizing leisure and consumption, see John Higham, "The Reorientation of American Culture in the 1890s," in his *Writing American History: Essays in Modern Scholarship* (Bloomington, IN, 1970), 73–102; and Warren I. Sussman, "Culture Heroes: Ford, Barton, Ruth," in his *Culture as History: The Transformation of American Society in the Twentieth Century* (New York, 1984), 122–49.

More recent works include John F. Kasson, *Amusing the Million: Coney Island at the Turn of the Century* (New York, 1978); Lary May, *Screening Out the Past: The Birth of Mass Culture and the Motion Picture Industry* (New York, 1980); Lewis A. Erenberg, *Steppin' Out: New York Nightlife and the Transformation of American Culture, 1890–1930* (Westport, CT, 1981); Kathy Peiss, *Cheap Amusements: Working Women and Leisure in Turn-of-the-Century New York* (Philadelphia, 1986); Roy Rosenzweig, *Eight Hours for What We Will*; Elliot J. Gorn, *The Manly Art: Bare-Knuckle Prize Fighting in America* (Ithaca, NY, 1986).

6. The case history of the "Kern" family can be found on 185–240 of "The Juvenile Court as a Community Institution in the Municipal Court of Roxbury District," Miriam Van Waters Papers, Harvard Law School Library, Box 14, file V. The names used here are pseudonyms and some details have been omitted to preserve confidentiality. Hereafter, only direct quotations are footnoted and references have been simplified to "The Juvenile Court as a Community Institution," MVWP, HLSL.

For examples of the use of case history material in the analysis of social welfare, see Michael B. Katz, *Poverty and Policy in American History* (New York, 1983), chapter 1; and Gordon, *Heroes*, passim.

7. "The Juvenile Court as a Community Institution," 194–95, MVWP, HLSL. For an interpretation of women's use of social welfare agencies, including the SPCC, to strengthen their hand in the family, see Gordon, *Heroes*, 294–97.

8. Mark H. Leff, "Consensus for Reform: The Mothers' Pension Campaign in the Progressive Era," *Social Service Review* 47 (September 1973): 397–417; Lynn Y. Weiner, *From Working Girl to Working Mother: The Female Labor Force in the United States, 1820–1980* (Chapel Hill, NC, 1985), 128–32; Gordon, *Heroes*, 102–7. Lubove, *The Professional Altruist*, remains the standard

account of professionalization in social work. On the continuing significance of these distinctions, see Michael B. Katz, *The Undeserving Poor: From the War on Poverty to the War on Welfare* (New York, 1989).

9. Weiner, *From Working Girl to Working Mother*, 120–22.

10. Schlossman and Wallach, "The Crime of Precocious Sexuality," 65–94; Gordon, *Heroes*, 138–41.

11. Holl, *Juvenile Reform in the Progressive Era.*

12. Peiss, *Cheap Amusements*, 164–71, 178–84; Paul Boyer, *Urban Masses and Moral Order in America, 1820–1920* (Cambridge, MA, 1978), 222–23; William Foote Whyte, *Street Corner Society* (Chicago, 1943), 102–4, 276; Francis G. Couvares, *The Remaking of Pittsburgh: Class and Culture in an Industrializing City, 1877–1919* (Albany, NY, 1984), 114–15; Virginia Yans-McLaughlin, *Family and Community: Italian Immigrants in Buffalo, 1880–1930* (Ithaca, NY, 1971), 137–41, 146–47.

13. "The Juvenile Court as a Community Institution," 187, MVWP, HLSL.

14. Whyte, *Street Corner Society*, 104–8, on the differences between street-corner and college boys.

15. Holl, *Juvenile Reform in the Progressive Era*, 188.

16. Gordon, *Heroes*, 216–17, on pelvic examinations.

17. Brenzel, *Daughters of the State*, 123–30; Eric C. Schneider, "In the Web of Class: Youth, Class, and Culture in Boston, 1840–1940," (Ph.D. diss., Boston University, 1980), chapter 5.

18. "The Juvenile Court as a Community Institution," 188, 190, 207, MVWP, HLSL.

19. Peter L. Tyer, " 'Denied the Power to Choose the Good': Sexuality and Mental Defect in American Medical Practice, 1850–1920," *Journal of Social History* 10 (June 1977): 472–89.

20. Peter C. Holloran, *Boston's Wayward Children: Social Services for Homeless Children, 1830–1930* (Rutherford, NJ, 1989), 132–36.

21. Sheldon Glueck and Eleanor T. Glueck, *One Thousand Juvenile Delinquents: Their Treatment by Clinic and Court* (Cambridge, MA, 1934), chapters 7 and 8.

22. This is contrary to the arguments in Jacques Donzelot, *The Policing of Families* (New York, 1979); Christopher Lasch, *Haven in a Heartless World: The Family Besieged* (New York, 1977); and idem, *The Culture of Narcissism: American Life in an Age of Diminishing Expectations* (New York, 1979).

23. "The Juvenile Court as a Community Institution," 231, MVWP, HLSL.

24. See Elizabeth Janeway, *Powers of the Weak* (New York, 1980).

25. James T. Patterson, *America's Struggle against Poverty, 1900–1980* (Cambridge, MA, 1981), 11–19; Alexander Keyssar, *Out of Work: The First Century of Unemployment in Massachusetts* (Cambridge, England, 1986), 320–24.

26. Yans-McLaughlin, *Family and Community*, 174–77, 193–94; Tamara K. Hareven, *Family Time and Industrial Time: The Relationship between the Family*

and Work in a New England Industrial Community (Cambridge, England, 1982), 73–74; John Bodnar, *The Transplanted: A History of Immigrants in Urban America* (Bloomington, IN, 1985), 71–83; S. J. Kleinberg, *The Shadow of the Mills: Working-Class Families in Pittsburgh, 1870–1907* (Pittsburgh, 1989), 129–32, 174–83, 268, 271–72; Claudia Goldin, "Family Strategies and the Family Economy in the Late Nineteenth Century: The Role of Secondary Workers," in *Philadelphia: Work, Space, Family, and Group Experience in the Nineteenth Century*, ed. Theodore Hershberg (New York, 1981), 277–310.

27. David Nasaw, *Children of the City: At Work and at Play* (New York, 1985).

28. David Nasaw, *Schooled to Order: A Social History of Public Schooling in the United States* (New York, 1979), 166–67.

29. Peter Knights, *The Plain People of Boston, 1830–1860* (New York, 1971).

30. The seminal work in the modern study of class is E. P. Thompson, *The Making of the English Working Class* (New York, 1963).

On insecurity, unemployment, and the uneven pace of development in the period covered by this book, see Alan Dawley, *Class and Community: The Industrial Revolution in Lynn* (Cambridge, MA, 1976), chapter 6; Susan Hirsch, *The Roots of the American Working Class: The Industrialization of Crafts in Newark, 1800–1860* (Philadelphia, 1978), chapter 2; Bruce Laurie, *Working People of Philadelphia, 1800–1850* (Philadelphia, 1980), chapter 1; Sean Wilentz, *Chants Democratic*, 108–29; Priscilla Ferguson Clement, *Welfare and the Poor in the Nineteenth-Century City, Philadelphia, 1800–1854* (Rutherford, NJ, 1985), chapter 1; Brian Greenberg, *Worker and Community: Response to Industrialization in a Nineteenth-Century American City, Albany, New York, 1850–1884* (Albany, NY, 1985), chapter 4; David Brody, *Workers in Industrial America: Essays on the Twentieth-Century Struggle* (New York, 1980), 3–14; David Montgomery, *Workers' Control in America* (Cambridge, England, 1980), chapter 1; Katz, *Poverty and Policy*, chapter 1; Keyssar, *Out of Work*, 59–76, 89–96.

The presence of female-headed households is also an indication of poverty and potential vulnerability. Between 1880 and 1910, approximately one Boston family (the census term until 1950) in five was female-headed, which did not include those families in which males were absent at least occasionally. This was probably an increase over earlier years. See Gordon, *Heroes*, 86 and 329, note 3.

Part 1: The Creation of Private and Public Charity

1. Thomas Malthus, *An Essay on the Principle of Population* (London, 1973), 214, 219, 221–22, 260. The possibility of "reform"—of teaching moral restraint to the poor—is developed in the second and subsequent editions of Malthus. See Gertrude Himmelfarb, *The Idea of Poverty: England in the Early Industrial Age* (New York, 1984), 113–19; Walter I. Trattner, *From Poor Law to Welfare State: A History of Social Welfare in America* (New York, 1974), 45–56;

Michael E. Rose, *The Relief of Poverty, 1834–1914* (London, 1972), 8–12; E. P. Thompson, *The Making of the English Working Class* (New York, 1963), 220–24, 266–68.

Obviously these trends were international and not a response to peculiarly American circumstances as is maintained in David J. Rothman, *The Discovery of the Asylum: Social Order and Disorder in the New Republic* (Boston, 1971).

2. Carl Bridenbaugh, *Cities in the Wilderness: The First Century of Urban Life in America, 1625–1742* (New York, 1938), 80–83, 233–35, 392–94; idem, *Cities in Revolt: Urban Life in America, 1743–1776* (New York, 1955), 124–26; Rothman, *Discovery of the Asylum*, 39–42; Douglas Lamar Jones, "The Strolling Poor: Transiency in Eighteenth-Century Massachusetts," *Journal of Social History* 8 (Spring 1975): 28–54; Gary B. Nash, *The Urban Crucible: Social Change, Political Consciousness, and the Origins of the American Revolution* (Cambridge, MA, 1979), 125–26, 184–97, 253–54.

1. Moral Entrepreneurs and the Invention of the Reformable Child

1. On poverty, see Alan Kulikoff, "The Progress of Inequality in Revolutionary Boston," *William and Mary Quarterly* XXVIII (July 1971): 380–84, 398–99; Samuel Rezneck, "The Depression of 1819–1822: A Social History," *American Historical Review* 39 (October 1933): 33; Peter R. Knights, *The Plain People of Boston, 1830–1860* (New York, 1971), 83, 88–89, 96; Edward Pessen, "The Egalitarian Myth and the American Social Reality: Wealth, Mobility, and Equality in the 'Era of the Common Man,' " *American Historical Review* 76 (October 1971): 1020–21; William H. Pease and Jane H. Pease, *The Web of Progress: Private Values and Public Styles in Boston and Charleston, 1828–1843* (New York, 1985), 23–24.

2. Howard S. Becker, *Outsiders: Studies in the Sociology of Deviance* (New York, 1963), 147–63. Becker provides a caricature of reformers; nonetheless, the concept of moral entrepreneurship remains valuable.

3. Redmond J. Barnett, "From Philanthropy to Reform: Poverty, Drunkenness, and the Social Order in Massachusetts, 1780–1825" (Ph.D. diss., Harvard University, 1973), 245–54.

4. The Moral Instruction Society was organized specifically to bring religious instruction to the poor; it did not aim its efforts at society at large and discover the poor later, as Smith Rosenberg maintains happened with early missionary societies in New York. See *Religion and the Rise of the American City: The New York City Mission Movement, 1812–1870* (Ithaca, NY, 1971), 9, 59, 91–93. Raymond A. Mohl, *Poverty in New York, 1783–1825* (New York, 1971), chapter 12; Barnett, "From Philanthropy to Reform," 259–69; Stanley K. Schultz, *The Culture Factory: Boston Public Schools, 1789–1860* (New York, 1973), 27–28; Barbara Meil Hobson, *Uneasy Virtue: The Politics of Prostitution and the American Reform Tradition* (New York, 1987), 20–21. Cutler was among Boston's wealthiest one hundred citizens in 1833, and Samuel T. Armstrong

made the top two hundred in 1848. See Edward Pessen, *Riches, Class, and Power before the Civil War* (Lexington, MA, 1973), 332–33. These men were Trinitarians, and despite their wealth, were not considered part of the Brahmin elite.

5. William Jenks's diary, November 25, 1821, Jenks Family Collections, Massachusetts Historical Society, Boston; Society for the Moral and Religious Instruction of the Poor (SMRIP), *Annual Report*, 1820, 14; idem, *Annual Report*, 1827, 20–21. The reports are in the Congregational Library, Boston. It is interesting to note that the missionaries were women; as with the Ministry to the Poor's volunteers, no mention is made of their identities. On the invisible but highly significant roles played by women in antebellum charity, see Lori D. Ginzberg, *Women and the Work of Benevolence: Morality, Politics and Class in the 19th-Century United States* (New Haven, CT, 1990), 36–46.

6. SMRIP, *Annual Report*, 1830, n.p.; idem, *Annual Report*, 1834, 11, 12, 17. See also Maria Kleinburd Baghdadi, "Protestants, Poverty, and Urban Growth: A Study of the Organization of Charity in Boston and New York, 1820–1865" (Ph.D. diss., Brown University, 1975), 50. Paul Boyer, in his chapters on tract societies and Sabbath schools, does not discuss the impact of the poor's demand for aid on moral reform societies. See *Urban Masses and Moral Order in America, 1820–1920* (Cambridge, MA, 1978), chapters 2 and 3. The Society reorganized in the 1840s as it became imbued with anti-Catholic zeal.

7. Tuckerman, *First Quarterly Report*, 1827, 4. Tuckerman's reports are in Widener Library, Harvard University.

Evidence that many status groups enrolled in reform movements is usually taken as evidence of their "middle-class" nature. See, for example, Boyer, *Urban Masses and Moral Order*, 60–61; Smith Rosenberg, *Religion and the Rise of the American City*, 8; Mary P. Ryan, *Cradle of the Middle Class: The Family in Oneida County, New York, 1790–1865* (Cambridge, England, 1981), 103–4; John S. Gilkeson, Jr., *Middle-Class Providence, 1820–1940* (Princeton, 1986), 9–10, 44–46, 53. But what the members of the movement share is a set of values, not a class position.

Others will point to the presence of elite members as evidence of social control. See, for example, Clifford S. Griffin, "Religious Benevolence as Social Control, 1815–1860," in *Ante-Bellum Reform*, ed. David Brion Davis (New York, 1967), 81–96; Mohl, *Poverty in New York*, 138, 193; Anthony F. C. Wallace, *Rockdale: The Growth of an American Village in the Early Industrial Revolution* (New York, 1972), 318–27; Paul G. Faler, *Mechanics and Manufacturers in the Early Industrial Revolution: Lynn, Massachusetts, 1780–1860* (Albany, NY, 1981), 102, 116–36; and Paul E. Johnson, *A Shopkeeper's Millennium: Society and Revivals in Rochester, New York, 1815–1837* (New York, 1978), 119–28, who stresses a combination of coercion and economic self-interest for workers adopting evangelical religion. (Faler modifies his position on 137, and in his articles, cited below, but the thrust of his argument in his book is undeniable.) Thus one is left with an interpretation that mistakes culture for class and one that poses the rest of society as dominated by the elite. Neither illuminates why different groups in society form cross-class alliances to achieve common ends.

Historians of the American working class have found that evangelicalism and the "industrial culture" it fostered led both to acquiescence in the leadership of the entrepreneurial class and rebellion in defense of working-class interests. See Paul Faler, "Cultural Aspects of the Industrial Revolution: Lynn, Massachusetts, Shoemakers and Industrial Morality, 1826–1840," *Labor History* 15 (Summer 1974): 390–92; Alan Dawley and Paul Faler, "Working-Class Culture and Politics in the Industrial Revolution: Sources of Loyalism and Rebellion," *Journal of Social History* 9 (June 1976): 468–69; Jill Siegel Dodd, "The Working Classes and the Temperance Movement in Ante-Bellum Boston," *Labor History* 19 (Fall 1978): 510–31; Bruce Laurie, *Working People of Philadelphia, 1800–1850* (Philadelphia, 1980), 42, 48–52, 122–24, 142–47, 168–203; Barbara M. Tucker, *Samuel Slater and the Origins of the American Textile Industry, 1790–1860* (Ithaca, NY, 1984), 181–84. For the post–Civil War period, see Herbert G. Gutman, "Protestantism and the American Labor Movement: The Christian Spirit in the Gilded Age," in his *Work, Culture, and Society in Industrializing America* (New York, 1977), 79–117.

8. Daniel T. McColgan, *Joseph Tuckerman, Pioneer in American Social Work* (Washington, DC, 1940), passim; Daniel Walker Howe, *The Unitarian Conscience: Harvard Moral Philosophy, 1805–1861* (Cambridge, MA, 1970), 140–41; Nathan Irvin Huggins, *Protestants against Poverty: Boston's Charities, 1870–1900* (Westport, CT, 1971), 29. David Rothman argues, incorrectly in my view, that Tuckerman could find no alternatives to the cohesive colonial order that had broken down. *The Discovery of the Asylum: Social Order and Disorder in the New Republic* (Boston, 1971), 178.

Other reformers questioned the marketplace more critically than Tuckerman, but they were fairly unusual. See Anne M. Boylan, "Women in Groups: An Analysis of Women's Benevolent Organizations in New York and Boston, 1797–1840," *Journal of American History* 71 (December 1984): 506, for the Boston Seamen's Aid Society's comments about wages paid to poor women.

9. McColgan, *Joseph Tuckerman*, 1–4, 23–31; Howe, *Unitarian Conscience*, 313.

10. Joseph Tuckerman, *First Semi-Annual Report*, 1830, 23; idem, *Second Semi-Annual Report*, 1831, 41; idem, *Letter to the Executive Committee of the Benevolent Fraternity of Churches* (Boston, 1834), 17; idem, *On the Elevation of the Poor*, ed. Edward Everett Hale (Boston, 1874), 29.

11. Joseph Tuckerman, *An Essay on the Wages Paid to Females for Their Labor* (Philadelphia, 1831), 46, 20–21; idem, *Gleams of Truth; or, Scenes from Real Life* (Boston, 1835), 21–22, 25; idem, *The Principles and Results of the Ministry at Large in Boston* (Boston, 1838), 119. On the increasing tendency toward moralism in the late 1810s and early 1820s, see Mohl, *Poverty in New York*, 159–70,

245–54. For the role of temperance in bourgeois culture, see Ian R. Tyrrell, *Sobering Up: From Temperance to Prohibition in Antebellum America, 1800–1860* (Westport, CT, 1979), 70–75; and Norman H. Clark, *Deliver Us from Evil: An Interpretation of American Prohibition* (New York, 1976), 12–13; and on the role of evangelical religion in bourgeois self-identification, see Johnson, *Shopkeeper's Millennium*, 8. For the relationship between poverty and intemperance, see Smith Rosenberg, *Religion and the Rise of the American City*, 94–95. Stanley Schultz is mistaken when he argues that Tuckerman blamed poverty on intemperance. See *Culture Factory*, 227.

12. Tuckerman, *Essay on Wages*, 26–27; Hobson, *Uneasy Virtue*, 51–61; Carroll Smith-Rosenberg, "Beauty, the Beast, and the Militant Woman: A Case Study in Sex Roles and Social Stress in Jacksonian America," in her *Disorderly Conduct: Visions of Gender in Victorian America* (New York, 1985), 109–28.

13. Tuckerman, *Principles and Results*, 280–81; idem, *On the Elevation of the Poor*, 68–69.

14. Tuckerman, *Principles and Results*, 14, 104.

15. See Tyrrell, *Sobering Up*, 129, for reformers' tendency to ignore economic causes of poverty. Tuckerman, *Essay on Wages*, 8, 10, 12–13, 21, 23, 37–40, 42; idem, *Principles and Results*, 300–301. See also the material reprinted in *On the Elevation of the Poor*, 85–87. For an exception to this, see Raymond Mohl's discussion of Mayor Livingston in *Poverty in New York*, 225–36.

16. Tuckerman, *Principles and Results*, 80, 294, 301. It is usual to note Thomas Chalmers's influence on Tuckerman and on the development of home visiting for the poor. See McColgan, *Joseph Tuckerman*, 115–16; Huggins, *Protestants against Poverty*, 17–19; Smith Rosenberg, *Religion and the Rise of the American City*, 260–61. However, Chalmers was a disciple of Malthus, a fact known widely enough to have Karl Marx refer to "Parson Malthus and his pupil, the arch-Parson Thomas Chalmers" in the first volume of *Capital*. See Stewart J. Brown, *Thomas Chalmers and the Godly Commonwealth in Scotland* (New York, 1982), 116. Tuckerman had a copy of *An Essay on the Principle of Population* in his library and eagerly visited Malthus on his trip to England in 1833–34. Howe, in *Unitarian Conscience*, 240, seems unaware of Malthus's influence on Tuckerman. Rothman also does not discuss Malthus and thus fails to see that Tuckerman and the advocates of the workhouse operated from the same rather than "very different" assumptions. *Discovery of the Asylum*, 178–79.

17. Francis Tiffany, *Charles Francis Barnard: A Sketch of His Life and Work* (Boston, 1895), 23; McColgan, *Joseph Tuckerman*, 200–201; Josiah P. Quincy, *Memoir of Rev. R. C. Waterston* (Cambridge, MA, 1893), 3–5. Again it is worth noting that the paid ministers who led the organization were male, while the volunteers, about whom nothing was written, were mostly women.

Several historians have tied "industrial morality" to the rise of manufacturing. See Johnson, *Shopkeeper's Millennium*, 137–38; Faler, *Mechanics and Manufacturers*, 103–4, 109–10; Tyrrell, *Sobering Up*, 97–98. Tuckerman's work was supported by some of New England's leading manufacturers: Patrick Tracy Jackson, Amos Lawrence, Abbott Lawrence, and Nathan Appleton. See Hale's introduction to *On the Elevation of the Poor*, 11. Nonetheless, given the social origins of the ministers, it is a mistake to overemphasize the role of manufacturers. See also Ryan, *Cradle of the Middle Class*, 98, 114.

18. Tuckerman, *Principles and Results*, 146–49; Anne M. Boylan, *Sunday School: The Formation of an American Institution, 1790–1880* (New Haven, CT, 1988), 33.

19. Tuckerman, *Second Semi-Annual Report*, 1829, 14–16; Massachusetts Commissioners on the Pauper System, *Report of the Commissioners Appointed by an Order of the House of Representatives, February 29, 1832, on the subject of the pauper system of the commonwealth of Massachusetts* House Doc. 6 (Boston, 1833), 40–42; Tuckerman, *On the Elevation of the Poor*, 174–75. Howe argues that Tuckerman's moralism and environmentalism were incompatible. See *Unitarian Conscience*, 250. Raymond Mohl makes a similar dichotomy between moralism and environmentalism in "Humanitarianism in the Preindustrial City: The New York Society for the Prevention of Pauperism, 1817–1823," *Journal of American History* 57 (December 1970): 576–99.

Smith Rosenberg, *Religion and the Rise of the American City*, 250–60, argues that Robert Hartley and the New York Association for Improving the Condition of the Poor remained optimistic that through character reformation they could eliminate pauperism. Tuckerman and the Boston Society for the Prevention of Pauperism evinced little optimism. The thrust of Tuckerman's report to the state was that the cost of relief and the numbers of the poor were becoming overwhelming. Charity organization was a defensive, not optimistic, strategy. The BSPP reports are in the Boston Public Library.

20. McColgan, *Joseph Tuckerman*, 244–53.

21. Association of Delegates from the Benevolent Societies of Boston, *First Annual Report*, 1835, 25–43. These reports are in the New York Public Library.

22. Tuckerman, *Letter to the Executive Committee*, 12.

23. Ibid., 15, 17; Baghdadi, "Protestants, Poverty, and Urban Growth," 143, 165–68.

24. Tuckerman, *Letter to the Executive Committee*, 12–13; Boston Society for the Prevention of Pauperism, *Annual Report*, 1851, 27. Baghdadi argues that relief-giving became bureaucratized around midcentury. See "Protestants, Poverty, and Urban Growth," 254–76.

25. Quoted in Tiffany, *Charles Francis Barnard*, 57.

26. Robert S. Pickett discusses the New York Society for the Prevention of Pauperism but seems unaware that the society moved from social welfare reform to juvenile reform and was not a juvenile reform association from its

inception. See his *House of Refuge: Origins of Juvenile Reform in New York, 1815–1857* (Syracuse, NY, 1969), 21–49, and compare to Mohl, "Humanitarianism in the Preindustrial City," 593–94.

Bernard Wishy, *The Child and the Republic: The Dawn of Modern American Child Nurture* (Philadelphia, 1968), 17–23, 32–33; Joseph F. Kett, *Rites of Passage: Adolescence in America, 1790 to the Present* (New York, 1977), 64–70; Daniel Walker Howe, "The Social Science of Horace Bushnell," *Journal of American History* 70 (September 1983): 310–13; Schultz, *Culture Factory*, 48–52; Ryan, *Cradle of the Middle Class*, 68–70, 99–102, 157–61; Boylan, *Sunday School*, 141–49; Thomas Walter Laqueur, *Religion and Respectability: Sunday Schools and Working Class Culture, 1780–1850* (New Haven, CT, 1976), 9–18.

For contemporary accounts, see R. C. Waterston, *Thoughts on Moral and Spiritual Culture* (Boston, 1842), 23–36; Walter Channing, *An Address on the Prevention of Pauperism* (Boston, 1843), 66; Frederick T. Gray, *Sunday School and Other Addresses* (Boston, 1852), 113–14.

27. Tuckerman, *First Semi-Annual Report*, 1830, 9; idem, *Second Semi-Annual Report*, 1831, 20–21. The most explicit contrast between the homes of the poor and the ideal bourgeois home is not in the early reports, but in *Principles and Results*, 64–76, published in 1838. Boyer, *Urban Masses and Moral Order*, 39–40.

28. Tuckerman, *First Semi-Annual Report*, 1830, 19; idem, *First Semi-Annual Report*, 1831, 14; idem, *Second Semi-Annual Report*, 1831, 13–14, 16; William Howe, *Address* (Boston, 1840), 4–5; Gray, *Sunday School*, 113.

29. Tuckerman, *First Semi-Annual Report*, 1831, 16–17; Schultz, *Culture Factory*, 261–71; Dean May and Maris A. Vinovskis, "A Ray of Millennial Light: Early Education and Social Reform in the Infant School Movement in Massachusetts, 1826–1840," in *Family and Kin in Urban Communities, 1700–1930*, ed. Tamara A. Hareven (New York, 1977), 69–76; Boylan, *Sunday School*, 19–20; Mohl, *Poverty in New York*, chapter 11; Carl F. Kaestle, *Pillars of the Republic: Common Schools and American Society, 1780–1860* (New York, 1983), 66–73, 76–82, 88–98, 100–103; idem, *The Evolution of an Urban School System: New York City, 1750–1850* (Cambridge, MA, 1973), 112–20.

30. SMRIP, *Annual Report*, 1823, 33; Joseph Tuckerman, *A Word to Fathers and Mothers* (Boston, 1828), 2–4; idem, *Second Semi-Annual Report*, 1828, 28–29; idem, *First Semi-Annual Report*, 1831, 14, 16–17, 22; idem, *Second Semi-Annual Report*, 1831, 31–32. For New York, see Mohl, *Poverty in New York*, 256–57.

31. On "traditionalist" culture, see Faler, "Cultural Aspects of the Industrial Revolution," 367–94; Dawley and Faler, "Working-Class Culture and Politics in the Industrial Revolution." 466–80; Laurie, *Working People of Philadelphia*, 53–66; idem, " 'Nothing on Compulsion': Life Styles of Philadelphia Artisans, 1820–1850," *Labor History* 15 (Summer 1974): 337–66; Gutman, "Work, Culture, and Society in Industrializing America, 1815–1919," in *Work, Culture, and Society*, 3–78.

SMRIP, *Annual Report*, 1817, 1; idem, *Annual Report*, 1822, 13; idem, *Annual Report*, 1826, 3; Michael B. Katz, *Class, Bureaucracy, and Schools: The Illusion of Educational Change in America* (New York, 1971), 10–11; David Nasaw, *Schooled to Order: A Social History of Public Schooling in the United States* (New York, 1979), 20–22; Kaestle, *Evolution of an Urban School System*, 164–66; Schultz, *Culture Factory*, 264–67.

For values taught in Sunday school, see Boyer, *Urban Masses and Moral Order*, 46–51; Boylan, *Sunday School*, 38, 52, 67–68; Anne Scott MacLeod, *A Moral Tale: Children's Fiction and American Culture, 1820–1860* (Hamden, CT, 1975), 28–29, 79, 91, 108. More generally, see Richard D. Mosier, *Making the American Mind: Social and Moral Ideas in the McGuffy Readers* (New York, 1947), chapters 4 and 5; and Daniel T. Rodgers, *The Work Ethic in Industrial America, 1850–1920* (Chicago, 1974), 129–32.

Boylan notes that the Lancastrian system was eventually abandoned for smaller, more informal classes, but this seems to have occurred as denominational Sunday schools catering to the children of church members replaced mission Sunday schools aimed at the working class. See *Sunday School*, 135–39, 150–52, 167.

32. This interpretation can be found in E. P. Thompson, *The Making of the English Working Class* (New York, 1963), 375–79; Wallace, *Rockdale*, 308–12, 318–22, 326; Tucker, *Samuel Slater*, 44, 75–76, 166–71; and to a lesser degree in Boyer, *Urban Masses and Moral Order*, 42–43.

33. See Boylan, *Sunday School*, 37–39; and Laqueur, *Religion and Respectability*, especially 28–29, 91–92, 94. Laqueur argues that Sunday schools were an integral part of working-class culture, were essential to the creation of a literate working class, and spread the religious culture and idiom drawn upon by working-class trade unionists and radicals. Boylan notes that Sunday schools did not become as intrinsic a part of American working-class culture as English schools did for the English working class. See 166–67.

34. SMRIP, *Annual Report*, 1827, 22; Schultz, *Culture Factory*, 24, 26–30; Boylan, *Sunday School*, 19–20, on the importance of educational services performed by the Sunday schools. Boyer discusses the number of children enrolled in Sunday schools in *Urban Masses and Moral Order*, 40–41. For the role of the wives of the directors of the SMRIP in advancing education for the poor, see May and Vinovskis, "A Ray of Millennial Light," 69–70.

J. Leslie Dunstan, *A Light to the City: 150 Years of the City Missionary Society of Boston, 1816–1966* (Boston, 1966), 165; and Boylan, *Sunday School*, 160, mention the less pious reasons why children attended Sunday schools. Laqueur, *Religion and Respectability*, 102–5, 123, 128, 148, 150, notes the importance of secular education among working-class clients of the Sunday schools.

35. Tiffany, *Charles Francis Barnard*, 101–21, 155–57.

36. Ibid., 64–67, 75–77, 124–25.

37. Boylan, *Sunday School*, 16, 18, 151–52, 167, shows the decline in out-

reach and the tendency to include the children of "middle-class" church members rather than mixed classes. On Barnard, see Baghdadi, "Protestants, Poverty, and Urban Growth," 251–55.

2. Public Welfare and the Public Reformatory

1. Robert A. McCaughey, *Josiah Quincy, 1772–1864: The Last Federalist* (Cambridge, MA, 1974); Roger Lane, *Policing the City: Boston, 1822–1885* (New York, 1971), 20–25; Josiah Quincy, *A Municipal History of the Town and City of Boston during Two Centuries* (Boston, 1852), 103, 105, 109; idem, *Remarks on Some of the Provisions of the Laws of Massachusetts Affecting Poverty, Vice, and Crime* (Cambridge, MA, 1822), passim. Raymond A. Mohl, "Humanitarianism in the Preindustrial City: The New York Society for the Prevention of Pauperism, 1817–1823," *Journal of American History* 57 (December 1970): 594–95, links the reformation of juveniles to the prevention of pauperism.

2. On the founding of the state reform school, see John Clark Wirkkala, "Juvenile Delinquency and Reform in Nineteenth-Century Massachusetts: The Formative Years in State Care, 1846–1879" (Ph.D. diss., Clark University, 1973), especially 25–38.

3. Sean Wilentz, *Chants Democratic: New York City and the Rise of the American Working Class, 1788–1850* (New York, 1984), 14–15, 62–63, 92–103, 237–48; Joyce Appleby, *Capitalism and a New Social Order: The Republican Vision of the 1790s* (New York, 1984), chapter 4.

4. Josiah Quincy, *Report of the Committee on the Pauper Laws of This Commonwealth* (Boston, 1821), 5–6, 8–10; Robert W. Kelso, *The History of Public Poor Relief in Massachusetts, 1620–1920* (Boston, 1922), 122–25. John Alexander has argued that punitive attitudes toward the poor were present in eighteenth-century Philadelphia. See John K. Alexander, *Render Them Submissive: Responses to Poverty in Philadelphia, 1760–1800* (Amherst, MA, 1980).

5. Boston, "Report of the Committee on the subject of Pauperism, at large, and on the expediency of erecting a Work House," March 12, 1821, *Boston Town Records* 37: 188–90; Kelso, *History of Poor Relief*, 117.

6. McCaughey, *Josiah Quincy*, 51–56, 79–82, 83–85, 89–95, 100–106; Andrew R. L. Cayton, "The Fragmentation of 'A Great Family': The Panic of 1819 and the Rise of the Middling Interest in Boston, 1818–1822," *Journal of the Early Republic* 2 (Summer 1982): 143–67; Ronald P. Formisano, "Boston, 1800–1840: From Deferential-Participant to Party Politics," in *Boston, 1700–1980: The Evolution of Urban Politics*, ed. Ronald P. Formisano and Constance K. Burns (Westport, CT, 1984), 36–41.

7. Quincy, *Municipal History*, 93–96, 138–43, 170–75; Prison Discipline Society of Boston, *Annual Report*, 1834, 105. Original reports are at the University of Delaware Library.

8. Boston, "Report of the Committee on the subject of Pauperism," 191.

9. Boston Society for the Moral and Religious Instruction of the Poor,

Annual Report, 1823, 5, Congregational Library, Boston. Joseph Tuckerman, *An Essay on the Wages Paid to Females for Their Labor* (Philadelphia, 1830), 43–49; Massachusetts Commissioners on the Pauper System, *Report of the Commissioners Appointed on Order of the House of Representatives, February 29, 1832, on the subject of the pauper system of the commonwealth of Massachusetts* House Doc. 6 (Boston, 1833), 19–20, 39, 40–42; Boston Society for the Prevention of Pauperism, *Annual Report*, 1851, 28–30, Boston Public Library; Frederick T. Gray, *Sunday School and Other Essays* (Boston, 1852), 107, 111–13.

M. J. Heale, "From City Fathers to Social Critics: Humanitarism and Government in New York, 1790–1860," *Journal of American History* 63 (June 1976): 21–41, discusses the relationship between public and private reform. On pauperism, see Gertrude Himmelfarb, *The Idea of Poverty: England in the Early Industrial Age* (New York, 1984), 163–65, 188, 397–99. On the poorhouse, Brian Gratton, *Urban Elders: Family, Work, and Welfare among Boston's Aged, 1890–1950* (Philadelphia, 1986), 128–32; idem, "The Invention of Social Work: Welfare Reform in the Antebellum City," *Urban and Social Change Review* 18 (1985): 3–8; Michael B. Katz, *In the Shadow of the Poorhouse: A Social History of Welfare in America* (New York, 1986), 11–13, 15–25; Paul Faler, "Cultural Aspects of the Industrial Revolution: Lynn, Massachusetts, Shoemakers and Industrial Morality, 1826–1860," *Labor History* 15 (Summer 1974): 388–89.

10. Blanche D. Coll, "The Baltimore Society for the Prevention of Pauperism, 1820–1822," *American Historical Review* 61 (October 1955): 81; Mohl, "Humanitarianism in the Preindustrial City," 578–84; M. J. Heale, "Humanitarianism in the Early Republic: The Moral Reformers of New York, 1776–1825," *Journal of American Studies* 2 (October 1968): 171–72; Priscilla Ferguson Clement, "The Philadelphia Welfare Crisis of the 1820s," *Pennsylvania Magazine of History and Biography* 105 (April 1981): 152–57, 161–64; Katz, *In the Shadow of the Poorhouse*, 40–42.

11. Quincy, *Municipal History*, 102–5.

12. Quincy, *Remarks*, 10–11, 13, 19–20; Boston, "Report of the Committee on the subject of Pauperism," 188; McCaughey, *Josiah Quincy*, 119. See also *Boston City Records* 4: 46–47.

13. David J. Rothman, *The Discovery of the Asylum: Social Order and Disorder in the New Republic* (Boston, 1971), passim; Max Weber, *The Theory of Social and Economic Organization*, trans. A. M. Henderson and Talcott Parsons (New York, 1964), 364–73. Boston, *Report of the Directors of the House for the Employment and Reformation of Juvenile Offenders* (Boston, 1827), 21–22; J. F. Richmond, "The House of Reformation," *New-England Magazine* 3 (July–December 1832): 384. All documents about the House of Reformation are located in the Boston Public Library. See also John R. Sutton, *Stubborn Children: Controlling Delinquency in the United States, 1640–1981* (Berkeley, CA, 1988), 82–83. Sutton emphasizes conflicts among Calvinist, Enlightenment, and Romantic worldviews as the source of disagreements over reformatory policies. He argues that Wells, along with the superintendents of the New York and

Philadelphia refuges, introduced romantic approaches to the reform of delinquents. I believe he overstates the similarities among the institutions and overemphasizes the philosophical sources of conflict.

14. Samuel Eliot, *Address in Commemoration of William Appleton, the Founder, and E. M. P. Wells, the Missionary of St. Stephen's Chapel, Boston* (Cambridge, MA, 1888), 14–15; Orlando Lewis, *The Development of American Prisons and Prison Customs, 1776–1845* (Montclair, NJ, 1967), 302.

15. Richmond, "House of Reformation," 384–85; Quincy, *Municipal History*, 107.

16. G. De Beaumont and A. De Toqueville [sic], *On the Penitentiary System in the United States and Its Application in France*, trans. Francis Leiber (Philadelphia, 1833), 114–21; Richmond, "House of Reformation," 384–85; Robert S. Pickett, *House of Refuge: Origins of Juvenile Reform in New York State, 1815–1857* (Syracuse, NY, 1969), 89–93; Joseph M. Hawes, *Children in Urban Society: Juvenile Delinquency in Nineteenth-Century America* (New York, 1971), 40–56. Compare to Negley K. Teeters, "The Early Days of the Philadelphia House of Refuge," *Pennsylvania History* 28 (April 1960): 165–87, and Steven L. Schlossman, *Love and the American Delinquent: The Theory and Practice of 'Progressive' Juvenile Justice, 1825–1920* (Chicago, 1977), 28–32. Clearly, not all reform efforts were cut from the same cloth, as is maintained in Rothman, *Discovery of the Asylum*, chapter 9.

17. Quincy, *Municipal History*, 108.

18. Ibid., 108; Boston, "Report on Prisons," City Doc. 21, 1838, 26–27.

19. Boston, *Report of the Standing Committee of the Common Council on the Subject of the House of Reformation for Juvenile Offenders* (Boston, 1832); Quincy, *Municipal History*, 108; Pickett, *House of Refuge*, 92–93; Hawes, *Children in Urban Society*, 52–53; Robert M. Mennel, *Thorns and Thistles: Juvenile Delinquents in the United States, 1825–1940* (Hanover, NH, 1973), 24–29.

20. Stanley K. Schultz, *The Culture Factory: Boston Public Schools, 1789–1860* (New York, 1973), 292–302.

21. Lewis, *American Prisons*, 319; Boston, "Report of the Committee . . . having reference to the creation of a new edifice," City Doc. 8, 1834, 2–3; idem, "Report of the Inspectors of Prisons," City Doc. 4, 1841, 5–6; idem, "Report of the Inspectors of Prisons," City Doc. 18, 1841, 39; idem, "Report of the Committee appointed to consider . . . that boys *only* be admitted to the House of Reformation," City Doc. 6, 1840, 5.

22. Schultz, *The Culture Factory*, 247, 249; Boston, "Report of the Committee on the Houses at South Boston," City Doc. 14, 1841, 3.

23. For the relatively benign interpretation of institutional decline, see Gerald N. Grob, *The State and the Mentally Ill: A History of Worcester State Hospital in Massachusetts, 1830–1920* (Chapel Hill, NC, 1966); idem, *Mental Institutions in America: Social Policy to 1875* (New York, 1973); and idem, *Mental Illness and American Society, 1875–1940* (Princeton, 1983). Rothman, *Discovery of the Asylum*, and idem, *Conscience and Convenience: The Asylum and Its Alternatives*

in Progressive America (Boston, 1980), stresses decisions made by reformers stemming from their fear of social disorder. For a persuasive critique of both positions, see Michael B. Katz, "Origins of the Institutional State," *Marxist Perspectives* 1 (Winter 1978): 6–22. Christopher Lasch, in "Origins of the Asylum," in his *The World of Nations: Reflections on American History, Politics, and Culture* (New York, 1973), 3–17, is more sharply critical of reform, seeing humanitarianism as creating a new form of repressive control over the individual. For a similar argument, see Michael Foucault, *Discipline and Punish: The Birth of the Prison* (New York, 1979). Lasch, in this essay and in his later work, dramatically overemphasizes the ability of institutions and reformers to control the lives of the individuals with whom they come in contact. Moreover, in this monolithic interpretation institutions have no history, for their functions were established at their inception. Sutton, *Stubborn Children*, 87–89, takes the Weberian position that system and bureaucracy replaces charismatic leadership.

24. Sutton, *Stubborn Children*, 87, argues that a Calvinist view of family triumphed over a romantic one, which I find unpersuasive.

25. Boston, *Report of the Committee to whom was referred the Memorial of the Directors of the House for the employment and reformation of Juvenile Offenders* (Boston, 1829), 4–5, 13; idem, "House of Reformation Report," City Doc. 8, 1838, 7–8. Richmond, "House of Reformation," 382–90, and Beaumont and Tocqueville, *On the Penitentiary System*, 114–21, do not discuss the girls, while, in its most extensive report on the House of Reformation, the Prison Discipline Society of Boston, *Annual Report*, 1829, 245–50, mentioned that 10 percent of the inmates were girls, but did not devote a single line to them.

26. Beaumont and Tocqueville, *On the Penitentiary System*, 123.

27. Boston, *Report of the Memorial Committee*, 11; idem, *Report of the Standing Committee*, appendix A, for statistics; Ann Butler, *Notes of Inmates in the Female Department of the House of Reformation at South Boston* (Boston, 1834), 29–30; Mennel, *Thorns and Thistles*, 16–17.

28. Boston, *Report of the Memorial Committee*, 11, 19; idem, *Report of the Standing Committee*, 15; idem, "Report of the Committee on a new edifice," City Doc. 8, 1834, 3.

29. Boston, "Annual Report of the Directors of the Houses of Industry, Correction, and Reformation," 1839, 9–10; idem, "Committee on boys only," City Doc. 6, 1840 8–9; idem, "Report of the Directors of the House of Reformation," City Doc. 6, 1841, 6.

30. Boston, "Report of the Directors of the House of Reformation," City Doc. 6, 1841, 6–8; idem, "Report of the Inspectors of Prisons," City Doc. 5, 1842, 12.

31. Boston, "Report of the Inspectors of Prisons," City Doc. 21, 1843, 10; idem, "Report of the Inspectors of Prison," City Doc. 2, 1844, 17; idem, "Annual Report of the Directors of the Houses of Industry and Reformation," City Doc. 27, 1851, 6–7; idem, "Report of the Inspectors of Prisons," City

Doc. 50, 1851, 21–23; idem, "Report of the Inspectors of Prisons," City Doc. 81, 1854, 19.

32. Barbara Meil Hobson, *Uneasy Virtue: The Politics of Prostitution and the American Reform Tradition* (New York, 1987), 117–18, 124–25; Ruth H. Bloch, "American Feminine Ideals in Transition: The Rise of the Moral Mother, 1785–1815," *Feminist Studies* 4 (1978): 101–26.

33. Hobson, *Uneasy Virtue*, 118–24; Christine R. Stansell, *City of Women: Sex and Class in New York, 1789–1860* (New York, 1986), 176–91.

The only works that deal extensively with female delinquents in the United States are Barbara M. Brenzel, *Daughters of the State: A Social Portrait of the First Reform School for Girls in North America, 1856–1905* (Cambridge, MA, 1983), and Steven Schlossman and Stephanie Wallach, "The Crime of Precocious Sexuality: Female Delinquency in the Progressive Era," *Harvard Educational Review* 48 (February 1978): 65–94. Schlossman and Wallach argue that female delinquency was recognized as a problem only in the Progressive era, while Brenzel ignores the House of Reformation. Her oversight is surprising since Samuel Gridley Howe's experience with the House of Reformation contributed to his anti-institutionalist position that helped shape the history of the girls' reform school. Robert Picket, *House of Refuge*, Joseph Hawes, *Children in Urban Society*, and Robert Mennel, *Thorns and Thistles*, discuss girls but do not use gender in their analyses, while David Rothman, *Discovery of the Asylum*, ignores the existence of female delinquents altogether.

34. Boston, "Committee on boys only," 4; in 1827 seventeen of forty-two boys were Irish; the shift was in perception, not clientele. See Boston, *Report of the Directors of the House of Reformation*, 18–19.

35. Oscar Handlin, *Boston's Immigrants, 1790–1880* (Cambridge, MA, 1941), 104–17, 243, 250–51, 256–57; Michael P. Conzen and George K. Lewis, *Boston: A Geographical Portrait* (Cambridge, MA, 1976), 25; Lawrence H. Fuchs, "Immigration through the Port of Boston," in *Forgotten Doors: The Other Ports of Entry to the United States*, ed. M. Mark Stolarik (Philadelphia, 1988), 17–20; Theodore Lyman, Jr., *Addresses Made to the City Council of Boston* (Boston, 1835), 17–24.

36. Wirkkala, "Delinquency and Reform," 25–38; Hawes, *Children in Urban Society*, 81–83; Michael B. Katz, *The Irony of Early School Reform: Educational Innovation in Mid–Nineteenth-Century Massachusetts* (Boston, 1968), 164–77; "Report and Resolve for the Erection of a State Manual Labor School," Senate Doc. 86, March 27, 1846. Published records of the state reform school are located at the Massachusetts State Library.

37. *Second Annual Report of the Trustees and Officers of the State Reform School for Boys*, 1849, 9–10, 28–29. Hereafter State Reform School, *Annual Report*. R. Richard Wohl, "The 'Country Boy' Myth and Its Place in American Urban Culture: The Nineteenth-Century Contribution," ed. Moses Rischin, *Perspectives in American History* 3 (1969): 77–156; Timothy L. Smith, "Protestant Schooling and American Nationality, 1800–1850," *Journal of American History*

53 (March 1967): 679–95; Carl F. Kaestle, *Pillars of the Republic: Common Schools and American Society, 1780–1860* (New York, 1983), 76–77, 80–83, 90–93; David B. Tyack, *The One Best System: A History of American Urban Education* (Cambridge, MA, 1974), 84–86.

38. Wirkkala, "Delinquency and Reform," 82–84.

39. State Reform School, *Annual Report*, 1860, 33.

40. Ibid., 1858, 51.

41. Ibid., 1855, 28.

42. Wirkkala, "Delinquency and Reform," 91–92.

43. State Reform School, *Annual Report*, 1856, 50.

44. Wirkkala, "Delinquency and Reform," 101–2, 104–6; State Reform School, *Annual Report*, 1855, 20–21.

45. State Reform School, *Annual Report*, 1849, 9–10; ibid., 1857, 4; Wirkkala, "Delinquency and Reform," 112–14.

46. State Reform School, *Annual Report*, 1852, 41; Joseph A. Allen, *Westboro' State Reform School Reminiscences* (Boston, 1877), 5–6, 38.

47. Wirkkala, "Delinquency and Reform," 114–17.

48. "Records of the Governor's Council," 1860, 184–91, ms., Massachusetts State Archives; Katz, *Irony of Early School Reform*, 198–99. For similar histories, see Schlossman, *Love and the American Delinquent*, 105–6; Pickett, *House of Refuge*, 72–75, 81–85, 144–49, 158–61; Mennel, *Thorns and Thistles*, 28–29, 61–62, 107–9; Hawes, *Children in Urban Society*, 47–48, 55–56, 134–35; Rothman, *Discovery of the Asylum*, 230–34; idem, *Conscience and Convenience*, 275–82; Teeters, "Early Days of the Philadelphia House of Refuge," 174–75.

Part 2: Domestic Reform

1. Steven L. Schlossman, *Love and the American Delinquent: The Theory and Practice of 'Progressive' Juvenile Justice, 1825–1920* (Chicago, 1977), 49–54; Thomas Bender, *Toward an Urban Vision: Ideas and Institutions in Nineteenth-Century America* (Baltimore, MD, 1975), 4–7; R. Richard Wohl, "The 'Country Boy' Myth and Its Place in American Urban Culture: The Nineteenth-Century Contribution," ed. Moses Rischin, *Perspectives in American History* 3 (1969): 77–156; John L. Thomas, "Romantic Reform in America, 1815–1865," *American Quarterly* 17 (Winter 1965): 656–81; Peter L. Tyor and Jamil Zainaldin, "Asylum and Society: An Approach to Institutional Change," *Journal of Social History* 13 (Fall 1979): 23–48; Susan E. Houston, "Victorian Origins of Juvenile Delinquency: A Canadian Experience," *History of Education Quarterly* 12 (Fall 1972): 254–80; Maria Kleinbard Baghdadi, "Protestants, Poverty, and Urban Growth: A Study of the Organization of Charity in Boston and New York, 1820–1865" (Ph.D. diss., Brown University, 1975), 269, 277–78.

2. Charles Loring Brace, *The Dangerous Classes of New York and Twenty Years Work Among Them* (New York, 1880), 400, 96.

David Rothman declares that the "Brace position" was not idiosyncratic and that "something of a school" formed around him, while dismissing this position in two paragraphs. See David J. Rothman, *Discovery of the Asylum: Social Order and Disorder in the New Republic* (Boston, 1971), 259–60. Rothman ignores the Massachusetts State Industrial School for Girls in *Discovery of the Asylum* and misdates the rise of alternatives to the asylum in *Conscience and Convenience: The Asylum and Its Alternatives in Progressive America* (Boston, 1980), 265.

    Charles Loring Brace and Samuel Gridley Howe have both been considered "anti-institutionalists," a curious label for individuals responsible for the creation and administration of many institutions. To be sure, they opposed the congregate institution, as did many others in mid–nineteenth-century America, but that does not make them anti-institutionalists. Paul Boyer argues that Brace was such an advocate of hard-boiled individualism that he thought even the family placed too many restraints on the individual. See Paul S. Boyer, *Urban Masses and Moral Order in America, 1820–1920* (Cambridge, MA, 1978), 99–101; Schlossman, *Love and the American Delinquent*, 42–49; Bender, *Toward an Urban Vision*, 136.

    3. Charles L. Brace, *The Best Method of Disposing of Our Pauper and Vagrant Children* (New York, 1859), 11–13; Bender, *Toward an Urban Vision*, 136–38, 142–44; Robert M. Mennel, *Thorns and Thistles: Juvenile Delinquents in the United States, 1825–1940* (Hanover, NH, 1973), 36; Daniel Walker Howe, "The Social Science of Horace Bushnell," *Journal of American History* 70 (September 1983): 310–13.

    4. John Higham, *From Boundlessness to Consolidation: The Transformation of American Culture, 1848–1860* (Ann Arbor, MI, 1969), 21–28; Norman H. Clark, *Deliver Us from Evil: An Interpretation of American Prohibition* (New York, 1976), 11–13; John Lukacs, "The Bourgeois Interior," *American Scholar* 39 (August 1970): 624–25; Boyer, *Urban Masses and Moral Order*, 83, 85–86; Kathryn Kish Sklar, *Catharine Beecher: A Study in Domesticity* (New York, 1976), 158–63; Mary P. Ryan, *Cradle of the Middle Class: The Family in Oneida County, New York, 1790–1865* (Cambridge, England, 1981), 146–85; Maxine van de Wetering, "The Popular Concept of 'Home' in Nineteenth-Century America," *Journal of American Studies* 8 (1984): 5–28; Ann Douglas, *The Femininization of American Culture* (New York, 1977), chapter 2; Colleen McDannell, *The Christian Home in Victorian America, 1840–1900* (Bloomington, IN, 1986), 6–8, 82–85, 92–93, 111–16, 128–36; Kathleen D. McCarthy, *Noblesse Oblige: Charity and Cultural Philanthropy in Chicago, 1849–1929* (Chicago, 1982), 29–33, 48–49; Carroll Smith-Rosenberg, "Beauty, the Beast, and the Militant Woman: A Case Study in Sex Roles and Social Stress in Jacksonian America," in *Disorderly Conduct: Visions of Gender in Victorian America*, ed. Carroll Smith-Rosenberg (New York, 1985), 118–19; idem, "The Cross and the Pedestal: Women, Anti-Ritualism, and the Emergence of the American Bourgeoisie," ibid., 133–34, 144–45, 150–51, 153–55; Lori D. Ginzberg,

Women and the Work of Benevolence: Morality, Politics and Class in the 19th-Century United States (New Haven, CT, 1990), 119–22.

5. Kenneth T. Jackson, *Crabgrass Frontier: The Suburbanization of the United States* (New York, 1985), 48–52, 58–61, 69–72; Gwendolyn Wright, *Building the Dream: A Social History of Housing in America* (Cambridge, MA, 1981), 75–77, 107–11; Clifford Edward Clark, Jr., *The American Family Home, 1800–1960* (Chapel Hill, NC, 1986), 29–32, 104–7; McDannell, *The Christian Home,* chapter 2.

3. Private Alternatives to the Asylum

1. Edith Rivers, "The Young Forgers; or, Homes and Prisons," in *Working and Trusting; or, Sketches Drawn from the Records of the Children's Mission* (Boston, 1859), 73–128.

2. Peter L. Tyor and Jamil Zainaldin, "Asylum and Society: An Approach to Institutional Change," *Journal of Social History* 13 (Fall 1979): 23–48. Steven L. Schlossman, *Love and the American Delinquent: The Theory and Practice of 'Progressive' Juvenile Justice, 1825–1920* (Chicago, 1977), 49–54, discusses the cult of domesticity as one of three influences on the farm/family reform school. The other two are the foreign examples of Mettray and Rauhe Haus and the "anti-institutionalism" of Charles Loring Brace and Samuel Gridley Howe. As the section below indicates, reformers began moving in the direction of farm/family institutions before the 1850s, when foreign examples became more influential.

3. Boston Farm School, "Report on the Establishment of a Farm School," 1832, 2–6; idem, *Annual Reports of the Managers and Officers of the Boston Asylum and Farm School,* 1852, 28–29; Boston Prison Discipline Society, *Annual Report,* 1834, 86–87; Dorothea Dix, *Remarks on Prisons and Prison Discipline in the United States* (Philadelphia, 1845), 92; Orlando F. Lewis, *The Development of American Prisons and Prison Customs, 1776–1845* (Montclair, NJ, 1967), 317–18; Robert S. Pickett, *House of Refuge: Origins of Juvenile Reform in New York State, 1815–1857* (Syracuse, NY, 1969), 93–95; Raymond W. Stanley, *The Four Thompsons of Boston Harbor, 1621–1965* (Boston, 1966), 37–43. The reports of the Boston Farm School are in the Massachusetts State Library, while those of the Prison Discipline Society are at the University of Delaware.

4. "Report on the Establishment of a Farm School," 5–6.

5. Children's Mission to the Children of the Destitute, *Annual Report,* 1850, 5; idem, *Annual Report,* 1853, 3–4; idem, *Annual Report,* 1863, 11; idem, "Account of the Proceedings at the Dedication of the Children's Mission's Home," March 17, 1867, 17; Robert M. Mennel, *Thorns and Thistles: Juvenile Delinquents in the United States, 1825–1940* (Hanover, NH, 1973), 41–42. The reports refer to "hundreds" placed each year; in 1858 they placed 175 youngsters. It is not clear whether both boys and girls were placed. The records of

the Children's Mission are at the Parents' and Children's Services of the Children's Mission.

6. R. Richard Wohl, "The 'Country Boy' Myth and Its Place in American Urban Culture: The Nineteenth-Century Contribution," ed. Moses Rischin, *Perspectives in American History* 3 (1969): 117; Mennel, *Thorns and Thistles*, 46–48; Miriam Z. Langsam, *Children West: A History of the Placing Out System of the New York Children's Aid Society, 1853–1890* (Madison, WI, 1964), chapter 5; Joseph M. Hawes, *Children in Urban Society: Juvenile Delinquency in Nineteenth-Century America* (New York, 1971), 103–5; Thomas Bender, *Toward an Urban Vision: Ideas and Institutions in Nineteenth-Century America* (Baltimore, MD, 1975), 145–47; Bruce Bellingham, " 'Little Wanderers': A Socio-Historical Study of the Nineteenth-Century Origins of Child Fostering and Adoption Reform, Based on Early Records of the New York Children's Aid Society (Ph.D. diss., University of Pennsylvania, 1984).

7. David Rothman downplays the importance of domestic reform as a rival to the congregate asylum in *Discovery of the Asylum: Social Order and Disorder in the New Republic* (Boston, 1971), 259–60, and in *Conscience and Convenience: The Asylum and Its Alternatives in Progressive America* (Boston, 1980), 265.

8. Bender, *Toward an Urban Vision*, 126–28, for similar debates on the local level, in Lowell, Massachusetts.

The only public family-style institution, besides the Massachusetts State Industrial School for Girls, which is discussed in chapter 4, was the Ohio Reform School for Boys. See Robert M. Mennel, " 'The Family System of Common Farmers': The Origins of Ohio's Reform Farm, 1840–1858," *Ohio History* 89 (Spring 1980): 125–56. Distinctions between private and public are a little arbitrary since many institutions that became public were started with private money. However, these institutions (such as the State Reform School for Boys in Massachusetts) always acted in a quasipublic fashion, while the private institutions were purely private in terms of controlling their own funding, admissions, and policy.

9. Bradford K. Pierce, "The Comparative Value of the Family and Congregate System in Reformatory Institutions Considered," *Proceedings of the Second Convention of Managers and Superintendents of Houses of Refuge and Schools of Reform in the United States of America* (New York, 1860), 128–29, 131; Charles Loring Brace, "Comments," *Proceedings of the First Convention of Managers and Superintendents of Houses of Refuge and Schools of Reform in the United States of America* (New York, 1858), 51; Bender, *Toward an Urban Vision*, 135–36.

10. Hawes, *Children in Urban Society*, 104–8; Bender, *Toward an Urban Vision*, 144–47; Langsam, *Children West*, chapter 5. For later critiques of Brace's placement policies, see Hastings H. Hart, "Placing-Out Children in the West," National Conference of Charities and Correction (hereafter, NCCC) *Proceedings* (1884): 143–50; Robert W. Hubbard, "Placing Out Children: Dangers of

Careless Methods," NCCC *Proceedings* (1899): 171–77; Lyman P. Alden, "The Shady Side of the 'Placing Out System'," NCCC *Proceedings* (1885): 201–10.

Bellingham found that the New York Children's Aid Society was far more careful about placements than contemporaries (and historians) have thought, and documented children's histories. See "Little Wanderers," 52–53, n. 3.

11. Pierce, "Comparative Value," 129; Brace, "Comments," 51; *Proceedings of the Second Convention*, 59; *Proceedings of the First Convention*, 16. Schlossman is not correct when he states that Brace was "not at all identified" with the family reform school. See *Love and the American Delinquent*, 226, n. 82. Schlossman argues (48–49) that Brace and Howe unintentionally pushed the family system forward as a compromise between the congregate institution and immediate placement. The farm/family model emerged as a compromise, but Brace, as the comments in the text show, and Howe, as the next chapter will indicate, were conscious of their parts in the process.

12. Children's Aid Society (hereafter CAS), *Annual Report, 1876–77*, 3; Rock Lawn Records Book, March 4, 1892, June 2, 1893; CAS, *Annual Report, 1885–86*, 6; idem, *Annual Report, 1878–79*, 3–4; idem, *Annual Report, 1877–78*, 3. Published and manuscript records of the CAS are at the Archives and Special Collections, Joseph P. Healey Library, University of Massachusetts at Boston.

13. Idem, "Its Origins and Objectives," 1.

14. Idem, Board of Directors Minutes, vol. 1, March 27, April 3, April 17, May 15, 1863. Also, idem, *Annual Report, 1865–66*, 8. While 1,482 boys were tried in police court, only eighty-eight were taken by the CAS. A brief history of the CAS can be found in Nathan Irving Huggins, *Protestants against Poverty: Boston's Charities, 1870–1900* (Westport, CT, 1971), 93–103.

15. CAS, *Annual Report, 1863–65*, 3; idem, Board of Directors Minutes, vol. 1, October 5, 1866; December 7, 1866.

16. Anne Kuhn, *The Mother's Role in Childhood Education* (New Haven, CT, 1947), passim; Anne Scott MacLeod, *A Moral Tale: Children's Fiction and American Culture, 1820–1860* (Hamden, CT, 1975), 29–31; Schlossman, *Love and the American Delinquent*, 49–53. Schlossman sees Victorian culture as "domesticating" the asylum; rather, reformers believing in domestic reform created an alternative to it. Steven Mintz, *A Prison of Expectations: The Family in Victorian Culture* (New York, 1983), 27–39; Bernard Wishy, *The Child and the Republic: The Dawn of Modern American Child Nurture* (Philadelphia, 1968), 17–49, 98–102; Mary P. Ryan, *Cradle of the Middle Class: The Family in Oneida County, 1790–1865* (Cambridge, England, 1981), 157–63. Carl N. Degler, *At Odds: Women and the Family in America from the Revolution to the Present* (New York, 1980), 86–102, stresses the continued emphasis on breaking the will more than these other authors, who emphasize the shift toward a more intense and long-term process of training and internalization of values.

While affectionate discipline may have become the dominant form of child rearing among bourgeois Protestant families in the mid–nineteenth century, elements of it were present in the seventeenth and eighteenth centuries. See Philip Greven, *The Protestant Temperament: Patterns of Child-Rearing, Religious Experience, and the Self in Early America* (New York, 1977). A fascinating account of developing a superego in young children can be found in Charles Strickland, "A Transcendentalist Father: The Child-Rearing Practices of Bronson Alcott," *Perspectives in American History* 3 (1969): 5–73.

17. CAS, *Annual Report*, 1863–65, 7–8, 10; idem, *Annual Report*, 1866–67, 3–4; Pine Farm Visitors Book no. 1, November 1867.

18. Pine Farm Visitors Book no. 1, January and June 1867, July 1870.

19. CAS, *Annual Report*, 1866–67, 3–4; Pine Farm Visitors Book no. 1, November 1867; Rock Lawn Records, January 4, 1889. All surnames are fictitious, as per my agreement with the Boston Children's Services Association, but I have attempted to preserve ethnic identity.

20. CAS, Board of Directors Minutes, vol. 1, April 6, 1866. The list of original founders and supporters bristles with Brahmins. Various members of the Lowell, Lawrence, Appleton, Shaw, Wigglesworth, Bowditch, Lee, Saltonstall, Endicott, Cabot, and Amory clans (among others) are listed in the first volume of the Board of Directors. Support such as this ensured the financial base of the CAS.

21. For a similar point, see David J. Rothman, *Conscience and Convenience*, especially 419–21.

22. Pine Farm Intake no. 523; Rock Lawn Records, May 3, 1897; Pine Farm Visitors Book no. 6, October 1892, January and February 1893.

23. Pine Farm Visitors Book no. 4, November 1884; Book no. 3, September 1879; Book no. 4, January 1885; Book no. 6, October 1893.

24. 30 percent had only mothers living, 17 percent had only fathers, 6 percent were orphaned, 6 percent had parents who were separated, and another 6 percent lived with a biological parent and a stepparent. The remaining 35 percent lived with two parents.

Bellingham, "Little Wanderers," chapter 5, also found that placement with the NYCAS was a matter of family strategy. He found 20 percent of his sampled children were orphaned (322).

The statistics are compiled from a systematic sample (n = 354) of boys accepted at Pine Farm between 1864 and 1895. I recorded every other record, but this is slightly more than half the total population, since boys who were readmitted had their records combined and were counted as only one case. I compiled a separate sample of Rock Lawn inmates (n = 83) but limited most discussions, except where indicated, to the Pine Farm sample because the records were far superior.

25. This is based on my sample of 354 Pine Farm boys; the percentages may not add up to a hundred because of rounding.

26. Pine Farm Visitors Book no. 4, February 1883, March 1885. For a complaint of ill treatment, see Book no. 3, December 1875; for recognition of

the problem, Book no. 2, August 1872. A general discussion of placement problems can be found in Hastings H. Hart, "Placing-Out Children in the West," NCCC *Proceedings* (1884): 143–50. The degree of movement meant that many boys disappeared from the records.

27. Committee on Pine Farm, February 3, 1892; Pine Farm Visitors Book no. 5, April 1888; Intake no. 11; CAS, *Annual Report*, 1889–90, 11; Committee on Placing Out, Minutes, August 5, 1896, 182. Statistics are based on combined systematic samples of Pine Farm and Rock Lawn boys. Rock Lawn is discussed below.

28. Rock Lawn Records, December 2, 1892, April 5, 1896. There is no evidence of discrimination within the institution.

29. James Oliver Horton and Lois E. Horton, *Black Bostonians: Family Life and Community Struggle in the Antebellum North* (New York, 1979), 9–12, 18–19, 35; Elizabeth Hafkin Pleck, *Black Migration and Poverty: Boston, 1865–1900* (New York, 1979), 163–66, 178, 187–92. There were sixteen blacks among 437 inmates in my combined Pine Farm-Rock Lawn sample.

Pleck maintains that blacks were not overrepresented in public institutions (189–90), but her data are scattered and contradicted by other sources. See Horton and Horton, *Black Bostonians*, 35; Peter C. Holloran, *Boston's Wayward Children: Social Services for Homeless Children, 1830–1930* (Rutherford, NJ, 1989), 142, 150.

30. Rock Lawn Records, March 6, 1891; Rock Lawn Intake no. 77; and Pine Farm Visitors Book no. 2, July 1873. See Pine Farm Intake nos. 148, 189, 206, and 475 for other examples. Bellingham, "Little Wanderers," 236–43 and 335, found that kin retrieved 11 percent of the children in places.

31. CAS, *Annual Report*, 1884–85, 15. The number of boys in the sample with criminal charges against them dropped from 27 percent in 1880–84 to 7 percent in 1885–89.

32. Pine Farm Visitors Book no. 4, committees for July 1882, October 1885.

33. Pine Farm Intake no. 457.

34. CAS, *Annual Report*, 1888–89, 12–13; Pine Farm Visitors Book no. 4, March 1886; Book no. 5, July 1888; Committee on Pine Farm, January 22, 1894.

35. CAS, Board of Directors Minutes, vol. 1, January 5, 1894; idem, *Annual Report*, 1893–94, 16–17.

36. Idem, Board of Directors Minutes, vol. 1, October 5, 1866; October 4, 1867; Pine Farm Visitors Book no. 2, December 1870 and April 1872; CAS, *Annual Report*, 1872–73, 6.

37. CAS, *Annual Report*, 1879–80, 4–5; idem, *Annual Report*, 1884–85, 8.

38. Huggins, *Protestants against Poverty*, 102–3; Roy Lubove, *The Professional Altruist: The Emergence of Social Work as a Career, 1880–1930* (New York, 1965), 43–45; F. M. Greg, "Placing Out Children," NCCC *Proceedings* (1892): 415; Sophie E. Minton, "Family Life versus Institution Life," in NCCC *Report*

of the Committee on the History of Child-Saving Work (1893), 37; J. M. Mulry, "The Care of Destitute and Neglected Children," NCCC *Proceedings* (1898): 168; Byron C. Mathews, "The Duty of the State to Dependent Children," NCCC *Proceedings* (1898): 371; Galen A. Merrill, "Some Recent Developments in Child-Saving," NCCC *Proceedings* (1900): 227; Hastings H. Hart, "Common Sense and Cooperation in Child Saving," NCCC *Proceedings* (1903): 181.

Pine Farm Visitors Book no. 6, December 1893; Committee on Pine Farm, March 15, 1890; February 28, April 29, 1896; CAS, *Annual Report*, 1895–96, 21; Rock Lawn Records, June 6, 1898.

39. LeRoy Ashby, *Saving the Waifs: Reformers and Dependent Children, 1890–1917* (Philadelphia, 1984), 10–11, 13–14, 18–31, 226, n. 30; Rothman, *Conscience and Convenience*, 261–62; Susan Tiffin, *In Whose Best Interest? Child Welfare Reform in the Progressive Era.* (Westport, CT, 1982), 61–64, 72–76, 92–10-6; Mennel, *Thorns and Thistles*, 109–14, 121; Michael B. Katz, *In the Shadow of the Poorhouse: A Social History of Welfare in America* (New York, 1986), 118–21.

40. Pine Farm Visitors Book no. 4, February 1883, November 1885, March 1886; CAS, *Annual Report*, 1886–87, 11–12; idem, *Annual Report*, 1888–89, 9; idem, *Annual Report*, 1889–90, 6. Also Huggins, *Protestants against Poverty*, 117–18; Homer Folks, *The Care of Destitute, Neglected, and Delinquent Children* (New York, 1911), 183; Henry W. Thurston, *The Dependent Child* (New York, 1930), 201.

41. Charles W. Birtwell, "Comments," in *The Care of Dependent, Neglected, and Wayward Children*, ed. Anna Garlin Spencer and Charles Birtwell (Chicago, 1893), 124.

42. W. P. Lynde, "Prevention in Some of Its Aspects," NCCC *Proceedings* (1879): 162–70; Clara T. Leonard, "Family Homes for Pauper and Dependent Children," NCCC *Proceedings* (1879): 170–78; Mulry, "Care of Destitute and Neglected Children," 168; Mathews, "Duty of the State," 371; William P. Letchworth, "Children of the State," NCCC *Proceedings* (1886): 142–43; Homer Folks, "The Care of Delinquent Children," NCCC *Proceedings* (1891): 137–38; Tiffin, *In Whose Best Interest?*, 92–94.

43. Tiffin, *In Whose Best Interest?*, 94.

44. Huggins, *Protestants against Poverty*, 99–103, 111, 130–31; CAS, *Annual Report*, 1889–90, 6; idem, *Annual Report*, 1890–91, 13; idem, *Annual Report*, 1891–93, 6; idem, "Illustrative Cases and Forms," 1899, n.p.; Gary R. Anderson, "Charles Birtwell," *Biographical Dictionary of Social Welfare in America*, ed. Walter I. Trattner (Westport, CT, 1986), 95–97.

45. Bellingham, "Little Wanderers," chapter 9, found that about 20 percent of placed children were, in effect, adopted by their families.

46. Mintz, *Prison of Expectations*, 14–16, 18–19; Paul E. Johnson, *A Shopkeeper's Millennium: Society and Revivals in Rochester, New York, 1815–1837* (New York, 1978), 43–48; Joseph F. Kett, *Rites of Passage: Adolescence in America, 1790 to the Present* (New York, 1977), 100–102, 114–15, 144–62, 168–70; Paula

Fass, *The Damned and the Beautiful: American Youth in the 1920s* (New York, 1977), 59–71; Michael Katz, *The People of Hamilton, Canada West* (Cambridge, MA, 1975), 303–5; Ryan, *Cradle of the Middle Class*, 155–56, 165–73, 177–79; Degler, *At Odds*, 180–86.

Viviana A. Zelizer, *Pricing the Priceless Child: The Changing Social Value of Children* (New York, 1985), 170–95, discusses the shift in foster care. As child labor became defined as illegitimate and children became valued for their emotional appeal, families took infants rather than older children. Maria Klein-burd Baghdadi notes the irony that reformers were placing children out at a time when the family was becoming smaller and more intimate. However, this occurs much later than in the period she covers. See "Protestants, Poverty, and Urban Growth: A Study of the Organization of Charity in Boston and New York, 1820–1865" (Ph.D. diss., Brown University, 1975), 279.

4. Domestic Reform and the Delinquent Girl

1. Barbara Welter, "The Cult of True Womanhood: 1820–1860," *American Quarterly* 18 (Summer 1966): 151–74; Gerda Lerner, "The Lady and the Mill Girl: Changes in the Status of Women in the Age of Jackson," *Midcontinent American Studies Journal* 10 (Spring 1969): 5–14; Nancy R. Cott, *The Bonds of Womanhood: "Woman's Sphere" in New England, 1780–1835* (New Haven, CT, 1977). An illuminating recent discussion of the doctrine of spheres is Linda K. Kerber, "Separate Spheres, Female Worlds, Woman's Place: The Rhetoric of Women's History," *Journal of American History* 75 (June 1988): 9–39.

On female criminality and arrest statistics, Estelle B. Freedman, *Their Sisters' Keepers: Women's Prison Reform in America, 1830–1930* (Ann Arbor, MI, 1981), 10–15; Barbara Meil Hobson, *Uneasy Virtue: The Politics of Prostitution and the American Reform Tradition* (New York, 1987), 115–17. On the redefinition of the streets and public space, Christine Stansell, *City of Women: Sex and Class in New York, 1789–1860* (New York, 1986), 190–94; Gunther Barth, *City People: The Rise of Modern City Culture in Nineteenth-Century America* (New York, 1980), 28–29, 129–30, 146–47; Hobson, *Uneasy Virtue*, 31–36; Kerry Wimshurst, "Control and Resistance: Reformatory School Girls in Late Nineteenth-Century South Australia," *Journal of Social History* 18 (Winter 1984): 275. Perry R. Duis, *The Saloon: Public Drinking in Chicago and Boston, 1880–1920* (Urbana, IL, 1983), 204–29, 234–40, discusses the effort to segregate public drinking and vice to specific areas of the city.

On increasing orderliness, Theodore Ferdinand, "The Criminal Patterns of Boston since 1849," *American Journal of Sociology* 73 (July 1967): 84–99; Roger Lane, "Urbanization and Criminal Violence in the Nineteenth Century," *Journal of Social History* 2 (December 1968): 156–63.

2. Carroll Smith-Rosenberg, "Beauty, the Beast, and the Militant Woman: A Case Study in Sex Roles and Social Stress in Jacksonian America," in *Disorderly Conduct: Visions of Gender in Victorian America*, ed. Carroll Smith-

Rosenberg (New York, 1985), 109–28; Freedman, *Their Sisters' Keepers*, 28–35, 40–47; Hobson, *Uneasy Virtue*, 49–60, 66–68, 124–30; Margaret Wyman, "The Rise of the Fallen Woman," *American Quarterly* 3 (Summer 1951): 167–77; W. David Lewis, *From Newgate to Dannemora: The Rise of the Penitentiary in New York, 1796–1848* (Ithaca, NY, 1965), 224–25; Lori D. Ginzberg, *Women and the Work of Benevolence: Morality, Politics, and Class in the 19th-Century United States* (New Haven, CT, 1990), 119–23; Nicole Hahn Rafter, *Partial Justice: Women in State Prisons 1800–1935* (Boston, 1985).

On the different streams of women's reform, see Nancy A. Hewitt, *Women's Activism and Social Change: Rochester, New York, 1822–1872* (Ithaca, NY, 1984), and Anne M. Boylan, "Women in Groups: An Analysis of Women's Benevolent Organizations in New York and Boston, 1797–1840," *Journal of American History* 71 (December 1984): 497–523; and idem, "Timid Girls, Venerable Women, and Dignified Matrons: Life Cycle Patterns among Organized Women in New York and Boston, 1797–1840," *American Quarterly* 38 (Winter 1986): 779–97.

3. *Eighth Annual Report of the Trustees of the State Industrial School for Girls*, Doc. 24, 1864, 3–4; *Tenth Annual Report of the Trustees of the State Industrial School for Girls*, Doc. 21, 1866, 4. Hereafter cited as Lancaster, *Annual Report*. These reports discuss the absence of proper family and home life in working-class neighborhoods. Published records of the State Industrial School for Girls are at the Massachusetts State Library, while manuscript records are at the Schlesinger Library, Radcliffe College.

Charles Loring Brace, *The Dangerous Classes of New York and Twenty Years Work among Them* (New York, 1880), 116, for a typical comment about street girls. Stansell, *City of Women*, 172–92, 193–97, 203–9.

"Report of the Commissioners for the Establishment of a State Reform School for Girls, under the Resolves of April 12, 1854," House Doc. 43, 1855, 23. *Acts and Resolves, 1855*, chapter 442, sec. 4, 838.

4. Stansell, *City of Women*, 180–85; Carroll Smith-Rosenberg, "Puberty to Menopause: The Cycle of Femininity in Nineteenth-Century America," in *Disorderly Conduct: Visions of Gender in Victorian America*, ed. Carroll Smith-Rosenberg (New York, 1985), especially 182–91; Charles E. Rosenberg and Carroll Smith-Rosenberg, "The Female Animal: Medical and Biological Views of Women," in *No Other Gods: On Science and American Social Thought*, ed. Charles E. Rosenberg (Baltimore, MD, 1976), 54–61.

5. Children's Aid Society, *Annual Report*, 1865–66, 10; Lancaster, *Annual Report*, 1879, 19; idem, *Annual Report*, 1858, 9. CAS records are available at the Archives and Special Collections, Joseph P. Healey Library, University of Massachusetts at Boston.

6. Freedman, *Their Sisters' Keepers*, 15–17; Wimshurst, "Control and Resistance," 277–78.

7. For the argument about separatism, see Freedman, *Their Sisters' Keepers*,

passim. On the incorporation of female reform into the larger culture, see Carroll Smith-Rosenberg, *Disorderly Conduct*, 173–76.

8. John Clark Wirkkala, "Juvenile Delinquency and Reform in Nineteenth-Century Massachusetts: The Formative Years in State Care, 1846–1879" (Ph.d. diss., Clark University, 1973), 44–50.

9. Wirkkala, "Delinquency and Reform," 50–53. Curiously, Barbara Brenzel, in her history of the Lancaster School, ignores the first commission. See Barbara M. Brenzel, *Daughters of the State: A Social Portrait of the First Reform School for Girls in North America, 1856–1905* (Cambridge, MA, 1983).

10. Harold Schwartz, *Samuel Gridley Howe: Social Reformer, 1801–1876* (Cambridge, MA, 1956); Samuel G. Howe, "Letter to William Appleton," December 25, 1850, 21, 22, 25, 27. Howe also noted that the type of institution he proposed could be managed exclusively by women. This letter was published together with a later one to the second state commission, which examined the issue again in 1854. See Samuel G. Howe, *A Letter to J. H. Wilkins, H. B. Rogers, and F. B. Fay, Commissioners of Massachusetts for the State Reform School for Girls* (Boston, 1854). See also Joseph M. Hawes, *Children in Urban Society: Juvenile Delinquency in Nineteenth-Century America* (New York, 1971), 84–85.

11. See Wirkkala, "Delinquency and Reform," 53–72, for a discussion of the Lancaster School's founding. An extensive discussion of the Fay Commission can be found in Brenzel, *Daughters of the State*, chapter 3. There is no direct evidence that the legislature was fearful of placing sexually active girls in families, but the issue was addressed by Samuel Gridley Howe and later by the Lancaster administration. See Howe, "Letter to Appleton," 31; and Lancaster, *Annual Report*, 1857, 21.

12. This is not to gainsay European influences or to make an argument for American exceptionalism. Certainly that part of David Rothman's thesis in *The Discovery of the Asylum: Social Order and Disorder in the New Republic* (Boston, 1971) can be dismissed. Steven L. Schlossman, *Love and the American Delinquent: The Theory and Practice of 'Progressive' Juvenile Justice, 1825–1920* (Chicago, 1977), 50, exaggerates by calling the family model a "foreign import." While aware of European efforts, the commissioners found their model literally at home. On the Fay Commission's analysis of foreign reform schools, see Brenzel, *Daughters of the State*, 50–64. There is also a general discussion in Robert M. Mennel, *Thorns and Thistles: Juvenile Delinquents in the United States, 1825–1940* (Hanover, NH, 1973), 52–54, and in Hawes, *Children in Urban Society*, 78–80. For the home in American culture, see Maxine van de Wetering, "The Popular Concept of 'Home' in Nineteenth-Century America," *Journal of American Studies* 18 (April 1984): 5–28.

13. Case no. 268. As per my agreement with the Division of Youth Services, Commonwealth of Massachusetts, all names are pseudonyms but ethnic identity is preserved.

14. Lancaster, *Annual Report*, 1857, 6, 31–32, 35; idem, *Annual Report*, 1864, 3–4; *Account of the Proceedings at the Inauguration of the State Industrial School for Girls, at Lancaster, Aug. 27, 1856* (Boston, 1856), 19, 48; Brenzel, *Daughters of the State*, 66–75.

15. Lancaster, *Annual Report*, 1857, 24, 35. The schedule is similar to that about a decade later, which specifically allowed one hour and twenty minutes for recess during the day. See Lancaster, *Annual Report*, 1868, 13. For the contrast with a private asylum, see Susan L. Porter, "The Benevolent Asylum — Image and Reality: The Care and Training of Female Orphans in Boston, 1800–1840" (Ph.D. diss., Boston University, 1984).

16. Lancaster, *Annual Report*, 1857, 12.

17. "Report of the Commissioners for the Establishment of a State Reform School for Girls," House Doc. 43, 1855, appendix, 29–48.

18. Lancaster, *Annual Report*, 1857, 61; idem, *Annual Report*, 1858, 10; idem, *Annual Report*, 1864, 18; idem, *Annual Report*, 1865, 19; Brenzel, *Daughters of the State*, 47–48. Barbara Brenzel argues that reformers confused poverty with criminality, as evidenced by their failure to distinguish between criminals and simple status offenders. See *Daughters of the State*, 70. This is true, but it misses an important point. The emphasis on distinguishing between "wanton" girls and all others, with only the former being excluded from Lancaster, reemphasizes that the Victorian definition of deviance focused exclusively on sex. All others could be saved and their inclusion in Lancaster should be taken as evidence of clarity of purpose.

19. Lancaster, *Annual Report*, 1857, 15–16; idem, *Annual Report*, 1860, 11; Brenzel, *Daughters of the State*, 76–80.

20. Brenzel notes this in *Daughters of the State*, 77. For the attitudes of one family toward a prostitute daughter, see Ruth Rosen and Sue Davidson, eds., *The Mamie Papers* (Old Westbury, NY, 1977), xxii–xxiv. Stansell, *City of Women*, 179–85, argues that prostitution was an economic and social choice working-class women made that turned an exploitative relationship into a potentially reciprocal one.

21. Hasia R. Diner, *Erin's Daughters in America: Irish Immigrant Women in the Nineteenth Century* (Baltimore, MD, 1983), 19–21, 46–48. Diner argues that Irish women so internalized codes against sexual activity that they needed few external constraints (22). That so many of the girls in Lancaster were Irish proves otherwise. Diner also comes to the curious conclusion that few former domestic servants were to be found among prostitutes (82). In fact, domestic service was the major prior occupation listed in William Sanger's survey of prostitution. See Hobson, *Uneasy Virtue*, 96.

22. Diner, *Erin's Daughters*, 12, 17, 21–22; Lancaster, *Annual Report*, 1857, 21.

23. Lancaster, *Annual Report*, 1859, 8; idem, *Annual Report*, 1861, 5, 16; Case nos. 2690, 2864, and 1933. Brenzel, *Daughters of the State*, 142–43. Bruce

Bellingham argues that it is not fair to judge "foster families" by standards of present-day affectionate families. However, this was the model officials held up in their pronouncements. See " 'Little Wanderers': A Socio-Historical Study of the Nineteenth-Century Origins of Child Fostering and Adoption Reform, Based on Early Records of the New York Children's Aid Society" (Ph.D. diss., University of Pennsylvania, 1984), 308–9.

24. These percentages are based on the tables in Carroll D. Wright, *The Working Girls of Boston* (Boston, 1889), 6–11.

25. See David M. Katzman, *Seven Days a Week: Women and Domestic Service in Industrializing America* (New York, 1978), chapter 2; Lynn Y. Weiner, *From Working Girl to Working Mother: The Female Labor Force in the United States, 1820–1980* (Chapel Hill, NC, 1985), 64–67; Virginia Yans-McLaughlin, *Family and Community: Italian Immigrants in Buffalo, 1880–1930* (Ithaca, NY, 1971), 53, 170, 203; Brenzel, *Daughters of the State*, 114–17, 138–41; Lancaster, *Annual Report*, 1875, 8.

Information about Lancaster's placements is based on a sample of 417 inmate cases originating in Boston between 1870 and 1939, out of a total Boston caseload of 1,529. Italian and Jewish girls comprised 9 and 7 percent, respectively, of the sample, with ethnicity determined by having a foreign-born father, unless the mother was foreign born and the father native.

26. Lancaster, *Annual Report*, 1868, 6; idem, *Annual Report*, 1874, 17; see also idem, *Annual Report*, 1862, 14; Hobson, *Uneasy Virtue*, 96–97; Freedman, *Their Sisters' Keepers*, 94.

27. Katzman, *Seven Days a Week*, 108–17; Lancaster, *Annual Report*, 1884, 22–24, for rules regulating girls in placement; idem, *Annual Report*, 1861, 14–15; Case no. 6976.

28. Brenzel, *Daughters of the State*, 143.

29. Case no. 970.

30. Case no. 951; Case no. 979; Lancaster, *Annual Report*, 1875, 6; "Report of the Commissioners," 23; Brenzel, *Daughters of the State*, 124–26. Barbara Brenzel argues that parents manipulated the entrance procedures to obtain a free, safe home for their daughters (135). It is doubtful that Lancaster officials felt themselves manipulated—they cooperated in the scheme. Their cooperation was due to their low opinions of working-class family life; these were precisely the reformable girls they hoped to get.

31. Case no. 866.

32. Case no. 1521.

33. These conclusions are based on my sample of case records and on comments by Lancaster officials, such as this one: "the number of those who had been guilty of actual immorality and of those who were in danger of becoming immoral seems to have increased, though the real facts in these cases must be sought from other sources than from the mittimus committing them to the school." See Lancaster, *Annual Report*, 1884, 15.

34. David J. Pivar, *Purity Crusade: Sexual Morality and Social Control, 1868–1900* (Westport, CT, 1973), 50–66, 99–117, 139–43; Freedman, *Their Sisters' Keepers,* 38–45.

35. Hobson, *Uneasy Virtue,* 124–27; Smith-Rosenberg, *Disorderly Conduct,* 173–75; Freedman, *Their Sisters' Keepers,* 46; Ginzberg, *Women and the Work of Benevolence,* 203–6.

36. Board of State Charities, *Annual Report,* 1865, xlvi, lxiv, lxxviii; idem, *Annual Report,* 1867, xx; idem, *Annual Report,* 1868, xxxi, xxxviii, xli–xlii. Board of State Charities reports are in the Massachusetts State Library.

37. Mennel, *Thorns and Thistles,* 91; Brenzel, *Daughters of the State,* 90–92; Michael B. Katz, *The Irony of Early School Reform: Educational Innovation in Mid–Nineteenth-Century Massachusetts* (Boston, 1968), 180–81.

38. Board of State Charities, *Annual Report,* 1865, xxiii, xxxvii; Wirkkala, "Delinquency and Reform," 195–96.

39. Wirkkala, "Delinquency and Reform," 191–212, appendix D, appendix F; Gardner Tufts, "The Massachusetts Statutes Relating to Juvenile Offenders and the Methods of Dealing with Them," National Conference of Charities and Corrections *Proceedings* (1880): 200–209; Board of State Charities, *Annual Report,* 1879, 55–56.

40. Lancaster, *Annual Report,* 1870, 18–19; idem, *Annual Report,* 1872, 4, 12; idem, *Annual Report,* 1874, 6, 7–9; idem, *Annual Report,* 1875, 13, 15; idem, *Annual Report,* 1876, 3.

41. Lancaster, *Annual Report,* 1874, 6; idem, *Annual Report,* 1875, 5; Brenzel, *Daughters of the State,* 131–32. The information on length of stay is based on my sample. When these records are stratified by decade, they show an increased length of stay beginning in the 1890s, but not until after 1910 did the mean length of stay increase to over two years.

42. Lancaster, *Annual Report,* 1879, 15–16; idem, *Annual Report,* 1883, 14, 16, 17–18, 19–20; idem, *Annual Report,* 1889, 92; idem, *Annual Report,* 1892, 25; Brenzel, *Daughters of the State,* 154–55.

43. Schwartz, *Samuel Gridley Howe,* 137–47, 275–76, for Howe's contribution to the institutionalization of the retarded. See also Peter L. Tyor, " 'Denied the Power to Choose the Good': Sexuality and Mental Defect in American Medical Practice, 1850–1920," *Journal of Social History* 10 (June 1977): 472–89; Peter L. Tyor and Leland V. Bell, *Caring for the Retarded in America: A History* (Westport, CT, 1984), 60–61, 68–69, 71–73, 80–84; Mark H. Haller, *Eugenics: Heriditarian Attitudes in American Thought* (New Brunswick, NJ, 1963) 22–24, 26–28, 33–36.

44. Lancaster, *Annual Report,* 1878, 7–8, 16; Wimshurst, "Control and Resistance," 279.

45. Lancaster, *Annual Report,* 1872, 10; idem, *Annual Report,* 1875, 8; idem, *Annual Report,* 1892, 20; Brenzel, *Daughters of the State,* 138–42.

5. Domestic Reform and the State Reform School for Boys

1. Allen's memoirs, upon which much of the following section is based, were published to coincide with an 1877 investigation of the reform school, which might suggest that they were self-serving. However, comparison with the annual reports Allen wrote at the time of his superintendency indicates their overall reliability. See Joseph A. Allen, *Westboro' State Reform School Reminiscences* (Boston, 1877).

See also the extensive review in Board of State Charities, *Annual Report*, 1864, 168–200. Board of State Charities reports are in the Massachusetts State Library. Allen is mentioned in Michael B. Katz's *The Irony of Early School Reform* (Boston, 1968), 188, 192–93, 198–99, but Katz misses the real impact of "family-style" reform.

2. Allen, *Westboro' Reminiscences*, 9–10, 13–14, 16, 17, 19, 20–21, 35, 43–44.

3. Ibid., 36–38, 45, 81.

4. Ibid., 65–67.

5. Ibid., 49–50. John Clark Wirkkala, "Juvenile Delinquency and Reform in Nineteenth-Century Massachusetts: The Formative Era in State Care, 1846–1879" (Ph.D. diss., Clark University, 1973), chapter 4. This point is made in David J. Rothman, *Conscience and Convenience: The Asylum and Its Alternatives in Progressive America* (Boston, 1980).

6. Letter from William Allen to the Governor and Council, May 16, 1861, "Public Criminal Institutions," Massachusetts Executive Department Letters, vol. 22, no. 72, Massachusetts State Archives; Wirkkala, "Delinquency and Reform," 118–19, 126–30.

7. Ibid., 163–68, 174–80, 188–90.

8. Ibid., 138–50.

9. Ibid., 123–24, 131–32.

10. Board of State Charities, *Annual Report*, 1872, 36–39. Wirkkala, "Delinquency and Reform," 158–59. See the discussion in Board of State Charities, *Annual Report*, 1865, lxxxii–lxxxv.

11. Board of State Charities, *Annual Report*, 1865, xliv–xlvii; idem, *Annual Report*, 1868, xxxii; idem, *Annual Report*, 1864, 175, 199; idem, *Annual Report*, 1867, 99–100.

12. Carl Siracusa, *A Mechanical People: Perceptions of the Industrial Order in Massachusetts, 1815–1880* (Middletown, CT, 1979), 22, 31.

13. Marvin Lazerson, *Origins of the Urban School: Public Education in Massachusetts, 1870–1915* (Cambridge, MA, 1975), 75–76, 81–83, 92–96, 111, 133–36; David B. Tyack, *The One Best System: A History of American Urban Education* (Cambridge, MA, 1974), 188–91; David Nasaw, *Schooled to Order: A Social History of Public Schooling in the United States* (New York, 1979), 116–17. Lazerson argues that manual training had to be divorced from its origins as training for defective or delinquent children before it became widely accepted.

226   5. THE STATE REFORM SCHOOL FOR BOYS

However, manual training appeared at Pine Farm, Lancaster, and Westborough at about the same time as he shows its adoption in public schools. On manual training in reform schools, see Robert M. Mennel, *Thorns and Thistles: Juvenile Delinquents in the United States, 1825–1940* (Hanover, NH, 1973), 102–5.

14. Lazerson, *Origins of the Urban School*, 101–3; Susan Tiffin, *In Whose Best Interest? Child Welfare Reform in the Progressive Era* (Westport, CT, 1982), 67–72; State Reform School, *Annual Report*, 1890, 10; idem, *Annual Report*, 1895, 19; idem, *Annual Report*, 1889, 9; idem, *Annual Report*, 1891, 59. Reports of the state reform school are in the Massachusetts State Library.

15. Gardner Tufts, "The Massachusetts Statutes Relating to Juvenile Offenders and the Methods of Dealing with Them," National Conference of Charities and Corrections *Proceedings* (1880): 200–9; Board of State Charities, *Annual Report*, 1869, 30; idem, *Annual Report*, 1879, 55–56.

16. Board of State Charities, *Annual Report*, 1872, lv; idem, *Annual Report*, 1868, xcix.

17. *Second Annual Report of the Trustees of the State Primary and Reform Schools*, 1880, 82–84. These reports are in the Massachusetts State Library.

18. Board of State Charities, *Annual Report*, 1878, 162; *Second Annual Report of the Trustees of the State Primary and Reform Schools*, 1880, 82. The percentages are derived from State Reform School for Boys, *Annual Report*, 1865, 30, 37; and *Second Annual Report of the Trustees of the State Primary and Reform Schools*, 1880, 75, 84.

19. For a similar process in Wisconsin, see Steven L. Schlossman, *Love and the American Delinquent: The Theory and Practice of 'Progressive' Juvenile Justice, 1825–1920* (Chicago, 1977), 99–123, and for Ohio, Robert M. Mennel, " 'The Family System of Common Farmers': The Early Years of Ohio's Reform Farm, 1858–1884," *Ohio History* 89 (Fall 1980): 312–21. Kerry Wimshurst argues in "Control and Resistance: Reformatory School Girls in Late Nineteenth-Century South Australia," *Journal of Social History* 18 (Winter 1984): 281–82, that girls resisted reformatory discipline more extensively than did boys, but my data indicate the opposite.

20. State Reform School, *Annual Report*, 1872, 3–4; Letter from Elizabeth Putnam to Governor Long, February 26, 1881, "State Institutions," Massachusetts Executive Department Letters, vol. 211, no. 50, Massachusetts State Archives.

21. Robert V. Bruce, *1877: Year of Violence* (Indianapolis, 1959).

22. Worcester *Gazette*, newspaper clipping, State Reform School Case Records, n.d. The case records are at Schlesinger Library, Radcliffe College. See also the Boston *Sunday Herald*, January 14, 1877 and the Boston *Daily Globe*, January 15, 1877.

23. Massachusetts General Court, "Report of the Committee on Public Charitable Institutions regarding the discipline of the State Reform School," House Doc. 285, 1877, 147–48, 250. Hereafter cited as 1877 Hearing.

24. 1877 Hearing, 582–83, 635, 665. See also 450; 501–3.

25. Ibid., 18, 75, 223–24, 232, 249. See also the testimony of the former assistant superintendent, William Phillips, 141–45.

26. Ibid., 19.

27. Ibid., 77, 33.

28. Ibid., 655, 538, 403. See Clifford R. Shaw, *The Jack-Roller, A Delinquent Boy's Own Story* (Chicago, 1930), 67, on other delinquents' reaction to trust boys, and 69, on sexual exploitation.

29. 1877 Hearing, 470, 655.

30. Ibid., 655, 475–76.

31. Ibid., 1–6.

32. State Reform School, *Annual Report*, 1883, 9–11, 80; idem, *Annual Report*, 1884, 8.

33. State Reform School, *Annual Report*, 1884, 79.

34. On hereditarianism and crime in the late nineteenth century, see Arthur E. Fink, *Causes of Crime* (Philadelphia, 1938), 108–33; Schlossman, *Love and the American Delinquent*, 107–8; Mennel, *Thorns and Thistles*, 83–92; Joseph M. Hawes, *Children in Urban Society: Juvenile Delinquency in Nineteenth-Century America* (New York, 1971), 191–98, 208–20; Anthony M. Platt, *The Child Savers: The Invention of Delinquency* (Chicago, 1969), 18–36.

35. *Sixth Annual Report of the Trustees of the State Primary and Reform Schools*, 1884, 7–8; *Seventh Annual Report of the Trustees of the State Primary and Reform Schools*, 1885, 12–13; Elizabeth Glendower Evans, "Statement from the Trustees of the State Primary and Reform Schools," in National Conference of Charities and Corrections, *Report of the Committee on the History of Child-Saving Work* (1893), 227–61. The quotation is from 239. See also Rothman, *Conscience and Convenience*, 282–84.

Part 3: The Organization of Welfare

1. Martin H. Slobodkin, "The Fort the Brahmins Built," *Boston Magazine* 68 (February 1976): 134, 118–19; Robert M. Fogelson, *America's Armories: Architecture, Society, and Public Order* (Cambridge, MA, 1989).

6. Catholic Welfare: Between Separatism and Accommodation

1. Anonymous, "Brands from the Burning," in *Light Dawning; or, Fruits of the Children's Mission* (Boston, 1856), 26–48. The quotations are from 34 and 40–41.

2. Robert H. Lord, John E. Sexton, and Edward T. Harrington, *History of the Archdiocese of Boston*, 3 vols. (Boston, 1945), 1: 761–80, 2:357–58; Donna Merwick, *Boston Priests, 1848–1910: A Study of Social and Intellectual Change* (Cambridge, MA, 1973), 3–4.

3. Fitzpatrick went to school with two mayors of Boston, Nathanial

Shurtleff and Frederic Prince, editor Thomas Brewer of the *Boston Atlas,* minister Henry Ward Beecher, the merchant-reformer Lewis Tappan, the author-reformer Edward Everett Hale, and the merchant George Cabot.

Oscar Handlin, *Boston's Immigrants: A Study in Acculturation* (New York, 1971), 180–84; Merwick, *Boston Priests,* 1–10; Thomas O'Connor, *Fitzpatrick's Boston, 1846–1866* (Boston, 1984), 7–8, 24, 49, 60–61.

4. Jay Dolan, *The Immigrant Church: New York's Irish and German Catholics, 1815–1865* (Notre Dame, IN, 1983), 3–4; Merwick, *Boston Priests,* 8–10, for the reaction to Irish immigrants. For Irish religious practices, see David Miller, "Irish Catholicism and the Great Famine," *Journal of Social History* 9 (Fall 1975): 81–98; and Sheridan Gilley, "The Roman Catholic Church and the Nineteenth-Century Irish Diaspora," *Journal of Ecclesiastical History* 35 (April 1984): 188–207. On the Irish clergy, see Emmet Larkin, "The Devotional Revolution in Ireland, 1850–1875," *American Historical Review* 77 (June 1972): 627–35.

Here the term "assimilation" is used to mean the integration of Boston's leading Catholics into the established social structure, while "acculturation" is used to mean the adoption of a new culture by Irish immigrants. See Milton M. Gordon, *Assimilation in American Life: The Role of Race, Religion, and National Origins* (New York, 1964), 60–83.

5. Handlin, *Boston's Immigrants,* 161–62; O'Connor, *Fitzpatrick's Boston,* 102–4.

6. *Pilot,* May 19, May 26, June 2, 1849.

7. John Higham draws the distinction between Catholic-Protestant tension, which was more or less constant, and nativism, which arose when Catholics seemed "dangerously foreign agents in national life." *Strangers in the Land: Patterns of American Nativism, 1860–1925* (New York, 1970), 5. However, the evidence from Boston suggests that Catholic-Protestant tension had diminished in the early nineteenth century.

8. For a general history, see Timothy L. Smith, *Revivalism and Reform: American Protestantism on the Eve of the Civil War* (New York, 1975), chapter 9. On Boston, see William B. Whiteside, *The Boston Y.M.C.A. and Community Need* (New York, 1951), 9–10, 19, 23.

9. Children's Mission to the Children of the Destitute, *Annual Report,* 1850, 6–7. The reports are at the Parents' and Children's Services of the Children's Mission.

10. Ray Allen Billington, *The Protestant Crusade: 1800–1860* (New York, 1952) 275–76; *Pilot,* August 6, 1853; Dolan, *Immigrant Church,* 129–39; Gail Farr Casterline, "St. Joseph's and St. Mary's: The Origins of Catholic Hospitals in Philadelphia," *Pennsylvania Magazine of History and Biography* 108 (July 1984): 289–314.

11. Missions were not an exclusively American phenomenon—similar revivals in postfamine Ireland sparked an upswelling of devotionalism. Jay P. Dolan, *Catholic Revivalism: The American Experience, 1830–1900* (Notre Dame,

IN, 1978), 22–24, 40–44, 60–62, 73–77, 105–8; Larkin, "Devotional Revolution," 644–49; Lord, et al., *History of the Archdiocese* 2:307, 749; Dolan, *Immigrant Church*, 54–55, 118–19.

12. Colleen McDannell, *The Christian Home in Victorian America, 1840–1900* (Bloomington, IN, 1986) 120–21, 123–25; Dolan, *Catholic Revivalism*, 42–43, 62–64, 156–61, 175–79, 189–91; idem, *Immigrant Church*, 52–63.

13. Thomas McAvoy argues that the Catholic clergy sought to keep their parishoners isolated from Protestant culture in order to protect them and preserve their religion. See Thomas T. McAvoy, "The Formation of the Catholic Minority in the United States, 1820–1860," *Review of Politics* 10 (January 1948): 13–34. However, as noted above, Irish immigrants were at best only nominally Catholic while the Church leadership had strong ties to Brahmin Boston and respected its culture. Oscar Handlin, by overlooking ethnic differences among Catholics and ignoring the key roles played by assimilationists, also overemphasizes the separatist intent of Catholic institutions. See *Boston's Immigrants*, 161–70. For a fine essay exploring the tension between assimilation and separatism, see Susan S. Walton, "To Preserve the Faith: Catholic Charities in Boston, 1870–1930," in *Catholic Boston: Studies in Religion and Community, 1870–1970*, ed. Robert E. Sullivan and James M. O'Toole (Boston, 1985), 67–119.

Michael B. Katz, *In the Shadow of the Poorhouse: A Social History of Welfare in America* (New York, 1986), 61–62, adopts the position that Catholic social welfare was more interested in relieving the poor than in reforming them. This is also the position of Jay Dolan, *Immigrant Church*, 122–28, but I think it is mistaken. See the discussion below.

On Irish Catholics' upward mobility, see Dennis P. Ryan, *Beyond the Ballot Box: A Social History of the Boston Irish, 1845–1917* (Rutherford, NJ, 1983), chapter 4.

14. George F. Haskins, *Report Historical, Statistical, and Financial of the House of the Angel Guardian* (Boston, 1864), 7–8. See A Friend of the House of the Angel Guardian [William D. Kelly], *The Life of Father Haskins* (Boston, 1899), 70–80, for the founding of the HAG.

15. Haskins, *Report*, 49–51.

16. Ibid., 21.

17. Ibid., 37–41.

18. Lawrence J. McCaffrey, *The Irish Diaspora in America* (Bloomington, IN, 1976), 63–66; Maldwyn Allen Jones, *American Immmigration* (Chicago, 1960), 121–23, 210–12. An exception to this was Boston's Home for Destitute Catholic Children, which did place children in foster homes. See Walton, "To Preserve the Faith," 70–71. Jay Dolan argues that a rural or pastoral ideal was part of Catholic reform after midcentury, but his evidence is weak and he admits that few children were placed in rural settings, that few children accepted these types of placements, and that the rural ideal was "more symbol than reality." See *Immigrant Church*, 138–39. On the House of the Angel

Guardian, see Peter C. Holloran, *Boston's Wayward Children: Social Services for Homeless Children, 1830–1930* (Rutherford, NJ, 1989), 86–91.

19. The HAG eventually became an orphanage, but the transition to long-term care occurred in the twentieth century. The sample is from the Register of the House of the Angel Guardian, Chancery of the Archdiocese of Boston Archives. Unfortunately the records contain very little information about individual cases. A similar independence toward private institutions was found by Bruce Bellingham, " 'Little Wanderers': A Socio-Historical Study of the Nineteenth-Century Origins of Child Fostering and Adoption Reform, Based on Early Records of the New York Children's Aid Society" (Ph.D. diss., University of Pennsylvania, 1984). See Holloran, *Boston's Wayward Children*, 90.

20. See Timothy L. Smith, "Protestant Schooling and American Nationality," *Journal of American History* 53 (March 1967): 679–95, for the identification between Protestantism and nationality.

21. Diane Ravitch, *The Great School Wars: New York City, 1805–1973* (New York, 1974), 3–84; and Michael Feldberg, *The Philadelphia Riots of 1844: A Study of Ethnic Conflict* (Westport, CT, 1975), 89–96.

22. For a discussion of the case, see Lord, et al., *History of the Archdiocese of Boston* 2:587–96; Richard J. Quinlan, "Growth and Development of Catholic Education in the Archdiocese of Boston," *Catholic Historical Review* XXII (April 1963): 34. The case is discussed briefly in Stanley K. Schultz, *The Culture Factory: Boston Public Schools, 1789–1860* (New York, 1973), 307–8, who quotes both Wall and Philbrick. See also O'Connor, *Fitzpatrick's Boston*, 110–16. O'Connor mistakenly calls the response of the children in the Eliot School "spontaneous" (115) and he overlooks Wiget's involvement entirely.

23. Lord, et al., *Boston Archdiocese* 2:596–601; O'Connor, *Fitzpatrick's Boston*, 115–16.

24. On Chicago schools in this period, see James W. Sanders, *The Education of an Urban Minority: Catholics in Chicago, 1833–1965* (New York, 1977), 24–29. Sanders also studied Boston parochial schools, and he argues that Boston Catholics built churches rather than schools in order to compete with Brahmin culture. See James W. Sanders, "Nineteenth-Century Boston Catholics and the School Question," University of Notre Dame, Working Paper Series, No. 2 (Fall 1977). While mixed feelings of competition and inferiority are certainly apparent, the unwillingness of the leadership to build schools, particularly in the face of criticism by some parish priests, is better explained by the larger context of desire for Irish acculturation. See O'Connor, *Fitzpatrick's Boston*, 49; and Merwick, *Boston Priests*, 64–73. For a similar phenomenon, see Timothy J. Meagher, " 'Irish All the Time': Ethnic Consciousness among the Irish in Worcester, Massachusetts, 1880–1905," *Journal of Social History* 19 (Winter 1985): 277–78.

25. O'Connor, *Fitzpatrick's Boston*, 117–18; Merwick, *Boston Priests*, 70–73, 87–89, 111–16. Scully is quoted on 72.

26. Handlin, *Boston's Immigrants*, 209–12; Higham, *Strangers in the Land*, 12–13.

27. Sam Bass Warner, *Streetcar Suburbs: The Process of Growth in Boston, 1870–1900* (Cambridge, MA, 1962), 65–66; Stephan Thernstrom, *The Other Bostonians: Poverty and Progress in the American Metropolis, 1880–1970*, (Cambridge, MA, 1973) 131–33; James Bernard Cullen, *The Story of the Irish in Boston* (Boston, 1889), 425–27; Dennis Clark, *The Irish in Philadelphia: Ten Generations of Urban Experience* (Philadelphia, 1973), 104, 144, 170; idem, "The Irish Catholics: A Postponed Perspective," in *Immigrants and Religion in Urban America* ed. Randall M. Miller and Thomas D. Marzik (Philadelphia, 1977), 58–60.

28. McCaffrey, *The Irish Diaspora*, 80, 138–40; Richard D. Cross, "The Irish," in *Ethnic Leadership in America*, ed. John Higham (Baltimore, MD, 1978), 182, 184, 189; James R. Green and Hugh Carter Donahue, *Boston's Workers: A Labor History* (Boston, 1979), 72–74, 78–87, 91–93; Meagher, "Irish All the Time," 280.

On the conservatism of Boston Irish Catholic leaders, particularly after the death of John Boyle O'Reilly, see Arthur Mann, *Yankee Reformers in an Urban Age: Social Reform in Boston, 1880–1900* (New York, 1954), chapter 2.

29. McDannell, *The Christian Home*, 58–68, 118–21, 138–42.

30. Larkin, "Devotional Revolution," 636, 639, 644, 648–49, 651–52; Robert D. Cross, *The Emergence of Liberal Catholicism in America* (Cambridge, MA, 1958), 1–8; Miller, "Irish Catholicism and the Great Famine," 91; McCaffery, *Irish Diaspora*, 72–77.

The Irish constituted about one-third of the immigrants entering the port of Boston between 1871 and 1880 and it seems reasonable to conclude that the new Irish had a major impact on Boston's Irish community. See Handlin, *Boston's Immigrants*, 264.

31. For a history of the Society, see Daniel T. McColgan, *A Century of Charity: The First One Hundred Years of the Society of St. Vincent de Paul in the United States*, 2 vols. (Milwaukee, WI, 1951); for a similar interpretation of the St. Vincent de Paul Society, see Walton, "To Preserve the Faith," especially 83–84.

32. St. Vincent de Paul Society, *Annual Report*, 1886, 6–8; Walton, "To Preserve the Faith," 67–68, 84–85. Another notable difference between Protestant and Catholic charitable efforts was the emphasis on male, rather than female, visiting among Catholics. St. Vincent de Paul Society records are at the St. Vincent de Paul Society, Boston.

33. St. Vincent de Paul Society, *Annual Report*, 1869, 3.

34. Ibid., 1886, 8; Walton, "To Preserve the Faith," 82–84; *Pilot*, November 27, 1880, as quoted in Mann, *Yankee Reformers in the Urban Age*, 26. Along similar lines, see George J. Gillespie, "A Plea for the Boys' Clubs," *St. Vincent de Paul Quarterly* 9 (November 1904): 309–14.

35. Thomas M. Mulry, "The Society of St. Vincent de Paul in the Charity

232

7. THE CHARITY NETWORK

Organization Movement," in *American Catholic Thought on Social Questions*, ed.
Aaron I. Abell (Indianapolis, IN, 1968), 178, 180–81; St. Vincent de Paul
Society, *Annual Report*, 1870, 5; Walton, "To Preserve the Faith," 88; Aaron
I. Abell, *American Catholicism and Social Action: A Search for Social Justice, 1865–
1950* (Garden City, NY, 1960), 125–26.

36. St. Vincent de Paul Society, *Annual Report*, 1887, 5; idem, *Annual
Report*, 1888, 5–6; idem, *Annual Report*, 1891, 10; Walton, "To Preserve the
Faith," 87; McColgan, *Century of Charity* 1:334.

37. Higham, *Strangers in the Land*, 86–87; Donald L. Kinzer, *An Episode in
Anti-Catholicism: The American Protective Association* (Seattle, WA, 1964),
186–87.

7. The Charity Network

1. Anonymous, *Boston By-Ways to Hell: A Visit to the Dens of North Street*
(Boston, 1867), 5–18. The quotation is from 16–17.

2. Hanover Street Home Mission, Record Book 1, n.d., June 14, 1865,
May 20, 1867, April 13, 1868, January 25, 1869, March 9, 1871; Record Book
2, January 14, 1878. The records of the Hanover Street Mission and the North
End Mission are in the Archives and Special Collections, Joseph P. Healey
Library, University of Massachusetts at Boston.

3. "The North End Mission," *North End Mission Magazine* 1 (April 1872):
2. On the role of women and charity, see Susan Porter Benson, "Business
Heads and Sympathizing Hearts: The Women of the Providence Employment
Society, 1837–1858," *Journal of Social History* 12 (Winter 1978): 302–12; John
T. Cumbler, "The Politics of Charity: Gender and Class in Late Nineteenth-
Century Charity Policy," *Journal of Social History* 14 (Fall 1980): 99–111;
William Leach, *True Love and Perfect Union: The Feminist Reform of Sex and
Society* (New York, 1980), 298–99, 320–21, 343–44.

4. Kathleen D. McCarthy, in *Noblesse Oblige: Charity and Cultural Philanthropy in Chicago, 1849–1929* (Chicago, 1982), 29–32, argues that in the Gilded
Age home visiting was discouraged. Patronesses became board members and
disengaged from the day-to-day work of their organizations. The Mission
seems to have been an exception to this.

See "The North End Mission," *North End Mission Magazine* 1 (January
1872): 16–17; "The Portuguese in Boston," *North End Mission Magazine* 2 (July
1873): 67–70; North End Mission, *The North Street Beacon Light*, (Boston, 1874),
3; idem, *Annual Report*, 1870, 18; idem, *Annual Report*, 1876, 8, 12–13, 16;
idem, *Annual Report*, 1878, 11; newspaper clipping, *Boston Post*, n.d.

5. "The North End Mission," *North End Mission Magazine* 1 (April 1872):
2; North End Mission, *North Street Beacon Light* 3; "The Portuguese in Boston,"
65; "The North End Mission," *North End Mission Magazine* 1 (January 1872):
17; North End Mission, *Annual Report*, 1903, 11.

6. Aaron I. Abell, *The Urban Impact on American Protestantism, 1865–1900* (Hamden, England, 1962), 71–75, 97, 139, 147–61; Arthur Mann, *Yankee Reformers in the Urban Age: Social Reform in Boston, 1880–1900* (Cambridge, MA, 1954), 75–77; Henry F. May, *Protestant Churches and Industrial America* (New York, 1949), 91–111, 163–66, 170–81; Robert H. Bremner, *From the Depths: The Discovery of Poverty in the United States* (New York, 1956), 57–60.

Paul Boyer, in *Urban Masses and Moral Order in America, 1820–1920* (Cambridge, MA, 1978), 134–39, contrasts the urban missions with the institutional churches. As the North End Mission shows, the two approaches were by no means exclusive and, as Nathan Huggins shows in *Protestants against Poverty: Boston's Charities, 1870–1900* (Westport, CT, 1971), 48–51, the North End Mission was only one of several religious agencies that adopted a social ethic. Boyer overlooks the trend toward the delivery of social services. For a work that emphasizes the shift toward social service in a slightly earlier period, see Carroll Smith-Rosenberg, *Religion and the Rise of the American City: The New York City Mission Movement, 1812–1870* (Ithaca, NY, 1971).

7. On the struggle to control popular recreation, see Stephen Hardy, *How Boston Played: Sport, Recreation, and Community, 1865–1915* (Boston, 1982), chapter 3; and Roy Rosenzweig, *Eight Hours for What We Will: Workers and Leisure in an Industrial City, 1870–1920* (Cambridge, England, 1983), chapter 5.

8. Children's Aid Society, *Annual Report*, 1885–86, 8–10; idem, *Annual Report*, 1886–87, 11–12; idem, *Annual Report*, 1887–88, 4, 14; idem, *Annual Report*, 1889–90, 11–12; idem, *Annual Report*, 1891–93, 6; Huggins, *Protestants against Poverty*, 98–102. CAS reports are in the Archives and Special Collections, Joseph P. Healey Library, University of Massachusetts at Boston.

9. Charles W. Birtwell, "Home Libraries" (reprint from the Proceedings of the International Congress of Charities, Corrections, and Philanthropy, Chicago, June 15, 1893), 4–8. On the expansion of work with children in their homes, see Huggins, *Protestants against Poverty*, 102–3; and LeRoy Ashby, *Saving the Waifs: Reformers and Dependent Children, 1890–1917* (Philadelphia, 1984), chapter 2.

10. This in fact was the criticism mounted against manual education after 1900. See Marvin Lazerson, *Origins of the Urban School: Public Education in Massachusetts, 1870–1915* (Cambridge, MA, 1971), chapter 5.

On the theory of manual training and physical exercise, see Dominick Cavallo, *Muscles and Morals: Organized Playgrounds and Urban Reform, 1880–1920* (Philadelphia, 1981), 50–51, 55–72, 76–81; Lazerson, *Urban School*, 76, 95–96; David Nasaw, *Schooled to Order: A Social History of Public Schooling in the United States* (New York, 1979), 115–17. See also David I. Macleod, *Building Character in the American Boy: The Boy Scouts, YMCA, and Their Forerunners* (Madison, WI, 1983), 44–50, 63, 70–71. Macleod notes that concerns about masculinity led to increased emphasis on physical activity among the middle class.

11. North Bennet Street Industrial School (NBIS), *Annual Report*, 1880–81, 10–12, 14–16, 17, 20; Lazerson, *Urban School*, 116–18. NBIS records are at Schlesinger Library, Radcliffe College.

12. NBIS, *Annual Report*, 1880–81, 22–23; idem, *Annual Report*, 1881–87, 5–6, 8–9, 11. Lazerson, *Urban School*, 118–24, discusses the relationship to the school system.

13. NBIS, *Annual Report*, 1887–88, 5; Marian Lawrence Peabody, *To Be Young Was Very Heaven* (Boston, 1967), 147; NBIS, *Annual Report*, 1888–89, 22, 23–24; idem, *Annual Report*, 1897–98, 11.

14. William Jewett Tucker, "The Andover House in Boston," in *The Poor in Great Cities*, ed. Robert A. Woods (New York, 1895; rep. ed., New York, 1971), 186; Andover House Association, *Annual Report*, 1894, 2; Robert A. Woods and Albert J. Kennedy, *The Settlement Horizon: A National Estimate* (New York, 1922), 67; South End House, *Annual Report*, 1907, 10. Andover House and South End House reports are in the Boston Public Library.

15. Birtwell, "Home Libraries," 8; South End House, *Annual Report*, 1900, 10; CAS, *Annual Report*, 1887–88, 14; idem, *Annual Report*, 1893–94, 28. For further evidence from a slightly later period, see CAS, Central Committee Minutes, vol. 4, May 7, 1912, 25–26.

Coercive reform and voluntary reform were linked organizationally. Charles Birtwell (Children's Aid Society), Robert Treat Paine (Associated Charities and the Children's Aid Society), Robert Woods and William Cole (South End House), G. Stanley Hall, (president of Clark University and father of the child study movement), and Edward E. Hale (founder of Lend a Hand societies and prolific author), were all prominent members of the Watch and Ward Society, which, together with the Law and Order League, sought to secure enforcement of liquor, gambling, and vice laws. See Roger Lane, *Policing the City: Boston, 1822–1885* (New York, 1971), 214–17.

16. On boxing and Sullivan's career, see Hardy, *How Boston Played*, 169–79; Michael T. Isenberg, *John L. Sullivan and His America* (Urbana, IL, 1988), especially 226–36; and James J. Corbett's amusing autobiography, *The Roar of the Crowd* (London, 1925; repr. Arno, 1976).

My general interpretation of crime as an avenue of mobility comes from Daniel Bell, "Crime as an American Way of Life," *Antioch Review* XIII (Summer 1953): 131–54. On the ties between sports, politics, and the underworld, see Mark H. Haller, "Urban Crime and Criminal Justice: The Chicago Case," *Journal of American History* 57 (December 1970): 619–35; and idem, "Organized Crime in Urban Society: Chicago in the Twentieth Century," *Journal of Social History* 5 (Winter 1971–72): 210–34; and David R. Johnson, *Policing the Urban Underworld: The Impact of Crime on the Development of the American Police, 1800–1887* (Philadelphia, 1979), chapter 6.

17. This account of Ida Eldridge and the founding of the Ellis Center is taken from an anonymous, handwritten, undated, unpaginated manuscript history in the Ellis Center files, Ellis Memorial Center, Boston.

18. Macleod, *Building Character*, 65–68; Ellis Memorial Center, *Report*, 1896–97, 19; idem, *Report*, 1906–07, 11; Richard C. Edwards, *Contested Terrain: The Transformation of the Workplace in the Twentieth Century* (New York, 1979).

19. George M. Fredrickson, *The Inner Civil War: Northern Intellectuals and the Crisis of the Union* (New York, 1965), 104–12, 162–65, 211–15; Lori D. Ginzberg, *Women and the Work of Benevolence: Morality, Politics, and Class in the 19th-Century United States* (New Haven, CT, 1990), 172–73, 192–200; McCarthy, *Noblesse Oblige*, 61–71. On the heightened consciousness of the urban poor in the Gilded Age, see Boyer, *Urban Masses and Moral Order*, 124–31.

20. See Frank D. Watson, *The Charity Organization Society Movement in the United States* (New York, 1922), 72–76, 178–79, for the background to the Associated Charities in Boston and their debt to Tuckerman. See also Mrs. James T. Fields, *How to Help the Poor* (Boston, 1883), 15–18; Associated Charities, "Constitution" (Boston, 1879), 6–7; idem, *Annual Report*, 1889, 17–20; Huggins, *Protestants against Poverty*, 60–62, 70–79. For the classification of the poor, see Associated Charities, "Hints to a Conference" (February 1880), 2–3. Associated Charities reports are at the Boston Public Library.

21. Roy Lubove, *The Professional Altruist: The Emergence of Social Work as a Career, 1880–1930* (New York, 1975), 1–21, Robert Bremner, *From the Depths: The Discovery of Poverty in the United States* (New York, 1956), 46–85, and Huggins, *Protestants against Poverty*, 57–79, examine the COS to trace the emergence of modern social welfare. This interpretation overemphasizes the admittedly modern organizational aspect of the COS at the expense of its traditional ideology. This is also the case in Ginzberg, *Women and the Work of Benevolence*, 197. Kenneth L. Kusmer, "The Functions of Organized Charity in the Progressive Era: Chicago as a Case Study," *Journal of American History* 60 (December 1973), in an otherwise acute analysis, writes that the charity workers in the COS did not distinguish between worthy and unworthy poor (661–62) but his evidence is thin and contradicted by other studies. McCarthy, *Noblesse Oblige*, 67–71, studies the Chicago COS, which was not organized until 1883, but deemphasizes the importance of friendly visiting and personal contact between wealthy and poor.

My interpretation is most similar to those of Boyer, *Urban Masses and Moral Order*, 143–61, and Michael B. Katz, *In the Shadow of the Poorhouse: A Social History of Welfare in America* (New York, 1986), 66–84, who focus on the contradictions between visiting and investigating the poor and discuss the ultimate failure of the movement. My interpretation is influenced by Thomas L. Haskell, *The Emergence of Professional Social Science: The American Social Science Association and the Nineteenth-Century Crisis of Authority* (Urbana, IL, 1977), 27–47.

It is worth noting that Edward Everett Hale, one of the founders of the Associated Charities, republished some of Joseph Tuckerman's essays in *On the Elevation of the Poor* (1874) in an effort to spark charity organization.

However, Hale, who intended the essays to be a handbook for charity workers, excluded most of Tuckerman's essays that were sympathetic to the poor.

22. Of course, the Associated Charities itself did not provide assistance, but coordinated the visiting and almsgiving of others.
Fields, *How to Help the Poor*, 23–25; Gareth Stedman Jones, *Outcast London: A Study in the Relationship between Classes in Victorian Society* (Harmondsworth, England, 1976), 251–58; Katz, *In the Shadow of the Poorhouse*, 70–71; Boyer, *Urban Masses and Moral Order*, 149–53.
Lubove, *Professional Altruist*, 12–16; Boyer, *Urban Masses and Moral Order*, 148–52; McCarthy, *Noblesse Oblige*, 67–71; and Bremner, *From the Depths*, 51–57, overlook the relationship between the restriction of outdoor relief and the rise of organized charity.

23. Associated Charities, "Circular Letter to Sewing Societies," October 1879, n.p.; idem, "Rules and Suggestions for Visitors of the Associated Charities," 2–5; idem, "Constitution" (Boston, 1879), 3–4; Boyer, *Urban Masses and Moral Order*, 146–47.

24. Richard Harmond, "Robert Treat Paine," in *Biographical Dictionary of Social Welfare in America*, ed. Walter I. Trattner (Westport, CT, 1986), 583–85; Sam B. Warner, Jr., *Streetcar Suburbs: The Process of Growth in Boston, 1870–1900* (Cambridge, MA, 1962), 101–6; Robert Treat Paine, "Address to Workingmen's Clubs," May 28, 1889, 2–3, 6, Box 9, Robert Treat Paine Papers, Massachusetts Historical Society.

25. Lowell is quoted in Fields, *How to Help the Poor*, 44; Robert Treat Paine, "Address," February 26, 1879, 8, Robert Treat Paine Papers, Massachusetts Historical Society; Octavia Hill, "A Few Words to Volunteer Visitors among the Poor," in *Essays by Octavia Hill* ed. Associated Charities (Boston, 1880), 13; Fields, *How to Help the Poor*, 102–3. For the attack on outdoor relief, see Raymond A. Mohl, "The Abolition of Public Relief, 1870–1900: A Critique of the Piven-Cloward Thesis," in *Social Welfare or Social Control?*, ed. Walter I. Trattner (Knoxville, TN, 1983), 35–50. Ironically, expenditures on outdoor relief in Boston increased even as the number of relief recipients declined. See Amos G. Warner, *American Charities*, rev. ed. (New York, 1908), 238.

26. Robert Treat Paine, "Address," February 26, 1879, 6, Robert Treat Paine Papers, Massachusetts Historical Society; Paine to Frothingham, quoted in Huggins, *Protestants against Poverty*, 65; Fields, *How to Help the Poor*, 63–64; Associated Charities, "Investigation," February 1895, 4.

27. Jane Addams, *Democracy and Social Ethics* (New York, 1902), 27–28; Lubove, *Professional Altruist*, 16–20, 23.

28. Lubove, *Professional Altruist*, 40–43, 49–52, 158–59; Kusmer, "Functions of Organized Charity," 671–72; McCarthy, *Noblesse Oblige*, 136; Katz, *In the Shadow of the Poorhouse*, 164–66; Boyer, *Urban Masses and Moral Order*, 154–58; Huggins, *Protestants against Poverty*, 148–49. On the impact of the 1893–97 depression in creating a constituency for reform, see David P. Thelan, *The*

New Citizenship: Origins of Progressivism in Wisconsin, 1885–1900 (Columbia, MO, 1972), particularly chapter 6.

29. For evidence of immigrants discriminating among social welfare agencies, see Olivier Zunz, *The Changing Face of Inequality: Urbanization, Industrial Development, and Immigrants in Detroit, 1880–1920* (Chicago, 1982), 270–79. On use of settlements by different types of neighborhood adolescents, see William Foote Whyte, *Street Corner Society* (Chicago, 1943), 25–27, 98–100. Most immigrants and working-class people formed alternative cultures rather than oppositional ones. That is, they did not choose to oppose the hegemonic culture but to find a place within it for the expression of alternative values. For the discussion of alternative and oppositional cultures, see Raymond Williams, "Base and Superstructure in Marxist Cultural Theory," *New Left Review* 82 (December 1973): 3–16. For a study using this distinction, see Rosenzweig, *Eight Hours for What We Will.*

30. Edward E. Hale, *If Jesus Came to Boston* (Boston, 1894), see chapter 2.

31. B. O. Flower, *Civilization's Inferno; or, Studies in the Social Cellar* (Boston, 1893), 36–37, 107–8, 201–2.

32. Jean Holloway, *Edward Everett Hale: A Biography* (Austin, TX, 1956), 115, for his early charity reform efforts. Mann, *Yankee Reformers,* 163–71, discusses Flower.

Part 4: Expertise and Scientific Reform

1. LeRoy Ashby, *Saving the Waifs: Reformers and Dependent Children, 1890–1917* (Philadelphia, 1984), 11–13; Susan Tiffin, *In Whose Best Interest? Child Welfare Reform in the Progressive Era* (Westport, CT, 1982), 7–8; Michael B. Katz, *In the Shadow of the Poorhouse: A Social History of Welfare in America* (New York, 1986), 113–29; David J. Rothman, *Conscience and Convenience: The Asylum and Its Alternatives in Progressive America* (Boston, 1980), 206–10.

2. My interpretation of Progressivism is indebted to Clyde Griffen, "The Progressive Ethos," in *The Development of an American Culture,* ed. Stanley Coben and Lorman Ratner (New York, 1983), 144–80; Stanley P. Caine, "The Origins of Progressivism," in *The Progressive Era,* ed. Lewis L. Gould (Syracuse, NY, 1974), 11–34; and Norman H. Clark, *Deliver Us From Evil: An Interpretation of American Prohibition* (New York, 1976).

On the sentimentalization of children, see Viviana A. Zelizer, *Pricing the Priceless Child: The Changing Social Value of Children* (New York, 1985). Zelizer argues that sentimentalization occurred by the mid–nineteenth century in the middle class, while working-class children actually became more valuable as opportunities for industrial employment expanded after the 1870s. By the 1930s, sentimental, rather than monetary, valuation of children characterized all classes. Zelizer's discussion of causation is inadequate, however. She argues that attitudinal change was the product of "sacralization" in which children became invested with "sentimental or religious meaning" (11). This simply begs the question.

On declining opportunities for child labor, see Alba Edwards, *Comparative Occupation Statistics for the United States, 1870–1940* (Washington, DC, 1943), 92; Paul Osterman, "Education and Labor Markets at the Turn of the Century," *Politics and Society* IX (1979): 103–22; and Selwyn K. Troen, "The Discovery of the Adolescent by American Educational Reformers, 1900–1920: An Economic Perspective," in *Schooling and Society: Studies in the History of Education*, ed. Lawrence Stone (Baltimore, MD, 1976), 239–51. David Nasaw argues that street trading was economically unnecessary for working-class families, and he sees the struggle over street trading as both a conflict within the family over youthful independence and between working-class children and reformers who were concerned about their precocity. See *Children of the City: At Work and At Play* (New York, 1985), 42–47, 126–27, 130–37.

On the impact of hereditarian and environmental thought on criminology, see Anthony M. Platt, *The Child Savers: The Invention of Delinquency* (Chicago, 1969), 18–36; and Ellen Ryerson, *The Best-Laid Plans: America's Juvenile Court Experiment* (New York, 1978), 21–27.

The standard work on Hall is Dorothy Ross, *G. Stanley Hall: The Psychologist as Prophet* (Chicago, 1972).

3. On efforts to curb child labor, see Walter I. Trattner, *Crusade for the Children: A History of the National Child Labor Committee and Child Labor Reform in America* (Chicago, 1970); and Jeremy P. Felt, *Hostages of Fortune: Child Labor Reform in New York State* (Syracuse, NY, 1965). On mothers' pensions, see Mark H. Leff, "Consensus for Reform: The Mothers' Pension Campaign in the Progressive Era," *Social Service Review* 47 (September 1973): 397–417. On the role of social welfare agencies in creating a constituency for reform, see John R. Sutton, *Stubborn Children: Controlling Delinquency in the United States, 1640–1981* (Berkeley, CA, 1988), 133–44.

On the role of the state, see Katz, *In the Shadow of the Poorhouse*, 121–24. Katz (124) asks how reformers managed to retain their belief in the benign state, but this is the wrong question. In the Progressive era reformers captured the state, or at least made it responsive to their concerns. Questioning the benevolence of the state would have meant questioning the validity of their entire endeavor. See Rothman, *Conscience and Convenience*, 43–54.

While I emphasize state activity in reform, it should not be concluded that state efforts replaced voluntary reform. See Ashby, *Saving the Waifs*, passim.

8. The Juvenile Court: Triumph of Progressivism

1. On the difference between social and structural reform, see Melvin G. Holli, *Reform in Detroit: Hazen S. Pingree and Urban Politics* (New York, 1969), 157–81.

2. For a largely exaggerated view of the power of the court (and the

therapeutic state in general) to control families, see Christopher Lasch, *The Culture of Narcissism: American Life in an Age of Diminishing Expectations* (New York, 1979), 271–75.

David J. Rothman argues in *Conscience and Convenience: The Asylum and Its Alternatives in Progressive America* (Boston, 1980) that reformers revolutionized social policy between 1900 and 1920 with instruments such as the juvenile court. This is true for the South and the West but an exaggeration for older urban areas. Rothman is right in noting that there were many juvenile courts and in directing attention away from the Chicago court and from Denver's Ben Lindsey. Anthony M. Platt, *The Child Savers: The Invention of Delinquency* (Chicago, 1969), 139, and Ellen Ryerson, *The Best-Laid Plans: America's Juvenile Court Experiment* (New York, 1978), 43–44, see the court as a successful effort to bring into official review conduct that had previously been handled informally. However, the whole basis of the antebellum refuge/asylum movement was to bring noncriminal behavior under adult supervision and to incarcerate children who had the potential to become criminals.

Appraisals of the court arguing for continuity in practice can be found in Robert M. Mennel, *Thorns and Thistles: Juvenile Delinquents in the United States, 1825–1940* (Hanover, NH, 1973), 144; Sanford J. Fox, "Juvenile Justice Reform: An Historical Perspective," *Stanford Law Review* 22 (June 1970): 1221–22; J. Lawrence Schultz, "The Cycle of Juvenile Court History," *Crime and Delinquency* 19 (October 1973): 468–69; and John R. Sutton, *Stubborn Children: Controlling Delinquency in the United States, 1640–1981* (Berkeley, CA, 1988), 122.

3. For separate trials and the procedures established in 1869 and 1870, see Gardiner Tufts, "The Massachusetts Statutes Relating to Juvenile Offenders and the Methods of Dealing with Them," National Conference of Charities and Corrections (hereafter NCCC) *Proceedings* (1880): 200–209; and John Clark Wirkkala, "Juvenile Delinquency and Reform in Nineteenth-Century Massachusetts: The Formative Era in State Care, 1846–1896" (Ph.D. diss., Clark University, 1973), 213–21. On probation, see National Probation Association, *John Augustus, First Probation Officer* (New York, 1939), 13–14, 33–35; and N. S. Timasheff, *One Hundred Years of Probation, 1841–1941*, 2 parts (New York, 1941), 1: 7–10. A convenient collection of juvenile court legislation is Hastings H. Hart, *Juvenile Court Laws in the United States* (New York, 1910). See also Peter C. Holloran, *Boston's Wayward Children: Social Services for Homeless Children, 1830–1930* (Rutherford, NJ, 1989), 197–99.

4. Many historians have noted that social welfare agencies played a key role in the passage of juvenile court legislation, but only David Rothman and Sanford Fox have looked at their institutional interest in advancing the court. See Platt, *Child Savers*, 75–100; Ryerson, *Best-Laid Plans*, 31–33; Mennel, *Thorns and Thistles*, 130–35; Joseph M. Hawes, *Children in Urban Society: Juvenile Delinquency in Nineteenth-Century America* (New York, 1971), 163–68, 177–78; David John Hogan, *Class and Reform: School and Society in Chicago, 1880–*

1930 (Philadelphia, 1985), 60–62. In contrast, see Rothman, *Conscience and Convenience*, 225–28; and Fox, "Juvenile Justice Reform," 1225–28. Sutton, in *Stubborn Children*, 133–44, sees the charity organization movement as creating an ideological climate within which the juvenile court could be adopted.

Steven L. Schlossman, *Love and the American Delinquent: The Theory and Practice of 'Progressive' Juvenile Justice* (Chicago, 1977), 69–78, after dismissing the usual interpretation of the court as a product of new, environmentalist social-scientific thought, argues that the court must be seen in the context of a new appreciation of the sanctity of the family and the necessity for preserving it. Progressives certainly advanced reforms designed to preserve the family, the juvenile court among them, but this is not a sufficient explanation for its adoption.

Both Platt and Fox agree that the juvenile court bill in Illinois entrenched sectarian agencies in the justice system and they see this as part of the essentially conservative nature of the court. However, this ignores the point that in the nineteenth century "public" institutions were largely Protestant in character and that Catholic welfare institutions were developed to defend Catholic children from Protestant proselytism. In Massachusetts, the agreement to send Catholic children to Catholic institutions and Catholic foster families, in so far as it was possible, was a major advance when considered from a religiously pluralistic perspective.

St. Vincent de Paul Society, *Annual Report*, 1888, 6; idem, *Annual Report*, 1891, 10; idem, *Annual Report*, 1903, 8; idem, *Annual Report*, 1904, 11; idem, *Annual Report*, 1907, 12. These records are at the St. Vincent de Paul Society, Boston. Children's Aid Society, *Annual Report*, 1889–90, 11–12; idem, "Report of the Committee on Probation Agency, October 1st, 1903 to October 1st, 1904," 3–4; idem, "Children's Aid Society Notes," 1905, 4–5; idem, *Annual Report*, 1904–05, 16; idem, Central Committee Minutes, vol. 3, August 27, 1907, 15. These records are at the Archives and Special Collections, Joseph P. Healey Library, University of Massachusetts at Boston. Carleton J. Lewis, "The Probation System," NCCC *Proceedings* (1897): 38–46. Judge Baker Foundation, *Harvey Humphrey Baker: Upbuilder of the Juvenile Court* (Boston, 1920), 41.

5. Schlossman, *Love and the American Delinquent*, 8–17; and Robert M. Mennel, "Origins of the Juvenile Court: Changing Perspectives on the Legal Rights of Juvenile Delinquents," *Crime and Delinquency* 18 (January 1972): 68–78. Ryerson, in *Best-Laid Plans*, 64–68, and Hogan, in *Class and Reform*, 62–63, maintain that the extension of *parens patriae* to delinquents in the juvenile court acts removed a whole class of offenders from criminal process. This is correct, but the whole trend in nineteenth-century law and practice was to blur distinctions between delinquent and dependent children. The juvenile court bills were simply the last step in the process.

6. Hart, *Juvenile Court Laws*, 47–50; Joseph Lee, "Report from Massachu-

setts," NCCC *Proceedings* (1905): 57; idem, "Report from Massachusetts," NCCC *Proceedings* (1906): 36–37.

7. Interview with Lee M. Friedman, Miriam Van Waters Papers, Harvard Law School Library, Box 8, File 2. Mr. Friedman lobbied for and helped draft the juvenile court legislation. Hereafter the collection is cited as MVWP, HLSL. Constance K. Burns, "The Irony of Progressive Reform: Boston, 1898–1910," in *Boston, 1700–1980: The Evolution of Urban Politics*, ed. Ronald P. Formisano and Constance K. Burns (Westport, CT, 1984), 133–64; and Charles H. Trout, "Curley of Boston: The Search for Irish Legitimacy," ibid., 165–95; Holloran, *Boston's Wayward Children*, 224–25.

8. John C. Burnham, "Oral History Interviews of William Healy and Augusta Bronner," Houghton Library, Harvard University (1960, 1961), 63; Baker Foundation, *Baker*, 32, 91; Herbert H. Lou, *Juvenile Courts in the United States* (Chapel Hill, NC, 1927), 155.

9. Lou, *Juvenile Courts*, 118.

10. Baker Foundation, *Baker*, 109, 110–11, 114, 115. Katherine F. Lenroot and Emma O. Lundberg, *Juvenile Courts at Work: A Study of the Organization and Methods of Ten Courts*, Children's Bureau Publication No. 141 (Washington, DC, 1925), 28. Hannah Kent Schoff, *The Wayward Child: A Study of the Causes of Crime* (Indianapolis, IN, 1915), 215. Miriam Van Waters, "The Juvenile Court from the Child's Viewpoint: A Glimpse into the Future," in *The Child, the Clinic, and the Court*, ed. Jane Addams (New York, 1925), 223–24; Charles W. Hoffman, "Organization of Family Courts, with Special Reference to the Juvenile Court," ibid., 258, 262; Ben B. Lindsey, "Colorado's Contribution to the Juvenile Court," ibid., 285–86. Platt, *Child Savers*, 142–43. On the role of science and medicine in Progressivism, see John C. Burnham, "The Cultural Interpretation of the Progressive Movement," in *Paths into American Culture: Psychology, Medicine, and Morals*, ed. John C. Burnham (Philadelphia, 1988), 223–24.

11. Paul Starr, *The Social Transformation of American Medicine* (New York, 1982), 189–94; Christopher Lasch, *The New Radicalism in America, 1889–1963: The Intellectual as Social Type* (New York, 1965), 155–62; and John Chynoweth Burnham, "The New Psychology: From Narcissism to Social Control," in *Change and Continuity in Twentieth-Century America: The 1920s*, ed. John Braeman, Robert H. Bremner, and David Brody (Columbus, OH, 1968), 392–97. Holloran relates the use of the medical model to the greater prestige accorded medicine. That may be true but it ignores the ideological implications of the analogy. See Holloran, *Boston's Wayward Children*, 223. For evidence on the juvenile court and adjustment, see Miriam Van Waters, *Youth in Conflict* (New York, 1926).

12. Baker Foundation, *Baker*, 114–15; Lou, *Juvenile Courts*, 113–14, 116–18.

13. Baker Foundation, *Baker*, 2–4; on Cabot, see *Who Was Who in America:*

A Companion Volume to Who's Who in America (1897–1942) (Chicago, 1942), 1: 181.

The comments on ethnicity are based on my sample of juvenile court records. The sample consists of 450 probation investigations from the years 1907, 1917, 1927, and 1937. Every tenth case was selected from 1907 (n = 130) and 1917 (n = 120); in order to produce a useful sample size for 1927 and 1937, a hundred cases were read for each year, representing a sample of every seventh case for 1927 and every sixth case for 1937. While this overweights the latter two years, the records are used for illustrative rather statistical purposes. The table of random numbers was used to select docket numbers within each year. However, not every case receiving a docket number had a probation investigation. Furthermore, many records were missing. When a selected docket number could not be found, the next available one was substituted. All probation records are located at the Boston Juvenile Court.

Ethnicity was determined by father's birthplace, unless the mother was foreign born and the father native. The leading ethnic groups were Italians (31 percent), American-born whites (18 percent), Jews (15 percent), Irish (11 percent), Canadians (7 percent), African-Americans (3 percent), and Poles (3 percent). The remaining 12 percent came from various groups but no group equaled 3 percent.

14. Baker Foundation, *Baker*, 51–54; Lenroot and Lundberg, *Juvenile Courts at Work*, 43–44.

15. Lenroot and Lundberg, *Juvenile Courts at Work*, 58–62, 80–83.

16. Baker Foundation, *Baker*, 109–11.

17. Ibid., 111–14. The figures on pleas and convictions are my calculations based on the tables entitled "Boston Juvenile Court," in Massachusetts, *Prison Commissioners' Report*, 1907, 112–13; 1908, 142–43; 1909, 136–37; 1910, 144–45; 1911, 138–39; 1912, 134–35; 1913, 148–49; 1914, 146–47; 1915, 148–49; and Bureau of Prisons, *Criminal Prosecutions*, 1916, 138–39. These reports are in the Boston Public Library. Lenroot and Lundberg, *Juvenile Courts at Work*, 134.

Cabot's methods were very similar to Baker's. See Frederick P. Cabot, *The Juvenile Delinquent* (Boston, 1918), 2–5; and M. A. De Wolfe Howe, *The Children's Judge: Frederick Pickering Cabot* (Boston, 1932), 64.

18. Baker Foundation, *Baker*, 32, 39–40; Lenroot and Lundberg, *Juvenile Courts at Work*, 90–91, 96, 99–103; Lou, *Juvenile Courts*, 150–51; Mennel, *Thorns and Thistles*, 162–67; Hawes, *Children in Urban Society*, 250–56. The statistics on probation and informal supervision are based on the Massachusetts *Prison Commissioners' Report* and the Bureau of Prisons *Criminal Prosecutions*, cited above.

19. Case nos. 10373, 10321, 10658, 10699. As per my agreement with the Boston Juvenile Court, all names are pseudonyms.

20. Case no. 10369.

21. Case no. 670.

22. Case no. 10080.

23. Case no. 10202.

24. Case nos. 10080 and 10669.

25. Lenroot and Lundberg, *Juvenile Courts at Work*, 173, 175–78, 185, 193.

26. Rothman, *Conscience and Convenience*, 251–52, 257, argues that probation extended the reach of the court, but he does not go as far as Christopher Lasch, who states in *The Culture of Narcissism* that probation extended the power of the state into "every corner of society" (273). Platt also concludes in *Child Savers* that the court brought into government control behavior that earlier had been ignored. Platt does not discuss the eighty years of child-saving before 1900 in which reformers sought through both public and private means to control the non-criminal but culturally offensive behavior of working-class children. In 1907, a staff of three probation officers did pretrial investigations for approximately thirteen hundred cases besides supervising delinquents placed on probation during that and the previous year. Not all of these were new offenders, but still the caseload was unmanageable; hence, the ten-minute-per-week visit. Holloran, *Boston's Wayward Children*, 226–27, notes the declining status of probation officers and the difficulty in attracting trained individuals for the job, which became a political sinecure.

27. Rothman, *Conscience and Convenience*, 238–43. Rothman entitles his chapter "The Cult of Judicial Personality." While he is right in pointing out the celebrity status of judges such as Ben Lindsey, the figure of the charismatic reformer is as old as the reformatory itself. Mennel, *Thorns and Thistles*, 135, mentions but does not explore the role of masculinity in the court. For evidence of the latter, see Richard S. Tuthill, "History of the Children's Court in Chicago," in *Children's Courts in the United States: Their Origin, Development, and Results*, ed. Samuel J. Barrows, House of Representatives Doc. No. 701 (Washington, DC, 1904), 3; Ben B. Lindsey, "Additional Report on Methods and Results," ibid., 107–9; George W. Stubbs, "The Mission of the Juvenile Court of Indianapolis," ibid., 150–51, 153; Baker Foundation, *Baker*, 110–11.

28. Judge Ben B. Lindsey and Wainwright Evans, *The Revolt of Modern Youth* (Garden City, NY, 1925), 39, 40–41, 115–16.

29. Baker Foundation, *Baker*, 118. "He Understands Boys," newspaper clipping, Cabot File, Boston Juvenile Court. Roy Cushman, the probation officer who wrote the introduction to the Baker Foundation publication on Baker, claims that Baker was effective with girls (5), but does not offer any evidence for the claim. The evidence in the court records suggests Baker shared Cabot's discomfort. See Holloran, *Boston's Wayward Children*, 219.

30. Lenroot and Lundberg, *Juvenile Courts at Work*, 58, 61–62, 96, 103, 153; Holloran, *Boston's Wayward Children*, 217.

31. There were seventy-two girls' cases in a sample of 450, but in five cases the charges were missing.

32. Case no. 306.

33. Case no. 10503. Only 2 percent of 378 boys in the sample were charged with lewdness or fornication, 3 percent with stubbornness, and 3 percent with running away. These same offenses constituted 47 percent of the girls' charges.

34. Steven Schlossman and Stephanie Wallach, "The Crime of Precocious Sexuality: Female Juvenile Delinquency in the Progressive Era," *Harvard Educational Review* 48 (February 1978): 71–75; Sophonisba P. Breckinridge and Edith Abbott, *The Delinquent Child and the Home* (New York, 1912), 35–41; Barbara Meil Hobson, *Uneasy Virtue: The Politics of Prostitution and the American Reform Tradition* (New York, 1987), 193–99.

Lenroot and Lundberg, *Juvenile Courts at Work*, 153, gives comparative incarceration rates. The rates differed tremendously among the courts, depending on the number of cases dealt with informally. A court, such as Boston's, that handled few cases informally would naturally incarcerate a much smaller percentage of the defendants appearing before it because of the large number of trivial cases. When the Harvard Crime Survey studied the juvenile court in 1927–28, it found that 20 percent of the female delinquents and 4 percent of the males were committed. Harvard Crime Survey, "Preliminary Report," 51–52, MVWP, HLSL, Box 1, File 1.

35. See chapter 4 and Barbara M. Brenzel, *Daughters of the State: A Social Portrait of the First Reform School for Girls in North America, 1856–1905* (Cambridge, MA, 1983), for a discussion of the use of state facilities by parents seeking to control their daughters. On attitudes toward women in Italian culture, see Virginia Yans-McLaughlin, *Family and Community: Italian Immigrants in Buffalo, 1880–1930* (Ithaca, NY, 1971), 170–73, 202-7.

36. Case no. 25786.

37. Hobson, *Uneasy Virtue*, 139–41; Linda Gordon, *Heroes of Their Own Lives: The Politics and History of Family Violence, Boston, 1880–1960* (New York, 1988), 102–8, 136–41, 187–92; Lynn Y. Weiner, *From Working Girl to Working Mother: The Female Labor Force in the United States, 1820–1980* (Chapel Hill, NC, 1985), 92–93; Yans-McLaughlin, *Family and Community*, 189–92; Selwyn K. Troen, "The Discovery of the Adolescent by American Educational Reformers, 1900–1920: An Economic Perspective," in *Schooling and Society: Studies in the History of Education*, ed. Lawrence Stone (Baltimore, MD, 1976), 239–51; David Nasaw, *Children of the City: At Work and at Play* (New York, 1985), 113–14, 132–37; Nancy J. Tomes, "Dynamic Psychiatry and the Female Delinquent," paper delivered at the Annual Meeting of the Organization of American Historians, 1983, 21–28.

38. James R. McGovern, "The American Woman's Pre–World War I Freedom in Manners and Morals," *Journal of American History* 55 (September 1968): 315–33. McGovern's view of a sexual revolution has been challenged by Daniel Scott Smith, "The Dating of the American Sexual Revolution: Evidence and Interpretation," in *The American Family in Social-Historical Perspective*, ed. Michael Gordon (New York, 1973), 321–35. Smith argues that the change occurred gradually and that middle-class women were catching up with work-

ing-class ones in their sexual practices (332). Kathy Peiss, in *Cheap Amusements: Working Women and Leisure in Turn-of-the-Century New York* (Philadelphia, 1986), argues that a new heterosexual culture emerged among working-class women and forced the middle class to respond to it.

On the challenge to traditional culture offered by bourgeois youth, see Paula S. Fass, *The Damned and the Beautiful: American Youth in the 1920s* (New York, 1977); John Kasson, *Amusing the Million: Coney Island at the Turn of the Century* (New York, 1978); and Lewis Erenberg, *Steppin' Out: New York Nightlife and the Transformation of American Culture, 1890–1930* (Westport, CT, 1981).

39. Case no. 10782.

40. Case nos. 657 and 10424.

41. Alexander Keyssar, *Out of Work: The First Century of Unemployment in Massachusetts* (Cambridge, England, 1986), appendix A.

42. Philip Davis, *Street-land: Its Little People and Big Problems* (Boston, 1915), 72–74.

43. Both the Harvard Crime Survey and the Children's Bureau investigators found 4 percent of the boys and 20 percent and 14 percent, respectively, of the girls were incarcerated. I found a higher percentage of delinquents incarcerated because of the nature of my sample. The records available were those of probation officers' investigations of the home rather than records of all children appearing before the court. In addition, any folder with a missing record was skipped for the next available one, and together this weighted the sample toward cases handled formally and considered serious enough to be investigated.

44. Lindsey, "Additional Report on Methods and Results," 71; David Nasaw, *Children of the City*, passim; Viviana A. Zelizer, *Pricing the Priceless Child: The Changing Social Value of Children* (New York, 1985), 32–52; Joseph F. Kett, *Rites of Passage: Adolescence in America, 1790 to the Present* (New York, 1977), 226–27.

45. Baker Foundation, *Baker*, 22–23. The categories of truancy, ordinance, and statutory violations, and gambling were considered together.

46. Ibid., 100–101.

47. Weiner, *From Working Girl to Working Mother*, 92–93; Stephen Hardy, *How Boston Played: Sport, Recreation, and Community, 1865–1915* (Boston, 1982), 97–98, 101–104; Zelizer, *Pricing the Priceless Child*, 32–35, 39–43; Paul Boyer, *Urban Masses and Moral Order in America, 1820–1920* (Cambridge, MA, 1978), 243–50; Nasaw, *Children of the City*, 152–57, 187–94; Paul Osterman, "Education and Labor Markets at the Turn of the Century," *Politics and Society* IX (1979): 103–22; Selwyn K. Troen, "The Discovery of the Adolescent by American Educational Reformers," 239–51. On Boston, see Davis, *Street-land*, 210–20. It is interesting to note that Joseph Lee and the Massachusetts Civic League were lobbyists for both the playground movement and the juvenile court.

48. Case no. 596.

49. See, for example, case nos. 563, 653, 10202.

9. Child Guidance and the Court

1. William Healy, Augusta F. Bronner, and Myra E. Shimberg, "The Close of Another Chapter in Criminology," *Mental Hygiene* XIX (April 1935): 208–22; John J. Perkins, *Common Sense and Bad Boys and Other Essays* (Boston, 1946), 19–20.

2. John Chynoweth Burnham, "Psychiatry, Psychology, and the Progressive Movement," *American Quarterly* 12 (1960): 457–65; and idem, "The New Psychology: From Narcissism to Social Control," in *Change and Continuity in Twentieth-Century America: The 1920s*, ed. John Braeman, Robert H. Bremner, and David Brody (Columbus, OH, 1968), 351–98; Margo Horn, *Before It's Too Late: The Child Guidance Movement in the United States, 1922–1945* (Philadelphia, 1989), 19–22, 29–30; Theresa R. Richardson, *The Century of the Child: The Mental Hygiene Movement and Social Policy in the United States and Canada* (Albany, NY, 1989).

3. Massachusetts Industrial School for Boys, *Annual Report*, 1924, 14; Trustees of the Massachusetts Training Schools, *Annual Report*, 1927, 6; idem, *Annual Report*, 1933, 22; State Reform School for Boys, *Annual Report*, 1939, 5. These reports are in the Massachusetts State Library. William Healy, *The Practical Value of Scientific Study of Juvenile Delinquents*, Children's Bureau Publication No. 96 (Washington, DC, 1922), 9–13. David Rothman, *Conscience and Convenience: The Asylum and Its Alternatives in Progressive America* (Boston, 1980), 231–34, 267–68, 274–75.

4. William Healy and Augusta F. Bronner, "The Child Guidance Clinic: Birth and Growth of an Idea," in *Orthopsychiatry, 1923–1948: Retrospect and Prospect*, ed. Lawson G. Lowrey (Menosha, WI, 1948), 20–24, 33–34; George S. Stevenson and Geddes Smith, *Child Guidance Clinics: A Quarter-Century of Development* (New York, 1934), 20–23; Margo Horn, "The Moral Message of Child Guidance, 1925–1945," *Journal of Social History* 18 (Fall 1984): 25–26; Richardson, *Century of the Child*, chapter 7.

5. Kathleen W. Jones, "William Healy," in *Biographical Dictionary of Social Welfare in America*, ed. Walter I. Trattner (Westport, CT, 1986), 364–69; Rothman, *Conscience and Convenience*, 54–56, 307, 311; Robert M. Mennel, *Thorns and Thistles: Juvenile Delinquents in the United States, 1825–1940* (Hanover, NH, 1973), 158–61; Jon Snodgrass, "The American Criminological Tradition: Portraits of the Men and Ideology in a Discipline" (Ph.D. diss., University of Pennsylvania, 1972), 58–61. Healy was also influenced by Adolf Meyer, who emphasized the interaction of mind and body and rejected the overly physiological approach to mental disorder traditional among neurologists. See *Conscience and Convenience*, 302–6.

6. John C. Burnham, "Augusta Fox Bronner," in *Notable American Women:*

The Modern Period, ed. Barbara Sicherman and Carol Hurd Green (Cambridge, MA, 1980), 108–9. Augusta Bronner's approach to delinquency, not surprisingly, was very similar to Healy's. See, for example, Augusta F. Bronner, "The Contribution of Science to a Program for Treatment of Juvenile Delinquency," in *The Child, the Clinic, and the Court*, ed. Jane Addams (New York, 1925), 75–92.

7. Healy and Bronner, "The Child Guidance Clinic," 16, 19, 27–28; and William Healy, *The Individual Delinquent: A Textbook of Diagnosis and Prognosis for All Concerned in Understanding Offenders* (Boston, 1915), 22. To see the progression in Healy's work, compare *The Individual Delinquent* with *Mental Conflicts and Misconduct* (Boston, 1917).

8. Bronner, "Contribution of Science," 77–79, 83.

9. William Healy and Augusta F. Bronner, *New Light on Delinquency and Its Treatment* (New Haven, CT, 1936), 147–50; Bronner, "Contribution of Science," 83–84.

10. Horn, *Before It's Too Late*, 136–45.

11. Case no. 10122. The Brennan case was not unique. See also case nos. 10202, 10731, and 10788. These cases are from the 1917 subset of my sample of juvenile court cases described in note 13, 242 and are located in the Boston Juvenile Court.

12. Healy, *The Individual Delinquent*, 188–89.

13. Linda Gordon, *Heroes of Their Own Lives: The Politics and History of Family Violence, Boston, 1880–1960* (New York, 1988), 124–27, 152–55; Mennel, *Thorns and Thistles*, 166–67; Snodgrass, "American Criminological Tradition," 104–8.

14. For an example of how cultural biases shaped social science, see Michael B. Katz's reanalysis of survey data about almshouse users in *Poverty and Policy in American History* (New York, 1983), 90–133.

15. Judge Baker Foundation, *Case Study Number Seven*, Series 1 (Boston, 1922).

16. Snodgrass, "American Criminological Tradition," 60, on Freud's influence on Healy.

17. Nancy Tomes discovered that while 86 percent of the boys in her sample arrived via public authorities, only 35 percent of the girls did so. Fifty-six percent of the girls were referred by private social welfare agencies as compared to 9 percent of the boys. Families brought 7 percent of the girls and 5 percent of the boys. See Nancy J. Tomes, "Dynamic Psychiatry and the Female Delinquent," paper delivered at the Annual Meeting of the Organization of American Historians, 1983, 28a, table 2.

18. Judge Baker Foundation, *Case Study Number 9*, Series 1 (Boston, 1922), quotations from 13, 14, 19, 21, 25.

19. Barbara Meil Hobson, *Uneasy Virtue: The Politics of Prostitution and the American Reform Tradition* (New York, 1987), 184–89; Paula Fass, *The Damned and the Beautiful: American Youth in the 1920s* (New York, 1977), 260–76; Joan

Jacobs Brumberg, " 'Ruined' Girls: Changing Community Responses to Illegitimacy in Upstate New York, 1890–1920," *Journal of Social History* 18 (Winter 1984): 249–50.

20. Roy Lubove, *The Professional Altruist: The Emergence of Social Work as a Career, 1880–1930* (New York, 1975), 76–89; Stevenson and Smith, *Child Guidance Clinics*, 12–13; Hobson, *Uneasy Virtue*, 187.

21. Horn, *Before It's Too Late*, 149–53; Stevenson and Smith, *Child Guidance Clinics*, 89; Samuel W. Hartwell, *Fifty-five "Bad" Boys* (New York, 1931), 14–22.

22. Hartwell, *Fifty-five "Bad" Boys*, 136–42.

23. Ibid., 356.

24. Gordon, *Heroes*, 159–60, 221–22, 240–49.

25. See Horn, *Before It's Too Late*, 169–71, for the declining length and effectiveness of treatment. Of the one thousand delinquents studied by Sheldon Glueck and Eleanor Glueck, 80 percent had a single diagnostic visit to the clinic. See *One Thousand Juvenile Delinquents: Their Treatment by Court and Clinic* (Cambridge, MA, 1934), 111.

26. William Healy and Augusta F. Bronner, *Delinquents and Criminals: Their Making and Unmaking, Studies in Two American Cities* (New York, 1926), 28–29, 61, 188–90, 203–4.

27. William Healy, Augusta F. Bronner, Edith M. H. Baylor, and J. Prentice Murphy, *Reconstructing Behavior in Youth: A Study of Problem Children in Foster Families* (New York, 1929), 232–33, 245, 253.

28. Bella Boone Beard, *Juvenile Probation: An Analysis of the Case Records of Five Hundred Children Studied at the Judge Baker Guidance Clinic and Placed on Probation in the Juvenile Court of Boston* (New York, 1934), 42, 57, 108, 111, 131–32, 147, 157.

29. Glueck and Glueck, *One Thousand Juvenile Delinquents*, 66, 69, 79, 85, 86–87, 88, 102.

30. Ibid., 151–52. For the implication that the court could be abolished, see Richard C. Cabot, "1000 Delinquent Boys: First Findings of the Harvard Law School's Survey of Crime," *Survey* (February 15, 1934): 38–40.

31. Glueck and Glueck, *One Thousand Juvenile Delinquents*, 119–25, 133–45.

32. For a different point of view, see Christopher Lasch, *The Culture of Narcissism: American Life in an Age of Diminishing Expectations* (New York, 1979), especially 271–75; and Jacques Donzelot, *The Policing of Families* (New York, 1979).

33. Glueck and Glueck, *One Thousand Juvenile Delinquents*, 171, 174.

34. Ibid., 241–79; Cabot, "1000 Delinquent Boys," 38–40.

35. Harry L. Eastman, "1000 Delinquent Boys," *Survey* (June 15, 1934): 199–200, as well as other correspondence in the same issue.

36. Thomas D. Eliot, "Suppressed Premises Underlying the Glueck Controversy," *Journal of Criminal Law and Criminology* 26 (1935): 22–33.

37. Healy, Bronner, and Shimberg, "The Close of Another Chapter in Criminology," 217, 220, 221.

Conclusion: The Failure of Cultural Reform

1. The Boston Foundation, *In the Midst of Plenty: A Profile of Boston and Its Poor* (Boston, 1989), 39–48.

Index

Dependence, 69; fear of, 32–33; redefined by moral entrepreneurs, 33
Deviance. *See* Female delinquency; Hereditarianism; Moral entrepreneurs;
Poverty; Psychological approaches to
delinquency
Domestic reform, 51–90, 117–18, 133,
179, 214 n7; abandoned as reform
model, 107; advantages for boys from
'superior parentage,' 106; concludes
with state welfare bureaucracy, 91;
criticism of congregate asylums, 56–
57; defined, 51, 56; evolution of, 54–
56; failures with African-Americans
and Catholics, 62–64, 71; manual or
vocational training as alternative, 95,
96–99; pastoral ideal, 51–52; placement policy, 62, 68–71, 86–87; pro-
duces theory for reforming girls, 74,
79; put in brief practice at Westborough School, 91–94, 101, 107
Domestic service: for Lancaster girls, 81–
84; Lancaster trustee views toward, 90;
sexual exploitation, 82
Domesticity, 83; among Catholics, 80–
81, 123; brought into public realm, 86;
defined, 73
Dominant culture: defined, 195 n5

Eiler, Herbert, case of, 180–81
Eldridge, Ida, 136–37
Eliot School, 120
Eliot, Thomas, 186
Ellis Memorial Center (boys' club), 136–
37
Emerson, George, 91
Ex parte Crouse, 150

Family: entry into by reformers, 135–36,
140–41, 185, 187; and domesticity, 73;
locus of women's activity, 73; negotia-
tions with agencies, 137; Lancaster
School as substitute, 74, 77–78; seen
as source for juvenile misconduct, 74,
80, 173–81, 187; resistance to reform,
8–11, 18, 64, 137–38, 148, 165, 169;
smaller and more intimate, 70–71;

working-class family life described, 27,
45, 142
Family economy, 11, 80, 147, 164–65,
166
Family style institutions, 53, 71, 118;
criticized as artificial, 69–70; as "dangerous and pernicious," 86–87; history
and aims, 52–54; Lancaster School as
architectural and organizational model,
76; part of prison system, 106–7; undermined by immediate placement, 53,
66–67, 88–89, 100–101, 105; versus
congregate asylum, 56–57
Family Welfare Society, 3, 6, 7
Fay, Francis, 75, 76
Fay Commission, 76
Feeble mindedness. *See* Hereditarianism
Female delinquency, 43, 73–74, 79–80,
163; creation of separate incarceral system, 73, 88–89, 90; defined as sexual
activity, 8, 85, 161–63, 177–79; and
institutional fear of "moral contagion,"
43–44, 67–68, 72; notion of "fallen
woman," 73; reformers view of, 73–
74, 160, 163. *See also* State Industrial
School for Girls (Lancaster)
Fenwick, Benedict, 113
Fields, Annie, 140; *How to Help the Poor*,
141
Fitzpatrick, John, 113, 119–21
Flower, Benjamin (*Civilization's Inferno*),
142–43
Freud, Sigmund, 172

Gender, 42; and juvenile court, 158–59;
reform, 200 n5, 200 n17, 210 n33,
231 n32
George Junior Republic, 5, 7, 10, 11
Girls, 8, 41–42, 142; agents for cultural
transmission, 59–60, 72–74; court
charges against, 73, 162–63; influence
on delinquents, 43; institutional arrangements for, 43–45, 67–68, 76–80,
130; left vulnerable by family, 74, 80;
"saving one as worth saving ten boys,"
74; placement in domestic service, 81–
84; reform stress upon domestic rou-

Wall, Thomas: beaten, 120
Warren Street Church, 29
Washburn, Emory, 76
Waterston, Robert, 22
Wells, E.M.P. (Eleazar), 39, 40, 47, 54, 118; background and views, 38; exercises educational philosophy at Boston Farm School, 54–55; criticized for overgenerous reform, 40
Westborough. *See* State Reform School for Boys
Williams, John, 113, 119; on accommodation, 120–21
Women as reformers, 44–45, 58, 68, 73, 75, 86, 130–31; in Catholic domestic culture, 123; class differences among, 81–82, 131; refining influence, 59; transmission of values, 52

Worchester Child Guidance Clinic, 179
Workhouses, 31, 41; deterrent, 32, 36; and elimination of public relief, 23–24; site for girls' reformatory, 43
Working class, 73, 190; children, 93, 99, 107, 110, 118, 132, 133, 146, 158, 163, 166; families, 77, 165, 185; fear of, 57, 109, 125; limited choices for women, 82, 130–31, 175; periodic unemployment, 13–14, 21, 25, 166, 175, 190
Wright, Carroll, 82

Yankee farm families, 55, 62, 76; boys' experience in, 65
YMCA, 96
"The Young Forgers; or, Homes and Prisons," 53
YWCA, 86